Creating and Pl
Alpine Gardens

by Rex Murfitt

How to Build Small Rock Gardens and Work with Alpine Plants

B. B. Mackey Books
P. O. Box 475
Wayne, PA 19087
www.mackeybooks.com

⇛ Creating and Planting Alpine Gardens

All text, photos, editing and book design ©
Copyright 2005 by Rex Murfitt and Betty Mackey

Published by *B. B. Mackey Books, P. O. Box 475,
Wayne, PA 19087*

Library of Congress Cataloging-in-Publication Data

Murfitt, Rex.

  Creating and planting alpine gardens : how to build rock gardens and work with alpine plants / by Rex Murfitt.-- 1st ed.

    p. cm.

  ISBN 1-893443-07-8 (alk. paper)

  1. Alpine gardens. 2. Alpine garden plants. I. Title.

  SB459.M87 2005

  635.9'528--dc22

                    2004027544

Photo Credits:

Rex Murfitt: front cover, back cover, pp.1, 4, 5, 7, 8, 10,16,19, 29, 33, 34, 38, 46, 51, 53, 60 top, 77, 78, 81, 87, 92 (upper), 98, 100, 114, 116, 120 (upper), 121, 127, 137, 140 , 149, 151, 153, 159, 162 (upper), 166, 169, 180, 181, 182, 184, 188, 195, 199, 201, 203, 205, 216, 221, 223 (lower), 224, 246 (lower), 247 (upper), 250, 254, 260. gallery a (upper), d, f, g.

Betty Mackey: back cover (lower), pp. 2, 3, 4, 14, 22, 25, 26, 34 (upper), 44, 45, 47, 52, 67, 83, 88, 91, 92 (lower), 95, 110, 112, 120 (lower), 126, 130, 134, 147, 157, 162 (lower), 172, 173, 178, 186, 209, 212, 213, 218, 223 (upper), 242, 245, 246 (upper), 247 (lower), 251, 256. gallery a (lower), b, c, e, h.

Edward Mackey: pp. 9, 34 (lower), 189, 227, 232, 233, 275.

Alan Mackey: p. 226.

Anne Freeman: 268.

Tom Mackey: p. 145.

Netherlands Flowerbulb Association, p. 240.

Drawing Credits:

Rex Murfitt: pp. 39, 40,41,42,43, 54, 55, 56, 57, 60 bottom, 101, 104, 105, 117, 132, 157.

Betty Mackey: pp. 84, 228.

public domain: p. 170.

USDA-NRCS PLANTS Database/ Britton, N.L., and A. Brown. 1913. Illustrated Flora of the Northern States and Canada. Vol. 3: 452: p. 144.

Front cover photo: *Sempervivum octopodes*

Back cover photos: *Penstemon barrettiae* (upper); *Saxifraga iranica (lower)*

ISBN 1-893443-07-8

Find information about this and other titles from B. B. Mackey Books at the website, **www.mackeybooks.com**, or ask for a free booklist.

Introduction   5

Chapter One. Beginning an Alpine Garden   9

Chapter Two. The Nature of Rocks   23

Chapter Three. Building a Rock Garden   35

Chapter Four. Building Raised Beds   47

Chapter Five. Soil and Topdressing   61

Chapter Six. Alpine Plants in Containers   77

Chapter Seven. Rock Gardens Under Glass   99

Chapter Eight. Plant Talk   121

Chapter Nine. Herbaceous and Semi-Woody Plants   135

Chapter Ten. Small Bulbs   225

Chapter Eleven. Dwarf Trees and Shrubs   243

Resources   261

Sedum spathulifolium 'Cape Blanco'

The author's garden. Above, *Saxifraga hostii*, a meadow species,
growing in a raised bed; below, the rock garden in springtime.

Introduction

Saxifrages in the author's alpine house, in cast concrete containers

In creating the successful small rock garden, we aim to create our own piece of alpine landscape, bringing it down from the vast alpine wilderness and setting it into our own lowland gardens, where it should look as natural as possible. The esthetic and artistic issues, so difficult to put into words, go beyond horticultural techniques.

Every ounce of imagination and taste must be employed or the effect will miss the mark. The ideal rock garden gives the impression that it has been in place for hundreds of years. The rock formations look like pre-existing outcrops, and the plants appear to be naturally occurring colonies, thriving in their bright and rocky environment.

This is a tall order, I know. I hope the following pages will explain and simplify the complex factors involved, and help you achieve a truly beautiful and satisfying alpine garden. The introductory chapters give background on the nature of rocky places and alpine plants. Types of rocks for use in building outcrops and natural looking strata are described in the second chapter. The third chapter gets into practical matters of rock placement and garden making.

This book is designed to reveal the hours of pleasure that this form of gardening offers. It pays particular attention to gardeners with limited space and time, not overlooking experienced gardeners who are seeking smaller gardens.

⇛ Creating and Planting Alpine Gardens

The informal lines of a rock garden are not ideal for every situation or the choice of every gardener. Possibly the formal lines of a raised bed would go better with the arrangement of the property. There are endless ways the surface and sides of a raised bed can be landscaped and planted to create a truly unique garden. Chapter 4 tells how to make and use raised beds and garden walls.

In Chapter 5 there are explanations about soil elements and soil mixtures, organic matter, and top dressing for the garden and for containers. Proportional soil recipes for different purposes are included here.

At homes with very little space for a garden of any kind, a gardener can often find just a few square feet for displaying a trough. With alpine plants, a complex miniature garden can be created within. Lots of alpine plants can be grown in containers, artfully fitted into very small spaces such as window sills and balconies. It is possible to have a small yet satisfactory garden on the hard surface of a patio or the vertical surface of a retaining wall. A few choice plants will even grow in small holes drilled into certain types of soft stone. Container gardening with alpines is discussed in Chapter 6.

This book is based upon rock gardening and rock plants but it is by no means restricted to them. I recognize that there are those who do not want to involve themselves in hauling in rocks, soils, and heavy materials although I am not one of them.

To me, the ultimate in gardening enjoyment comes from my cool greenhouse, the alpine house, which permits virtually year round gardening. It is ideal for the active gardener and the handyman who loves to invent or make things. You'll find more information on alpine houses and cold frames in Chapter 7.

The rest of the book concentrates on plants. It offers a look at winter hardiness and summer damage, planting techniques, care and maintenance of plants, and the preferences and idiosyncracies of alpine plants.

Plant Talk offers discussions about handling alpine and rock plants. Those listed in Chapters 9, 10, and 11 have been chosen for their hardiness, longevity, dwarf habit, perennial nature, abundant flowers, and general garden worthiness. These selections are usually available at nurseries even though in some cases it might require some searching. The emphasis is upon plants that are trouble-free, provided a good try is made to follow my recommended cultural practices. Once in a while I have included plants that are definitely a challenge to grow, for, after all, who wants gardening to be too easy. The rewards are great for those who succeed with them.

The plant chapters are a compressed discussion of a complex subject. I reluctantly had to exclude some popular plants to keep the size of this book within limits, but I have recommended more detailed books specializing in different plant genera or subjects. I know you will enjoy reading them and they will help you enormously to select plants as you progress with your new garden.

I have been fortunate enough to know many of their authors. Some are experts with whom I have studied or worked, and others are highly respected plants people. I am pleased to call many of them my friends. The book concludes with a bibliography and index.

It is my hope that this book will inspire gardeners, especially those who feel frustrated about gardening in smaller spaces. Many of us spend our lives happily building a garden and just when it reaches a state of maturity, so do we. We may have to rule out further strenuous garden work. Many of us find it hard to face the future cheerfully without contact with plants and gardens. There are no books that I know of that were written to help us to withdraw from our gardens.

Over the last few years a couple of my friends had to give up their gardens and move into much smaller accommodations. It was not long before they began to develop gardens in their new abodes.

One was limited to a raised planter which was an architectural element of his townhouse site. He soon tired of growing tomatoes and needed something more challenging. The other man never had any doubt about what he was going to create. An expert rock gardener for many years, he was going to make another rock garden. The fact that his townhouse had only a small garden area composed of solid rock did not deter him for one moment.

The experiences of these two friends got me thinking about people in similar positions who might benefit from a book about small but challenging gardens. There are lots of busy younger people who also live on such properties, and there are gardeners of all ages who live in cities, towns, and townhouses who would like to do some serious gardening despite limitations of space or time.

Rock and alpine gardens can be the answer, and there is no size limit on them. I hope that you will use this book to bring a wonderful touch of nature to your garden space, whether it is large or small.

Rocks, *Sempervivum* 'Mayfair', and a small pool make a wonderful combination.

1. Beginning an Alpine Garden

Have you become entranced with the gemlike beauty of alpine plants? The charm of small plants artfully arranged in a mountain-like landscape is hard to match. If you are interested in learning to grow alpines well in a small rock garden or in containers, even if you have little or no experience, this book is for you. We shall first concentrate on the site and its potential development into simpler rock garden designs such as outcrops, valleys, and small gorges.

The excitement of planning and building an alpine garden often encourages haste, so, before you begin, there are practical matters to consider about the site and the materials needed. Once you find the right site, you can develop its existing features in the most natural and attractive manner.

Designing From Nature

Where do we go to get ideas for rock gardens? The logical place to start is with nature itself. Observe the countryside when walking. You will often find natural outcroppings of rock to study along lake shores, seashores, highways, riverbanks, and woodlands. The cliffs and gorges illustrate nature's way with rock. As you drive along, notice the roadsides. Look for old cuts through rock that have healed and weathered after the builders' blasting. Do you feel you are driving through an actual rock garden? Granted, it is planted with grass, weeds and trees, but scale it down and you have a miniature gorge.

Those responsible for building parkways and turnpikes are rock gardeners on a grand scale. Notice how they leave interesting rock outcroppings wherever possible, and plant a few shrubs or evergreen trees near particularly handsome ledges. Once the wildflowers establish, there is a rock garden.

Highway cuts reveal the layered structure of rock.

The seashore and lakeside are pleasant places to study nature's rock gardening. Look at cliffs and rocky shorelines. See how the rocks have just tumbled there? Notice how this debris, known as talus or scree, has fallen from above and collected in a sloping mound at the base of cliffs. A few large slabs protrude here and there and wild flowers flourish. Vacation time presents opportunities to visit the mountains—the Rockies, the Cascades, the Adirondacks, the White Mountains, or even the Alps. You can study alpine gardens as they should be, complete with flowers. Make notes and take photographs.

Observe the ways of rocks, and the strata running through them. Note the effect of waterfalls, even if the water has ceased to flow after the spring runoff has ended.

Look at the lakeshore and pools, both large and small. Notice how the rocks settle naturally. Rocky sites are often haphazard: large and small stones are mixed; they are not graded into uniform sizes.

See how different kinds of plants select their homes and how some prefer to grow in crevices, on scree slopes or in shallow dry soils. Others choose damp streamside soils or they prefer deep soil, while others survive on the rocks in practically no soil.

Do not get overwhelmed by the options. The following sections will help you decide where to place an alpine garden, and which styles or features will blend with your home and landscape.

Selecting the Best Sites

Finding a pleasant site should be your first consideration. Is it warm and agreeable and light and airy? Or is it damp, sunken, or heavily shaded, with no air movement? Is it overshadowed by buildings? If the site does not feel comfortable, then it is no place for a rock garden or alpine plants.

Exposure. All plants need sunlight and good air circulation, especially those floriferous dwarf plants from the mountains: to be successful they must have at least half a day of bright sunlight. Choose a site that offers a healthy exposure. You are looking for a spot where there are no closely overhanging trees or overgrowing shrubs. Nonetheless, a tree that casts just a bit of light shade during hot weather is an advantage. Put yourself in the plant's place: on a hot summer day, some shade will be appreciated.

To evaluate the site, visit it several times a day and record the sun and shade patterns. Any information of this type will be valuable to you when planting time comes.

Overhangs. During your initial site appraisal, note the extent of overhanging roofs, balconies, and eaves. Overhangs of this type will prevent life-giving rain from falling on the garden. However, overhangs can be utilized to provide us with dry spots if we wish to grow drought resistant or drought-loving plants.

With enough sunlight, many of the silvery gray, Mediterranean-style plants that love the sun will thrive in the dry patch under an overhang. Moreover, they stand a greater chance of making it through the winter if they are kept dry. Problems occur when plants must reach for light. They all grow in one direction, toward the light, becoming weak and floppy. If the overhang is high enough for you to stand under without banging your head, it will probably allow enough light for plants such as *Helichrysum*, *Teucrium*, and some of the larger native buckwheats. *Eriogonum* makes a striking display under such conditions.

Drainage. Your site must be free of standing water. The existing soil, whatever its present quality, should be capable of draining surplus water away. The first step is to make sure you have a site which is well above the water table and conducive to good drainage.

Many attractive potential sites are unsuitable because they are waterlogged, which leads to root rot and other problems. In many cases, drainage problems are caused by recent construction work, where the natural drainage was disturbed. It is vital to find a method of draining the site. All too often, the garden space in recently constructed properties proves to have been a convenient site for stashing debris including lumps of concrete, tin cans, lumber, and other construction rubbish. To add insult to injury, this sad heap is usually mixed with the most awful clay soil imaginable.

But the site can be improved. Surplus surface water can be directed away from the garden site with drainage pipes or with correct grading. The construction rubble can be hauled away or leveled in order to provide a base for the rock garden.

Disappointing sites. Alpines are not ground cover plants for difficult places. Many would-be rock gardeners have been permanently discouraged from further rock gardening because of bad advice, such as, "Nothing will grow there! Build an alpine garden in the problem corner." Of course, alpines will quickly die unless conditions are right for them. My advice is to avoid those heavily shaded or dry places that are filled with masses of tree roots. Avoid any wet and shady places, too. When faced with these problems, do not consider alpine plants as a solution, but seek alternative types of plants that are suited for these spots.

Many kinds of plants are naturally equipped to accept a site in full exposure to the elements, while others are able to adapt. On the other hand, places where the wind whips around buildings and along passages, and those drafty corners where cold, drying winds prevail, are particularly hard on alpine plants, especially during winter and the thawing and freezing spells of early spring.

Access. When planning your rock garden, take a good look at the access routes to the garden site. Can the soil, rock, and gravel required for the garden be conveniently trucked to the site? Such an important convenience is easily overlooked. On the morning of a delivery, it would be devastating to realize that a truckload of soil and rock has to be wheelbarrowed across the dining room carpet.

Types of Sites

The preceding pages have described settings where a rock garden would be successful and warned of sites that would present problems. It is not always possible to obtain an ideal site and sometimes we must compromise. The next few pages are intended to help you recognize topographic features of a property that hold promise as sites for alpine gardens. Once identified, such features can be exploited and used to advantage in a particular rock garden style. Some plants are more tolerant than others of conditions that are less than perfect, and their individual attributes are considered in the plant directory section toward the end of this book.

Gentle slopes. Without a doubt, gentle slopes are ideal. Slopes lend themselves to rock gardens and they reduce physical effort, for they require far less stone and imported topsoil. There is less danger of soil erosion in the first heavy rainstorm, since a gently sloping garden settles easily and will not slide. This helps your garden to look more natural in its setting.

The woodland's edge. An interesting rock garden can be made where the site is at the edge of a wooded area, and a lawn would be impractical. It would not require a lot of stone to convert this kind of site into a meadow with a meandering path that invites a stroll through the alpine flowers.

12

Paved or impermeable surfaces. If your garden is limited to paved surfaces, you can still have a rock garden. Subject to the layout of the property, drainage, and convenience of access, it is possible to build a small rock garden right on the pavement (see page 00). I have seen several delightful gardens built on solid bedrock where the surplus water drains away.

Often, exposed solid rock is mounded in a gently convex shape. If so, it does not present a drainage problem, so go ahead and place your garden rocks right on the bare solid rock, making sure they are stable. Fit the new stones as close to the solid rock as you can, leaving the smallest possible crevices between the base rock and the stones, and also among the stones. Large crevices ruin the natural appearance. Smaller crevices are ideal homes for many alpine plants such as sedums and sempervivums.

Problems will occur if you place soil in depressions from which water cannot escape. This will produce stagnant soil, which is certain death to many plants. Where improving the drainage is not possible, rethink your plan and see if the low spots can be exploited to your advantage. Rearrange the rocks and leave the low spots as natural pools. When they dry up in summer, that's perfectly natural. Alpine meadows are home to lots of vernal pools.

Where the area is composed of stone or concrete paving, it is always possible to remove some of the pavers at intervals and plant in the spaces. This is a very effective way of enjoying alpines. Alpines can thrive in limited amounts of soil. If improved, even the gravel base under the pavers is acceptable to some plants, particularly to bright, colorful, fragrant thymes. The main thing is, be sure the desired alpine garden will not be sitting on solid, impervious clay, or nothing will survive. Remove six to eight inches of clay and replace it with rock garden soil (see page 65).

The removal of certain pavers is both an effective and a relatively simple way of creating an alpine garden. However, remember that you will want chairs and tables, and there will also be lots of foot traffic, so plan accordingly.

Another way to have an alpine garden on a solid surface is to use containers (see Chapter 6). Fascinating displays can be created by using pots of plants, trough gardens, and planted rocks. One advantage of this choice is that nothing is permanent and any mistakes can easily be corrected as you become more experienced.

Areas next to a wall or building. Almost every gardener has at some time or other developed gardens around the foundations of

buildings and walls. Small rock plantings are ideal for such locations. The plants and flowers will be conveniently close to the dwelling, and can be enjoyed.

Traditional shrubby foundation plantings become a problem after a few years because the shrubs grow and obscure windows, cutting off light and making maintenance around the house difficult. How often have you witnessed two sentinel conifers planted on each side of a doorway or entrance? Over the years, they grow to such a degree that they block access.

Moreover, there is always one specimen that grows too fast and takes over, sometimes killing or crowding the other plants.

This does not happen if the borders are planted with well behaved rock garden plants. There are dwarf forms of many of the plants normally used in these situations: pines, cedars, and spruces, as well as dwarf broad-leaved evergreens such as rhododendrons.

But even among these dwarfs, some are capable of outgrowing their space. To prevent this, first determine the ultimate height and spread that you will allow a plant in your site to attain in a particular time limit, say ten years. Second, study books and catalogs for varieties whose growth is within the height and spread limits you have set. Finally, check with the supplier to be sure that the size is appropriate.

When it is obvious that a plant is going to outgrow its allotted space, the sooner it is dug up and replaced the easier it will be for all, including the plant.

Steep banks. It can be a difficult task to build a rock garden on a steep bank. Lots of stone is needed because most of the bank has to be retained with a wall-like structure. The stonework has to be solid and stable, with the stones fitting tightly together, one upon the other. Otherwise it could all collapse because of the pressure exerted by the soil.

There is the additional challenge of trying to make the rockwork look natural. Frequently the finished bank will look artificial because it lacks continuous flow or rhythm. If the steep bank is already stable, you should place large stones at strategic intervals up and down the site. Make every effort to be certain that every rock is settled well into the bank, with no possibility of it slipping. To make a convincing picture, rather than scatter them singly, group rocks in threes and fives. The bolder the stonework, the less the danger of the garden looking like a bank on which someone has scattered a few stones.

To Begin

Study the area where you plan to make the new garden, looking for existing features that lend themselves to rock garden design. Uneven contours or slightly rolling ground can be incorporated into the plan. Sloping banks are, generally, excellent rock garden sites. Check any rock peeping through the soil surface, for it may have great potential. A rock that barely shows may be part of an underlying natural outcrop of rock, or even a series of rock ledges. Who knows what may await the explorer! Occasionally the gardener is presented with a gift that becomes the foundation for a handsome piece of rock work.

Start your investigation in a relaxed way by scraping the soil away from the exposed rock with a trowel or small implement. If all is well and more rock is uncovered, then allow yourself to become more excited and run for the shovel. You may want to start some serious excavating. Don't get overly hopeful, for it could be only a stray lump of rock dumped there during the building process.

Before expending any more energy, it might be worth testing the exposed rock with a metal rod, much as rescuers do when searching for avalanche victims. In this case the rod can be driven with a heavy hammer. Take care that you do not drive the rod in so tightly that you cannot remove it; keep it loose. Once the area has been probed and you have an accurate idea of the depth and extent of the underlying rock, you can assess the effect it will have on your design.

If you clear the soil away from the rock, you will have to decide where to place the excavated soil. You can use it on the site, or perhaps you'll prefer to remove it from the site. Do not be too quick to get rid of decent soil, for you may need to use it later, as the project develops.

From ditch to ravine garden. Look around for any features, natural or manmade, that might be incorporated or expanded into a possible design. Any help we get from the existing terrain can make a world of difference in an otherwise featureless landscape.

For instance, there is nothing particularly appealing about an old, discarded ditch, but it provides a design opportunity. If you are sure that it no longer carries water and will not flood when it rains, you can consider developing it into a handsome ravine garden. It can be large or small. Much depends on what the ditch is like to start with and what space you have available for its development. There is always the option of just filling it in and forgetting about it, but you can make it into a ravine garden by widening the ditch and making the sides slope gently outward. Using the excavated soil, emphasize the newly improved contours.

Aubrieta, alyssum, and daphe are featured in this raised portion of Al and Shirley Smith's garden in Victoria, B.C.

Where rock is available it would be fun to make the ditch into a miniature gorge, since the major excavating work has already been done. Depending on the supply of stone and the skill and strength of the builder, the sides of the gorge can be built up like retaining walls. For stability, they should slope backward at an angle. Vertical walls may not have the strength to stand up by themselves. Once completed, the ravine or gorge will give you a gardening environment with several microclimates. The lower parts will be cool, great for primulas, hepaticas, and ferns.

A sunken garden. You might not think of making a sunken garden, but where features are scarce and the terrain is boring, it can be just the thing. To visualize it, imagine a square ornamental pond about twelve feet wide and two or three feet deep, but with no water in it. Then imagine setting it into a plain section of lawn.

Next it would need four stone retaining walls all around the inside of the "pool." These walls provide four different aspects for plants that enjoy growing in a sunny wall, and also space for those that require a north facing wall. Be sure to add two broad steps on one side and a matching set on the opposite side. Then you can enter at one end and leave by the other without having to spoil the stroll by retracing your steps.

The floor of the sunken garden could be of loose gravel or random paving. Needless to say, perfect drainage is vital. Once the garden is constructed, all that is needed for the finishing touch would be one or two trough gardens or planted containers, and some comfortable seating. I am not suggesting that everyone go out and build sunken gardens, but if your garden site needs a special feature, then digging a sunken garden can be just what is required. Who knows, it may already be half formed on the site, just needing completion and formalization.

Develop an old stream bed. Old stream beds are pretty rare finds, particularly on today's smaller properties, but if you are lucky enough to have one, you can develop it. A stream will have gentler banks than a manmade ditch, so right from the start a lot of the work is done. It should not take much work to retain the banks, so some of the rocks can be used in other ways. The fact that the stream no longer carries water is not a problem because the very shaping of the ground suggests its presence, and of course clever use of plants will only add to the illusion.

If you like, the banks of the stream bed can be regraded to a more gentle slope and the actual stream bed can be transformed into a path. Any rocks that are no longer required to hold the stream banks in place can be used to build several small outcroppings for rock plants.

Flat Sites

Where you find no existing physical features to be exploited, nothing but an empty, flat area, look upon this as a clean canvas ready to receive whatever design you wish to create. A small rock garden full of colorful little plants will add a great deal of appeal to such a spot.

In many sites, flat areas are the only choice for the gardener. There is nothing wrong with flat areas. They are likely to be small lawns, paved areas, or tiny private gardens, often fenced for privacy. Many properties come complete with a built-in, raised planter, so if you have one, consider it an advantage in your garden planning. Planters of this type are discussed in Chapter 4.

Let us examine small lawns. Typically they are of little ornamental value, are a pain in the neck to mow, and are too small to serve as a sitting area. Provided that the site meets the requirements for healthy plant growth, a small lawn can make an excellent space for an outcropping rock garden. If rocks do not appeal to you, it can easily be planted as an alpine lawn, with a mixture of rock plants running together to form an irregular carpet.

Dividers. The area between a lawn and a hard-surfaced patio is another potential site. A rock garden built as a divider between the lawn and the paved surface provides something to enjoy from the comfort of the patio.

Where conditions allow, a rock garden set against a background of evergreens creates a lovely feature in a secluded, private space. When selecting the hedge plants, keep in mind their ultimate size and spread. There is no reason why there cannot be two rock gardens, one on each side of the hedge. One garden will derive some shade and protection from the hedge while the other benefits from full sun.

In many urban areas, the driveways, parking areas, and footpaths are permanent, so there is little that can be done to soften their appearance or relocate them. The garden site is defined by them.

I visited such a garden in England recently, and was delighted with the way the hard surfaces had been modified. A very low edging was installed along the path that leads from the street to the front door, and a bed of alpine soil mixture was installed the length of the walk, slightly wider than the path. Instead of emphasizing the width of the path, the bed made it appear narrower. Once planted with a few dwarf shrubs and alpine plants the picture was complete.

Driveways dominate the scene and there is not much that can be done about it, so as a guest you would not expect to find yourself parking behind an alpine garden. But what a delight it was, visiting this garden, to behold a slice of alpine landscape in a raised planter near the car's door. It took only a few pieces of carefully placed stone, a couple of prostrate shrubs, an upright juniper, and a few rock plants—nothing too demanding—and there it was. On the walk to the house door, there was a similar planter between the house and the walkway—what a lovely welcome home.

Designing a Small Rock Garden

Many of us who have built a successful rock garden would find it practically impossible to draw a workable plan of it on paper. Sketches may show some of the artistic detail or explain the thoughts

This gardener has made the parking area more interesting with raised beds which are high enough to be seen from the driver's seat.

and ideas, but will not show all the details of the overall plan. There are certainly sketches and diagrams available that illustrate how to build with rock, and how to place each stone. However, because of the unlimited variations of garden sites and stones, every gardener has to be his or her own landscape architect, to some extent.

Before embarking on your detailed plans, be sure of the objective. The aim is to construct an attractive rock garden that will be an ideal setting for colorful alpine flowers. In so doing, we must provide plenty of planting space for the plants. A beautifully fashioned mountain landscape is not of much use if there is no room for plants. But the factors must be in balance. I remember Will Ingwersen* saying, during my apprenticeship, "Rockwork should be a complete picture in itself. Do not rely on the plants to cover poor design."

Avoid the temptation to produce a whole mountainside or duplicate the Matterhorn in your garden. You may smile, but this was the vogue in the early days of rock gardening. Back in the 1800's, whole mountains were built of imported stone, some of such scale that they required years of work to complete. White marble was used to represent snow, and gray limestone and quartz were used for the ice and glaciers.

Instead, concentrate on one small portion of a natural vista. Recreate or suggest a section of alpine meadow, a cliff, a tiny ravine, or part of a mountain stream. A bold outcrop of weathered rock is a popular theme, and one that is not difficult to make or to adapt to many situations or locations.

It might seem from reading these introductory pages that rock and alpine gardens are for owners of large properties, or those who are interested in building model mountains—people with time on their hands and boundless energy, plus a generous budget for hauling soil and rocks.

This is not so, for the tiniest garden can have all the advantages of the larger one and none of the disadvantages. The initial expense is considerably less. Maintenance, weeding, and watering take less effort, and there is time for extra little touches, such as removing dead flowers and general finicky trimming and pruning.

*Will Ingwersen was the longtime managing director of Birch Farm Hardy Plant Nursery in Sussex, England. Recognized as one of Britain's leading horticulturists, he held the Victoria Medal of Honour, the highest horticultural award in Britain. He was well known as a plant collector, nurseryman, and rock garden builder. I worked for him as a journeyman, learning alpine nursery work and rock garden construction.

Habitats. A miniature landscape can be fashioned to provide special habitats for plants that have particular preferences or are seen at their best growing in vertical crevices. Plants such as the *Ramonda* and *Haberlea*, the marvelous and tricky *Lewisia tweedii*, and the glorious rosettes of silver saxifrages all thrive with their crowns in the vertical position so no water can linger among the leaves and cause decay. Moreover, crevices can be fashioned to face different points of the compass, and gain more or less direct sunshine.

Effects can be created simply by planting one or two dwarf trees at the base of outcropping rocks. Suddenly the rocks seem to be towering cliffs with forest trees at their base. Take care not to ruin the effect by planting something nearby that will grow too lush. These same small cliffs can be clothed in plants that love to tumble down over rocks.

The placing of a few smaller stones to form a special little setting within the rock garden can accommodate tiny little species that seek the protection of nooks and crannies. Other varieties thrive in a crevice created by setting two flat stones side by side on the soil; the roots will be in the cool soil beneath while the tops enjoy the warmth of the stone.

Water features. A rocky torrent cascading down the mountain-side is magnificent. But it is not necessary to have water in the rock garden, lovely as it is. It is a lot of extra work and expense, and it requires installation by a professional. Don't allow the water feature to become the focus of the rock garden, as often happens.

A few fortunate gardeners do have running streams on their property, in which case they have very little problem. Perhaps there is a pool in the garden which can be readily converted into an alpine lake at the foot of a mountain peak, complete with a reflection.

There are infinite possibilities for the use of water in the rock garden, from large waterfalls cascading into pools to musical little falls trickling into a succession of tiny pools.

Japanese Styles

An alternative to having a water feature is to create a Japanese style dry stream bed and waterfall. In it, you use dry sand and gravel to suggest the presence of water. Such a design, planted with care using plants normally associated with water, works quite well, for the imagination will do the rest and complete the picture.

21

⇝≫ Creating and Planting Alpine Gardens

I have found books on Japanese garden styles to be extremely helpful when studying the use of round stones. They explain the principles of balance, contrasts, and a pleasing restfulness for their stone arrangements. If you are committed to the alpine theme, be careful not to be sidetracked by these ideas or your planned alpine garden will easily become a Japanese garden. However, if the Oriental theme fits your garden setting, then use it. It is still possible to grow alpine plants in such a scheme.

It is wise to avoid setting pointed rocks on end, like spires. Oriental landscape artists can carry it off, but in a small rock garden it looks too contrived. A stone usually settles on its broadest surface and heaviest side.

This huge, lichen-covered rock casts a serene mood over the garden.

2. The Nature of Rocks

A classic alpine garden style is to replicate natural outcroppings of rock, and planning to do this is a good place to begin. Outcropping rocks are dramatic and can be adapted to almost any angle or grade. Once a few basic rules are grasped, you can let your imagination have free rein, creating crevices, cliffs, and snug little corners in which to tuck choice plants.

Outcrops and strata. Natural outcroppings of rock, like icebergs floating in water, show only a fraction of the mass beneath the surface. Despite their weathered, crumbly appearance, they are solid and we must always strive to portray this in our gardens.

Often a rock formation shows definite strata like the grain in a piece of wood. We must be aware of this as we place the stones, for we want to ensure uniformity and continuity. Any severe deviation from an established line will throw the whole picture out of focus. The soil cover is part of the makeup of a natural rock formation and must be duplicated in the rock garden.

We must make our rocky outcrop emerge from the earth and at some point return to it. Beyond this, our objective is to form a series of gently rising terraces with bays and pockets to accommodate our alpine plants.

Designing with rocks. The rock itself plays an important part in the planning of a rock garden. The composition and appearance of the stone will dictate to some extent what type of garden can be built. It would be very simple to say you must use this or that kind of stone for your layout, but transportation charges would make the cost prohibitive for even the smallest rock garden. Use whatever stone is handy and purchase it as close to home as you can.

Professional builders of large rock gardens abide by the cardinal rule, 'use local stone.' The reason for this is that a magnificent structure of exquisitely placed limestone would be incongruous in granite boulder country. So would a sedimentary sandstone rock garden where limestone abounds. However, where you have a choice, remember that a porous stone such as sandstone or limestone absorbs moisture and slowly releases it to the plants, making it a kinder environment for plant roots. Where large projects are involved, local rock is often less expensive than rock that has to be transported from any distance. Nevertheless, the color and type of rock, its cost, and whether it is local or otherwise, are not overwhelmingly important factors for the relatively small projects we are considering, so take advantage of any attractive stone that comes along.

If you search for stone yourself, good places to look are undisturbed corners of abandoned quarries, as well as old country roads and neglected fields. It is wise to check ownership before actually removing stones. Look for rocks that have the look of age: mellow colors, cracks, fissures, mosses and lichens. Glaring white and light colors and the sharp, cold surfaces of quarried stone are hard to work with. Also, avoid pure white quartz and glassy crystal and other similar colorful items where possible, as they are hard to work into an alpine landscape.

It is a good idea not to mix different types of stone in one garden. In the gigantic scale, nature normally works beautifully with mixed rocks, but in the garden it just does not look right. If you have two varieties of rocks on hand, build two separate rock gardens.

When you choose each piece of stone, keep in mind that it has to pay for its space. The more rock surface you get, the better. Oblong pieces are good because they have a solid base that stabilizes nicely in the soil. Select pieces that are shaped in a way that makes it easy for you to connect them to other stones. One good face, or side, is enough because the remainder will be covered with soil.

Esthetic Use of Rock

Ever since the first rock gardening books were published, authors have cautioned us about the use of white stones. I suspect that they were referring to glaring white quartz or marble, but any shiny white stone incurred their displeasure. Their aversion probably originated from the reaction against Victorian garden grottoes and ferneries, where such things as pieces of broken statuary were welcome. These were the early days of the natural style of gardening advocated by Gertrude Jekyll (1843-1932) and William Robinson (1838-1935).

It is easy to understand what they objected to when they compared such gardens to the mountains, where acres of white rocks of various types can be seen. Nature creates landscapes on a vast scale, and a detail like the color of a rock is inconsequential. On a sunny day in the mountains there is considerable glare from light colored rocks. But it is not disagreeable because the glare is softened by the green from surrounding trees, shrubs, and ground-hugging plants. It is an attractive picture that would not be possible in the small lowland garden. Rock color is a matter to consider and not necessarily one to condemn in the small rock garden. I am certain there are artistic gardeners who create excellent rock gardens of white rocks, yet it is a challenge.

Many interestingly colored rocks and stones can be found among the suppliers who cater to interior decorators. There are a few choice stones supplied for fireplaces and various other applications in room decoration. The rock gardener would need to acquire them before they are cut and polished. They are beautiful and very tempting, and by all means pick one if it appeals so you. Find out whether it can withstand freezing and winter wetness.

Expertly placed rocks and plants at the Jardin Botanique du Montreal

Primary Types of Rock for Gardens

There is no one particular type of stone that is correct for rock garden building, but some rocks are more desirable that others.

Limestone. Consider using limestone, because many plants thrive when growing near this type of rock. If it has weathered surfaces rich with lichens and is water worn, so much the better. The soft, silvery-gray color will be very appealing. Limestone rock is usually quarried, which causes the pieces to be sharply angular and the surfaces severe and raw. If the color and consistency of a particular stone is appealing, and the supplier is local, then it is worth spending some time sorting through a pile. Select the ideal individual stones for the particular garden plan you have in mind.

Pick up any European book on rock gardening and you will find pictures of beautiful rock gardens constructed with a glorious soft gray rock so artistically fissured it is almost unbelievable. The picture will most likely be a garden made with water-worn Westmorland limestone. Reginald Farrer wrote of this stone that it "fits block-like together as sections of a jigsaw puzzle."

When searching for limestone, look for a pleasing soft gray color. The rocks should be hard enough to endure the rigors of winter, yet soft enough to show some degree of weathering, as displayed in the rounding of sharp edges and some eroding of the strata. It is this erosion that gives the stone strong character, a result of the contrast of light and shade.

There are similar limestones in North America. They are not always conveniently located, but if your project warrants it, it is worth the time and effort it takes to track them down.

Tufa. Tufa is very popular with the specialist alpine plant growers, for they have found that many of the difficult-to-grow alpine plants thrive in it. Roots inserted into holes drilled directly in the rock establish themselves in the porous rock and are perfectly happy. Some species are content to grow directly on the surface, making their own root penetration. There are many helpful and rewarding uses for tufa in the small garden, as we shall see. Strictly speaking, tufa is not a true rock although it certainly looks like rock. Consider selecting some tufa, for it is an excellent choice for rock gardening, particularly for the very small garden.

It is formed by the petrifying action of water containing large amounts of lime. The evaporation of the lime-rich water leaves behind deposits of magnesium and calcium carbonate on mosses, leaves, twigs, and other organic matter.

This 18-inch tufa rock makes an excellent home for sempervivums.

It forms a relatively light, porous, moisture-retentive but free-draining material, providing an ideal condition for roots. These very qualities make it attractive to mosses; a small amount of moss is natural and looks fine, but in shade and moisture it will soon become a nuisance. Recently quarried tufa has a soft surface but soon hardens with exposure to the air.

It is principally gray colored, and ranges from light to very dark gray. There is also a pleasant golden colored variety. Tufa is available in several grades. The very hard grade, good for building rock gardens, is durable and tough. The softer grades are the best to use for direct planting, as long as they are tough enough to overwinter without flaking and deteriorating. Whenever possible, deal with a reputable supplier and explain what you intend to do with the tufa so he can provide the most appropriate type.

Tufa may be expensive because of transportation costs, but for the special small garden where quantities will be smaller, it is a wise and economical choice.

Sandstone. Sandstone is a good choice for rock gardens, and it is one of my favorite rocks. I find it easy to work with. It is quarried and usually sold as blocks and slabs. Every effort should be made to visit the quarry and meet with the supplier and explain to him what you wish to build. Once he understands he will be in a better position to provide the shape and size of stone best suited to your job. Otherwise you could end up with irregularly shaped pieces that are impossible to join to make nice, tight crevices. Or you might have a selection of pieces too small to be of use.

Many people imagine a good rock garden stone as angular, jagged, and pointy; they are not aware that we have to fit them together to form a convincingly natural look.

Sandstone is a mellow looking stone ranging in color from reddish brown through russet and light browns to gray. The term sandstone encompasses a wide range of sedimentary rocks, from very soft ones to durable ones used for buildings and bridges. The famous York paving stones, featured in the great British gardens, are a type of sandstone. The Romans faced Hadrian's Wall with Northumberland sandstone, an indication of its durability.

The rock garden value of some sandstone lies in the strong and prominent strata lines, evidence of its creation from deposits of sediment. These horizontal layers are a valuable guide to follow as you build from one outcrop to the next. The angle and flow of these lines has to be consistent.

Sandstone does not have the striking appearance of some of the choicer limestones with their fretted and water-worn surfaces, but it is easy to work with and makes a very pleasing rock garden.

Freshly quarried, it tends to be soft and raw looking, but left to weather it quickly hardens. Some sandstones are inclined to break down and split when exposed to heavy rains and severe freezing. Moisture enters the stone through the stratification and expands due to the action of frost. In order to prevent this, obtain a high quality rock that is not too soft. When laying the stones in the garden, keep the strata lines horizontal so that rain cannot easily penetrate them.

Granite. Granite is undoubtedly the most readily obtainable stone, and in some regions is the only choice for a would-be rock gardener. If selected carefully, it can be one of the nicest to work with. It will blend with the most varied local conditions, and is acceptable to the plants. It usually lacks any pronounced strata. The biggest drawback is that granite is often supplied from quarries where it is blasted. Some people deem it a cold and inhospitable rock, unsuited for gardens.

Blasted rocks have irregular shapes with sharp angles and many facets. They are popular with masons who build stone walls and rock facings, using mortar to hold the rocks in place. They prefer this type of stone, for its many different shapes make for an appealing wall. The rock gardener, on the other hand, needs rocks that have at least one flat surface to serve as a base for the rock to settle solidly into the soil. In addition to a solid base, a rock garden stone needs at least one decent face; this face will be the one that is prominently exposed once the rock is set in place in the garden.

Irregular, sharply angular granite rocks are extremely difficult to fit together, but, in spite of this, many delightful gardens have been built with them. I have made several gardens using them. Because it is the underlying rock formation of Victoria, British Columbia, where I live, it is readily available locally.

Granite rocks are not quite as demanding in their placement as those with pronounced strata. Even the hardest granite will show some suggestion of character. Look for little cracks, fractures, or bands of slightly different color or texture. These will indicate to you the position in which a particular piece should be placed. Try to place these rocks with the cracks and lines in a horizontal direction, parallel with the ground. Nature can get away with anything, even vertical strata, but in the rock garden irregular strata lines only grate on the senses because they are too strong for the scene.

Featherock, a volcanic product, is lightweight but has sharp edges.

Other Suitable Rocks and Rock Substitutes

Limestone, granite, and tufa are the most popular materials, but they are not the only ones that can be used. There are several other types of rock that work admirably. Rocks and stones are like any other specialized field—they have a jumble of names. Like many of our favorite plants, stones have synonyms and colloquial names that add to the confusion.

The terms **travertine** and **tufa** are often confused. It is difficult to find references to the use of travertine in rock gardens, and when one is found it generally turns out to be tufa.

They are both crystalline limestone deposited in solution from ground and surface water. Tufa is often referred to as travertine and vice versa. Travertine is sometimes called calcareous tufa, and is much harder than tufa. It resembles marble, a close relative. I have used it on occasion to build indoor landscapes where relatively small quantities are required (it is quite expensive). Historically, travertine has been cut and used as a building stone and for other decorative purposes. Rustic looking fireplaces are often made of travertine. Brightly colored floor and wall tiles with a highly polished surface are another use.

Featherock and **pumice** are both volcanic products and are popular in all kinds of landscape situations, both indoors and out. Featherock is quarried and is available in a range of sizes. Very large

29

pieces can be specially ordered, but price and selection are considerations. It has become the favorite medium for several types of garden embellishments, including carved fountains, prepared waterfalls, and sculptured pieces. It is a convenient option for indoor gardens and lobbies.

Featherock. A lightweight quarried product, featherock is durable and weather resistant. It is available at many stone supply companies, where it may be viewed in tumbled mounds. It usually is sold as large, rounded lumps. Of course there is a full range of sizes from monsters to pieces the size of a loaf of bread. The color ranges from silvery gray to darker gray and charcoal, nearly black. Personally, I prefer the lighter colors, but have seen very nice rock gardens built with darker shades.

Like any natural product, featherock varies in texture. Some pieces have a coarse, pitted surface while others have a finer-grained appearance. Some pieces show prominent, darker colored strata lines running through the lumps, which can be very attractive in a garden. The choice of stones is very personal. As the texture and consistency are variable, it is worthwhile to discuss your plans with your supplier. Be sure to look over the stones carefully before you purchase them.

Most stockpiles of featherock I have seen provide stones with flat bases and flattened tops, which are the features needed for rock gardens. Individual stones are usually rounded on the sides. It is not the most hospitable rock due to the harsh, abrasive, glasslike texture of the surface. Good, strong gloves and goggles for eye protection are a must for handling it. It can be deceptive—only when you find a rash of minute cuts on your hand do you realize how sharp it is. A stray fragment in the eye does not bear contemplation.

Despite these drawbacks, featherock is the logical material to select for making a choice, small alpine garden in a prominent location. It is not unduly heavy, it is attractive, and it is available, but, I have to say, at a high cost.

Pumice. Pumice is a wonderful thing, but I am not sure it is practical. I have seen some lovely rock gardens made with it. Boyd Kline, one of the original proprietors of the Siskiyou Rare Plant Nursery, still maintains the original pumice garden which he built many years ago. Pumice is extremely lightweight and porous, and has a wide range of colors. It is very easy to handle pumice and drill holes in it for plantings. I have a dozen young seedlings of *Kelseya* *uniflora* growing in a football-sized piece; they have survived their second season. Invasion by moss must be expected. I do not know what the supply of landscape-sized pieces of pumice is, but collecting it from the desert is no longer acceptable!

Concrete. I would like to describe one other material for rock garden construction. Are you ready? It is concrete! Reginald A. Malby* was a leading horticultural photographer and a great rock gardener living in the London area. When faced with the task of obtaining suitable stone, he fabricated it, as he described in the following passage from his book:

"The difficulty in obtaining real stone led me to cast round for an efficient substitute, and I must say, after considerable experience I find that roughly broken blocks of cement concrete—such as are sometimes obtainable when the foundations of the London roads are being removed—are really very useful. In appearance it is suggestive of conglomerate—its light colour when dry being its chief disadvantage. I got over this, however, in a manner which I will explain later."

"I am quite aware of the advice so frequently given that on no account should anything but real stone be used, but I believe I can show that it is not a necessity with the vast number of Alpines, if not indeed with all of them."

I was fortunate enough to see Reginald Malby's garden in the early 1950's, while it was still maintained, and I was not aware that the rock was actually concrete until told. Depending on the size of the aggregates (the sands and gravels added to the concrete), the finished concrete can resemble a rock known as conglomerate. While not the most attractive of rocks, it is, at least, rock. The use of concrete lumps in the small rock garden may not be necessary since costs for small amounts of rock should not be prohibitive. On the other hand, if used properly it will be very effective.

Looking back, I wonder if such thick, large lumps of old concrete are available today. Sidewalks are only four inches thick these days. As I study the black and white photographs in Malby's book, I recall how truly effective the rock work in the garden was. Even taking into consideration that I was seeing it after it had had some forty years to mature, his rock garden was an amazing achievement.

Some of the lumps were enormous, large enough to require more than one man to move them around. The garden was not large, and it was surrounded by a high brick wall. The whole garden impressed

**The Story of My Rock Garden,* by Reginald A. Malby. Headley Brothers, London. 1912.

me with the masterly fashion in which the rocks were fitted together to form bold outcrops. The paths and steps were often set between small cliffs that were draped with sprawling plants. There was a steep-sided pool, and rockwork with mounds and bays. As you entered the rock garden from the house, it took a while to register the fact that you were constantly climbing uphill.

Do you wonder how he colored the concrete? He later wrote in his book, "I obtained the salt, Ferri-Perchloride [iron perchloride], and when four ounces of this is dissolved in approximately a gallon of water, and applied to the concrete lumps by the aid of a small brush or mop, the result is a rich, yellowish brown colour most acceptable in contrast to the varying greens of the foliage." Today you can find products for coloring concrete at building supply stores.

History teaches us other practices in which effective 'rocks' can be made from concrete. An early technique known as Pulhamite was pioneered by James Pulham, Sr., who lived from about 1788 to 1838. When faced with landscape contracts requiring significant rocks where none existed, he devised a system for manufacturing them on site. The Pulham family had considerable experience and familiarity with recently perfected Portland cement. And James Pulman, Sr., had the skills necessary to fabricate wonderful, huge artificial rocks by coating cement onto a shaped framework of old bricks and other discarded masonry.* The secret of his success lay in the skill with which the cement was hand-tooled. It was pure artistry that could convince the beholder it was real stone. Colors were supplied to match any natural rock.

There are photographs of some of their work. Mr. Graham Stewart Thomas OBE VMH DHM VMM, in his great book* on the history of the rock garden, provides two illustrations of Pulham's work built between 1868 and 1876 at Battersea Park, London. One is from an old engraving showing a grouping of massive rocks, and the second is a more recent photograph showing the rockwork as it is today.

Gunnite or Gunite. There is a specially formulated liquid concrete called gunnite, originally developed primarily for lining the inside of swimming pools. It is often sprayed onto unstable slopes for erosion control and regularly used in zoos and aquariums to create natural looking animal habitats with rocks, pools, and waterfalls.

Gunnite hardens when dry. Under pressure, it is sprayed onto a rigid framework of metal covered with wire netting shaped to

*The Rock Garden and Its Plants, Graham Stewart Thomas, 1989, published by Sagapress, Inc. in association with Timber Press.

Gunnite was used to create the rocklike structures around the pool.

resemble rocks. As it dries, it is hand-tooled and painted with whatever finish is required. Skilled craftsmen produce very realistic rock finishes.

The garden in the photo above shows a recently completed gunnite rock garden designed to take advantage of a redundant swimming pool. The 'rocks' were formed by bending and welding metal rods and metal pipe into the shape of rocks. The metal was covered with fine wire netting and coated with liquid concrete, which was sprayed on in several applications. The artificial rocks were set around the sides of the pool in a continuous sequence, completely hiding the square outlines of the pool. Special pockets for soil and planting were formed to accommodate foundation plantings of shrubs and vines that quickly blended the new work with the existing landscape. Gunnite rock gardens require experts in the field and are expensive, but provide a solution where conventional gardening is not possible.

Boulders

Boulders, regardless of their geological makeup, seldom lend themselves to the stratified outcrop design. They are usually found on rugged slopes tumbled together in large groups. In the garden they are ideally suited to a similar design.

When forced to use boulders in the rock garden, restraint is the watchword. It is better to use a dozen or so carefully selected stones than a hundred at random. Search for boulders that show the effects of exposure to the weather: lichens, mosses, rough or cracked surfaces. Use them on a sloping bank, grouped together in varying sizes. Never grade them uniformly. Some soil can be filled in behind to give the appearance of half buried rocks on a mountainside. When replacing round stones that have been moved or collected from the wild, endeavor to set them much as they were, with the weathered surfaces showing. The raw, new looking planes should be buried where they will not conflict with the pattern you are creating.

33

Above the tree line, at high elevations, alpine flowers enliven a meadow after the snow pack has melted.

This wooded slope in Pennsylvania has potential for a shaded rock garden because of the boulders.

34

3. Building a Rock Garden

In the previous chapter we discussed different kinds of rocks and stones. It is hard to say exactly what is a stone and what is a rock. I usually refer to rock when speaking of natural masses. I call an alpine garden a rock garden, not a stone garden. I call rock "stone" when it is being used as a building material, but sometimes switch around for the sake of variety.

Until this point, I have dealt with rock gardens and rocks in general terms, without considering their size. Now it is time to become practical and think about the kind of stone you will use for your garden. It's wise to practice with small stones before designing and building with large ones. Be sure to note the safety tips below.

Stone for an alpine garden. What color, type, size, and weight of stone should you choose? It depends on a number of practical and esthetic factors. Will you do the work yourself, or have it done by a contractor? If you plan to do your own stonework, your strength limits the size of stone you should purchase. Rocks are surprisingly heavy. Be aware that some very large pieces may be hidden in the middle of a pallet of stone. Before you can design your garden, you'll need a way to decide on the size of the rocks to use. Local availability and cost are also important considerations.

The scope of your project is in the hands of the designer, whether you take that role yourself or depend on a professional. There are many approaches, but in all of them, the ideal alpine garden is designed to grow plants, and lots of them. You do not want to build a magnificent rocky edifice without space for your plants.

Attractive outcrops. When planning an alpine garden, it is important to consider how outcropping rocks occur in nature. Natural outcrops show exposed rock faces, comparable to random steps marching uphill. Attractive outcrops are those where the rocks slope back into the earth and are partly hidden from view.

Natural rock outcroppings show only a fraction of the mass of rock still hidden beneath the soil. For the most part, these are largely vertical faces that have emerged from the soil, set at an angle dictated by the tilt of the strata. As we place our stones in our outcrop, we must constantly carry this angle in mind. As the rock garden grows higher, each successive layer must follow the same strata angle and disappear into the earth.

If the garden site is being built on a natural slope or bank it will be easy for the bulk of the slope to give the impression that the strata lines are continued within, unseen. When working on a flat site, there is no slope to utilize. Increase the angle of the outcrop strata so that the rocks disappear back into the soil in a much shorter distance.

Alternatively, one may retain a modest incline and abruptly end the rock garden, and build an informal wall or a gentle slope of soil at the edge of the rock garden. Whether this slope is sunny or shady, it will provide an excellent home for plants that prefer to have their crowns at an angle, such as the lewisias, silver saxifrages, and many of the primulas.

A Word on Safety

As we begin to discuss the practical side of making a rock garden, even a small one, we must consider safety. Workers in the landscaping, masonry, and construction industries follow many safety regulations and procedures, including protective clothing. Time is spent on learning the safest way to lift and move heavy objects, since serious injury can occur. Back injuries are often caused by improperly handling heavy objects. If you hire a contractor or workers to assist you, make sure that they follow safety precautions. They should also have their own insurance, or be covered under your homeowner policy. It is wise to double check this point before proceeding.

Construction workers are required to wear hard hats, steel-toed boots, and heavy duty gloves. Safety goggles are required when large amounts of rock or stones are being loaded and unloaded. Dust masks are necessary when mixing cement and soil amendments. If you take on these tasks, you should use the same safety measures.

I realize that this may sound like overkill to gardeners about to create a small rock garden. Nonetheless, I suggest that you study one of the many manuals on back injury prevention. They explain how to lift heavy objects by using the strength in the legs rather than using the back alone. Do not rush into the work or let enthusiasm for the project tempt you to overwork. Pace yourself. Remember what happens to those who overdo snow shoveling at the first snowfall!

Wear practical clothing. Kneepads are helpful. While I do not suggest that you rush out and buy a pair of steel-toed boots for a small job, you should wear sturdy footwear, not sneakers, rubber boots or other lightweight gear. When working, it is easy to let a rock slip, and it can land on your toes or fingers.

Fingers! What can I say, other than that you must wear good quality work gloves. They will not prevent a falling stone from trapping a finger, but they are better than nothing, and they prevent many abrasions.

Safety goggles are a good idea. The greatest danger comes when rocks are being loaded or unloaded. Rock chips fly off when least expected. Landscaping materials give off dusts and particles when being worked, particularly during windy weather.

Dust masks are recommended when mixing cement or spreading peat moss, sand, and fertilizers, not that fertilizer will be a major factor in our projects. Wear appropriate gear, and make sure it is safe and comfortable enough to permit you to do the job.

Building a Small Alpine Garden

To provide a useful example, in this chapter I describe setting rocks into place to make a small alpine garden measuring ten feet by ten feet. I arrived at this figure by going out to my own rock garden with a tape measure and isolating an area within it, one that I felt was complete and well balanced. It contains a good number of plants and the rocks are in scale.

This size is somewhat arbitrary, but anything less seems too small to hold enough plants to make the project worthwhile. If you do not have this much space you can always use several troughs (Chapter 6) or a raised bed (Chapter 4). For a larger rock garden than this, you can use more or larger rocks, and more outcroppings, but the principles are the same.

The stones in this ten-by-ten area are, on average, nine inches thick and 12 to 18 inches long. The width varies from eight to six inches, but this is not so critical because most of it will be hidden and out of sight. Just make sure the stone is wide enough to stay in position once it is in place. A narrow base can become unstable because there is so little contact with the soil.

Measuring stone. To measure a piece of stone, one must mentally visualize it as a square or oblong, since it is difficult to measure an irregular shape. This may seem complicated but once you have examined and measured a few rocks you will be able to spot good building stones.

Our small rock garden design for the ten-by-ten foot area has two outcrops, one above the other. The lower outcrop contains 15 stones, including three that exceed 18 inches in length, and the upper outcrop has 12 stones. So one would probably have to purchase at least 36 pieces of stone in order to get a good choice of stones. There will be more on making outcrops on page 40.

Purchasing stone. Rock and stone are often sold by weight, usually by the ton. If you plan to ask your supplier for "rock garden stone" he will probably ask you how many tons. How can you say, since one stone can weigh anything! Furthermore, he may, in good faith, send you a load of shapeless stones which he sees as rockery stone. These shapeless stones defy even the efforts of experts to turn them into a rock garden. The best way, where it is possible, is to pay a visit to the supplier and look things over for yourself. Try to pick out your own rock.

Large rocks make the best looking gardens and are easier to use in handsome designs. I would prefer having a few large stones to having lots of small ones. Small pieces of stone, on the other hand, can be made to appear as if they were one, by joining them together cleverly. It requires patience, time, and fuss to get it to look right. Look at each piece for any graining in the rock, or find cracks or some other feature that you can use to suggest that a piece belongs with the others when joined. Align the stones tightly, side by side, with cracks or lines running horizontally (for continuity) as you fit them together.

Rock for gardens is often sold by the pallet. Look for varied yet rectangular shapes in the size range you can handle.

Practicing with Stone

Before starting work on your actual rock garden, it is wise to practice placing stones. This will help you become familiar with their characteristics and enable you to handle them adeptly.

It does not matter where you do your practice. I pick a spot that is convenient to the rock pile and where it is easy to move stone around. It can be the actual rock garden site or any paved area. It is easier to switch stones around by sliding them on a hard surface. Just be careful with your fingers—do not get them between a rock and a hard place! This exercise familiarizes you with the stone you have to work with, helping you decide how to use it to the best advantage.

Choose two or three stones and study them; observe their weight, appearance, shape, size, and texture. Then choose an average specimen from your supply of building stones. It is a great temptation to start with the best looking pieces. Avoid doing this to prevent setting a standard that is hard to maintain.

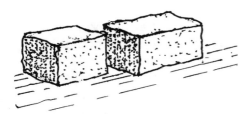

Place two stones together. Start your rock practice session with a nice oblong block. Set it on the ground with the side you have selected as the face toward you. Every piece has one particular side that appeals to the gardener as having the best features. Your choice of these features will define strata lines or provide a rugged quality.

Next select another stone. It may be a little thicker or thinner or larger or smaller; it does not matter. Now place it on the left of the first, arranged as if they were a unit.

What did you do? Did you put them end to end or side by side? By setting them end to end, then moving one stone back several inches, you gain two things. You are utilizing every inch of the face surface of each stone, and you begin to develop attractive features in your planting site. A valuable corner appears. Two different aspects are provided, plus a useful crevice.

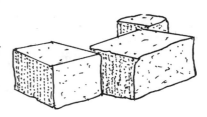

Then arrange the third stone to the right side of the first, end to end as before, but set back farther than the second stone. This adds variety. Now there are two corners, two more aspects, and two more crevices—not bad for a beginning! The stone supply is being used most economically, and each stone is used to the best advantage.

39

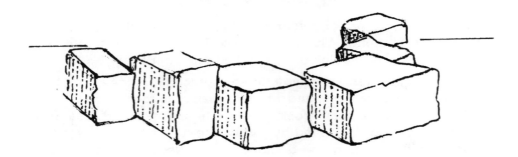

Place two more stones beside the second and third stones, and part of an outcrop begins to take shape. Experiment with several trial groups using easy-to-handle stones before attempting to build your garden with large ones. Vary the use of the long surface of each rock. Practice until you are familiar with the technique, because this is the way the whole garden will be built.

The rocks will begin to go together easily and effortlessly. With familiarity, ideas will come thick and fast. In all probability you will lay the stones perfectly level, as with steps. This is quite acceptable and may well suit the eventual design plan. However, tilting the stones slightly off the horizontal axis produces intriguing effects. Set the first stone, sometimes referred to as the keystone, several inches deeper into the soil at one end than at the other, thereby making it tilt. Set every successive stone parallel to the others, rigidly following the same angle. To be convincing, this angle need not be too great. Making it just a few degrees off horizontal is the most effective.

Building a Rocky Outcrop: First Steps

Select the keystone for the first outcrop, a good substantial rock, but not the biggest in the pile. Set the first permanent stone where you want the first outcrop to be. Start at the lowest part of the rock garden. It is likely that this is where a path or patio is located, and also the point from which the finished garden will be viewed. If the site is on a slope, however slight, always start at the bottom and work up the slope. If necessary, dig out a platform for the rock to sit on. By starting at the lowest part you will be digging into undisturbed soil, and so will have a solid base for the first stones.

Once the keystone is set into the ground, step back and study it. Is it at a slight angle, and does it face the direction from which the garden will be most viewed?

40

Then go ahead and add more stones, exactly as you did in the practice outcrop, but now take a little more time digging out a shallow bed for them to settle into. Adjust them to your satisfaction; step back to see the effect. If all looks well, continue to construct the outcrop, tipping each rock slightly backward so that any excess water automatically drains into the bulk of the rock garden.

This is very old advice based upon rock gardens built in rainy climates where rainwater can pour down the rock garden like a waterfall. No need to describe the damage this can cause! This applies equally well where irrigation is required; the water will drain back into the soil.

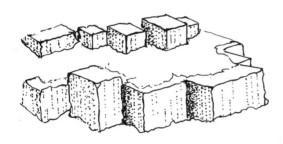

With the first outcrop well under way, envision your plan, since the shape or pattern the first outcrop has taken establishes a format that all subsequent work must follow. Just as the keystone dictates the shape of an individual outcrop, so the first outcrop sets a pattern for all others, whether you are making two outcrops as in our ten-by ten-foot design, or making more in a larger garden.

Before you get any farther, use stakes and string to protract or extend the lines of your keystone and first few rocks. This way, you can see in advance how the finished outcrop will look. It is easier to relocate stakes and strings than rocks and soil.

Recall the observations of outcrops in natural settings. There is invariably a certain regularity or uniformity to the exposed faces of the natural outcrops: they all face in one general direction. Imagine a hillside with layers of massive square blocks stacked several tiers high and covered with soil. Any rock that is visible has had the soil washed off. The exposed rocks are disintegrating because of the action of time and weather. The site has developed fissures, crevices, and slopes of loose, crumbled rock fragments.

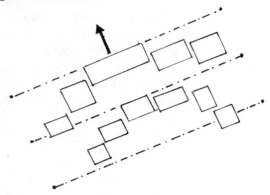

This bird's-eye-view of a rock garden layout shows the parallel lineup of the two outcrops (divided by the dotted lines). Additional outcrops would flow along the same lines.

Imagine our small stones to be these great rocks where only a tiny part of each one is visible. Our rocks must also give the impression that they are part of a solid mass below the surface. This can be achieved by ensuring that the bottom of each stone is completely buried in the soil and is invisible.

Building the garden by recreating a natural outcrop in too much detail is impractical and uses a lot of stone. Using so much rock occupies too much of the planting space. While maintaining the overall pattern of the rocky outcrops, just skip the occasional group of rocks. This is entirely in keeping with a rocky site, and the natural lines are retained.

Focus on building the lower outcrops before building any higher levels. As you select stones from the stockpile, vary the thickness to avoid uniformity. While outcrops are uniform to some extent, nature is not rigid, so a bit of variety is permissible. Relax a little and create interesting bays and irregularities in the faces of the outcrops.

When the arrangement of the stones meets your approval, it is time to fill the space behind the positioned stones with more prepared soil (see Chapter 5 on soil for alpines). Do this in several layers; carefully ram and pack soil into all the spaces and joints between the rocks. Pay particular attention to the base of each stone. It must be solid, with no inclination to wobble. Loose stones will lead to trouble later on, not to mention a twisted ankle. Practice has taught me to be methodical when packing soil, so be sure to pack soil firmly on all sides. A piece of two-by-four board is a convenient tool, and so is a pick handle. The smooth shaft of the handle makes it a comfortable tool to use, and its heavy end is great for pushing the soil under the stones.

Test the rocks for stability. Test the solidity of your structure by standing on the rock and gently trying to rock the stone. If it moves, repack the soil and tamp again. Try to get the ramming tool in at an angle of 35 degrees or so, for this guarantees that soil is being pushed and packed underneath the stone. When this operation is complete, add more soil to bring the level to the very top of the stones. Settle the soil by treading on it. Walk systematically back and forth over the whole outcrop, bringing your weight down hard on your heels for maximum pressure on the rocks. Pay particular attention to joints and corners.

There must be no cavities or air pockets, because after the planting is completed, roots can enter these voids, and plants happily growing may suddenly perish due to lack of contact with the soil. What's more, hollow spaces make excellent apartments for unpleasant tenants such as chipmunks, mice, and insects.

Once this back-filling and grading operation is completed, consider where you would like the higher outcrop or outcrops to be. Remember the outlines must follow the angles and be parallel with the earlier outcrops. Use stakes and string to do the layout.

Soil settlement. Before placing any stones in your planned alpine garden, determine whether the soil has been compacted enough to bear their weight. Any subsequent movement of stones will ruin your work. Settling can happen when 12 inches or more of soil has been added to the site. In such cases it is best to set in some foundation stones for the outcrop to rest upon. It is not necessary to use the best building stones for this job. Any rocky material will do, and the pieces will not be visible once the outcrop is completed. Use stones that are not good enough for the finished garden. Rounded stones, broken or angular pieces, or even lumps of broken concrete may be used. Place these foundations below the outcrops that will follow. Bury them just below the soil line where they will not be seen. To make a solid base, take the same care in firming these stones in place as the others. Spread a few inches of soil over them all to make a convenient bed for the main face stones of the visible outcrop that will be arranged on top of them.

In this cutaway view of a rock garden, the choice rocks have been placed with their faces showing. Other rocks are used for foundation or support (shown with dashes) and do not show. These can be chunks of concrete or broken or oddly shaped rocks.

43

Shaping the Alpine Garden

As each stone is set into position and your outcrops take shape, the rock garden construction site begins to resemble a wild mountain landscape, and all is going well. If your garden will be a large one with many outcrops, you can try a few variations for diversity. The informal nature of the weather-beaten outcrops can be enhanced by a slight change in the construction technique. Where stones of similar thickness were chosen, deliberately select some that are thinner. For instance, where a stone 24 inches thick would have been used, try using two thinner stones, each 12 inches thick, one on top of the other, so that they are roughly the height of the others, when combined. Set the top one a few inches back, just like building steps, packing a little soil between the stones as if making a sandwich. Later, an alpine plant will work its roots into this little crevice filled with soil.

If the stonework of a larger garden is beginning to look a bit repetitious now that several tiers of outcrops are in place, simply skip one of the outcrops entirely. In its place, allow the soil to flow in a graceful, fan-like slope between adjacent outcrops. This adds contours to the rock garden and suggests great cliffs with slopes of loose rock collected at their bases. It is not necessary to make your slide steep, since this would be difficult to plant and maintain. For an authentic touch, sink a few selected rocks randomly on the slope with just their tips peeping through the surface; they will make excellent stepping stones when planting time arrives.

By now, I hope that you see the beginning of a rock garden emerging from the pile of rocks and soil. During the construction you may have felt as if nothing made sense and your project would never be a rock garden. The rationale for setting the stones in place first, and then bringing the soil to the rocks, rather than trying to fit rocks into an existing soil pile, should now be apparent. Isolated rocks spread over a mound of soil can never have the convincing solidity of the same number of stones skillfully fitted together.

As the garden takes shape, a decision should be made about the ultimate height of the the rock garden. Since the first layers of the outcrop are in place, it is easier to visualize how additional height will look and how much higher you need to build. If the existing work is pleasing to the eye, additional height may not be required. Increased height, while it may provide a magnificent statement of artfully structured stone, will demand a greater supply of rock and soil. Before you continue building, make sure you know what you want to achieve.

The higher the rockwork is raised, the greater will be the tendency for the soil to dry out, which brings up an interesting point. If the garden is in an area that has too much rainfall, the extra height will afford more of the excellent drainage that many choice alpine plants require. Naturally, if the opposite is the case and rainfall is minimal, then dramatic rockwork must be forfeited in favor of good moisture management.

Rock gardens are not the only place to grow alpine plants. From here we go on to making raised beds. Additional options are described in the next few chapters.

Above, a dramatic trough with juniper and cotoneaster is well placed in the sunken garden of Beryl and Peter Bland, in Lancashire, England. Below, raised beds of New York fieldstone make a nice feature adjoining a parking area.

4. Building Raised Beds

A raised bed is a simple alternative to a rock garden, and much more straightforward to build. It makes a healthy and attractive setting for alpine plants, solving many site problems. Imagine a flowerbed created in the normal way. The soil in the bed is slightly higher than the surrounding soil level. If you encircle the whole bed with low walls built with rocks, and fill it with several more inches of prepared soil, you would have a basic type of raised bed. Not only do you have plants filling the bed, they can spill over the edges, draping downward and outward for more visual impact.

Why make raised beds? A raised bed allows you to have a rock garden in a site where a naturalistic slice of alpine scenery is completely out of place. Many houses today have limited garden space. The available site may be rigidly laid out with hard-surfaced paving. Often, there is an existing planter of some style, possibly attached to the main building.

While it is possible to build a small rock garden directly on a concrete surface, it still would not be in harmony with the property as

The author's raised bed houses his saxifrage collection, increasing his success with these challenging and exquisite plants. The metal pipes support shadecloth which protects the delicate flowers from excessive sun and heat, prolonging bloom time.

a whole. But in the same position, a neat, geometrical raised bed might be perfectly suitable. In addition, it is practical to use raised beds where good rock garden stone is not available or is outrageously expensive. Or perhaps you cannot tolerate rock gardens! It is reason enough.

Like containers, raised beds bring the planting level above any underlying problems such as terrible soil or poor drainage. They permit the building of gardens on impervious substrates such as concrete, paving, and solid rock. Raised beds allow a wide range of designs, including small, intimate plantings that combine with and unify townhouse garden spaces. Since the topsoil will be imported, total control over soil conditions can be maintained.

Besides, raised beds are faster to build than a complicated rock garden and offer a wider choice of planting schemes. It is expected that an alpine landscape would be planted with alpine plants, but a raised bed can safely be planted using a variety of plants. Above all, they are fun to research and develop.

A raised planting makes working with small plants much more comfortable, requiring less bending. The flowers are closer to eye level, making them easier to enjoy.

Planning a Raised Bed

A raised bed can be incorporated with the foundation planting of the house and any ancillary outbuildings. Garages, studios, cabanas, and the greenhouse are all potential sites for raised beds. The display produced by colorful plants can add an exciting new dimension to a dull corner.

Do not build directly against a building unless you are absolutely sure that no damage will be caused by banking a foot or so of soil against it. If there is any chance of damage, consult with a person qualified to advise on building construction. A safer choice would be to move the bed away from the building by a couple of feet or so. This means a fourth wall will be needed for a raised bed. However it will not demand the same attention to detail as the more visible walls. Chances are, when the project is complete the eye will flow right over the finished bed and not even be aware of the space between it and the building.

Approaches to doorways are great locations for raised beds. They might be placed on both sides of the path, or restricted to only one side. The vacant side could be a contrasting format, such as a simple flow of grass or a low planting of heather or pachysandra.

Parking areas often provide a spot that will accommodate a raised bed. The gardener will gain more planting space and a colorful feature that will enhance an otherwise uninteresting setting. However, vehicles may bump the bed and cause problems if the bed is too low to be easily seen from the car.

If no suitable spot can be found and you really would like a raised bed, go ahead and build one on the lawn! Take time to consider the lay of the land. Stake out your ideas with sticks and strings. Place the strings at the eventual height of the finished wall. Then the effects of the finished project can be studied before any work starts.

Perhaps a gracefully curving bed might be in keeping with the rest of the garden. Let the bed be large enough that its presence creates a meaningful impact, rather than appearing as an afterthought.

Making a preliminary layout will allow you to see any potential problems that a new addition may inflict on regular garden operations. Will it interrupt existing traffic patterns? Or create problems with the normal flow of lawn cutting? Are there any awkward corners to negotiate? What about the sprinkler system—will alterations be required to accommodate the addition?

Proportions: the height, width and length of a raised bed. I am not aware of any horticultural rules that govern the height of a raised bed, but a popular choice seems to be in the 18 to 24 inch range. At this height, most plant roots will be lifted above the problems that may prevail in the substrate. Providing there are none of the soil or drainage problems I have previously described, a 12- to 16-inch high wall is quite sufficient for general garden purposes. This is high enough to make a pleasant addition to your landscape.

The height of a raised bed is influenced by various factors. A primary one is cost. The higher the bed, the greater the expense due to the extra materials and labor for building higher, stronger walls which require more attention to footings and foundations.

The width of the raised bed, along with its location in the garden, affects the ease or difficulty of maintaining the plants within: weeding, pruning, and replanting. Three or four feet wide is a good size. Anything a lot narrower would hardly hold enough plants to justify the work to build it. A bed wider than five feet is too wide to reach into for garden tasks. Do not make the bed wider than can be conveniently reached into from one side or the other, for weeding will be easier if it can be handled without climbing all over the bed. The higher the walls, the less bending is needed, unless the bed is shaped in such a way that you must climb onto it for every minor task.

Avoid building small beds with long and narrow configurations; they are too reminiscent of more somber mounds. You will soon and repeatedly be reminded by well meaning visitors of exactly what they resemble.

Where you have a choice, lay the bed out running east to west. Then you will get northern and southern exposures which will provide a sunny side and a shadier one. The length will depend upon the job the bed is designed to achieve, so it may be self evident. However, it can easily become long enough to lose appeal and become dull and monotonous. To correct this, break the length and make it into two beds. Often the result of this division is more impressive than the original plan.

Keep in mind that raised beds need not be entirely geometrical, with right angles and straight lines, or completely square and level. True, if they are designed to conform to a formal plan, make sure they do so. But if an occasion presents itself, let the design run free. If trapezoids and trapeziums are appropriate, go ahead and use them. Flowing curves and round or kidney-shaped beds are all fair game. Raised beds make wonderful gardens when they follow the curves of a path or the sweep of a driveway, particularly on properties with limited space. These necessities have to remain, so why not embellish them with raised beds?

Building Materials

The choices of building materials for the walls of small raised beds are wide ranging. Natural stone is hard to beat, since it blends with most surroundings. Even in the most sophisticated setting, stone adds the feeling of harmony and permanence. Moreover, a good wall-building stone is relatively easy to work with, and no mortar is required. The stones are laid one on top of the other, with only a skim of soil mixture between each successive layer. Eight to twelve inches is a good average height for walls around small beds. It looks right and provides enough soil depth for alpine plants. An eight-inch wall is just the right height for easy construction. Its foundation preparation involves only a few inches of digging.

There are lovely flat stones available in many parts of the country. The best are about three or four inches thick and are completely flat and nicely squared. They are laid in successive layers.

If you fail to find good squared stones, practically any rocks will do providing they have one decent side to face the outside. They do not have to be large since the walls are not high and solidity is not the

A sand-filled plunge bed protects alpine plants from temperature fluctuations. This one contains part of the British National Collection of Silver Saxifrages, in the garden of Beryl and Peter Bland in Lancashire, England. A cover keeps it dry in winter.

prime concern. The walls are further supported by soil that is backfilled into the bed. Select the best and largest stones for the corners and use them to build extra strength into the structure. Strong corners give the whole project a reassuringly solid appearance.

Retaining walls built for garden projects do not always have to conform to the rigid lines we associate with typically vertical walls. We can build walls at an angle slanting back into the bed. This angle is referred to as the 'batter' of a wall. This is a useful practice when the only stones available are not easy to stack one on top of the other with any degree of stability. The wall is held up by the soil behind the reclining angle of the batter. Do not let this convenience lead you into hasty rockwork or the finished product will reflect it.

Rounded glacial boulders are often the only stone readily available. Unfortunately, they are not the easiest things to fashion into neat, crisp retaining walls. Under these circumstances it might be a good plan to modify the formal raised bed plan for an informally shaped raised bed outlined with skillfully placed boulders, which will make an attractive picture. Mounding and contouring the surface of the soil and strategically including a few larger boulders into it will draw the whole scheme together. The tricky part lies in placing the rocks that define and retain the bed. It is wise not to try to fit each boulder tightly to its neighbor in an unbroken chain around the bed. Vary the sizes. For instance, group three similarly sized stones together, then contrast them with several smaller ones. Let the stones fit together in an informal manner, and do not try to regiment them. When it comes to filling the bed with soil, use enough so that it can

51

flow around and cover as much of the outlining stones as possible. The bed will look less like a string of boulders when some of them are partly covered.

Other materials. There is a wide selection of manufactured concrete blocks made expressly for landscape projects. They are convenient and easy to work with, and suppliers provide a wealth of information on their selection and use. The thought of concrete blocks next to our little alpine plantings may cause shudders of distaste, but there are excellent products available in a range of textures and colors. A visit to a supplier at the planning stage will give you a look at many options. Rather than use a single layer of large blocks to form the bed, use several layers of thinner blocks because it will make a more appealing wall.

These same suppliers will probably carry a line of wooden products, sometimes called landscape timbers or railroad ties, though they have never seen a railroad. They are in convenient lengths, usually six or eight feet. They are about four inches thick and have been pressure treated with a preservative. They are quick and easy to use and make an acceptable low wall. There are also wood lookalike products made of plastic.

Broken concrete slabs from sidewalks and roads and other demolition projects make an acceptable wall-building material. Before you reject the thought of using second-hand broken concrete, consider that sidewalks usually come in a uniform four-inch thickness and are easy to work with. Slabs break into workable sizes, and they are often free.

With them, you can produce a nicely squared, neat, tidy wall. With only one edge of the slab showing, it is not readily recognized as second-hand concrete, particularly when the raised bed has been planted and established.

Construction

Begin by marking the outline of the proposed bed with stakes and strings. It is a good plan to use small wooden stakes to mark the exact location of each corner. These will clearly show you where the bed will be, and the stakes will indicate the outside or face of the walls that comprise the bed.

When you are completely satisfied with the layout, the first stage of construction will be to set the steel rods (used or old 3/4-inch water pipe is often used) that will act as guides in the actual placement of each stone. These pipes can be of any convenient length, provided that they are a foot or so taller than the finished height of the bed.

Place the rods exactly where the corner stones will be, at the four corners of the raised bed. Before driving them into the ground, lean them back slightly into the bed to provide a guide for the batter of the wall. Then tie a string to the two rods that you have decided will be the front wall, stretching it tight. The string can be raised as the wall grows, and if every stone that is set just touches the string, the wall will be straight and level.

Walls built without mortar are known as drystacked or drystone. For added strength they are always built to lean backward, into the mass of the raised bed. This is called the batter of a wall and it usually slopes five to ten degrees. On low walls of quality stone, the batter need not be excessive.

Once the degree of batter has been decided, the rods are adjusted to slope back at the desired angle, so that later, as the strings are raised with the laying of additional layers of stone, the correct angle is automatically maintained.

Before the wall can be built, you have the task of excavating to create a solid foundation for the walls of the bed. This is accomplished by removing all loose soil from the base of the wall until you uncover solid, undisturbed soil. You must avoid pockets of loose soil which will cause settlement after the wall is complete. The amount of excavation required will vary according to the previous use of the site. If you are lucky, the foundation will require only a few inches of digging. While you are at it, make the foundation trench just a few inches wider than the finished wall.

Next, lay down a six-inch layer of crushed rock. Pieces from three-eighths to half an inch are a good size. Level off and pack down the crushed rock. This will make a solid base for the walls and permit drainage for walls up to three feet high.

Building straight walls. The most effective way to build a perfectly straight and level wall is by laying one course at a time, the full length of each wall. Run a string between two corner stakes along one of the longer walls. Set it at the estimated average height of your supply of stone.

In the beginning, keep the line level by measuring up from the ground. As the wall grows, measure from the top of the last completed course. Use a device called a line level. This is a small spirit level that is hung from the guide strings, referred to as the line. This makes it possible to adjust the line and keep it perfectly level as you construct the wall.

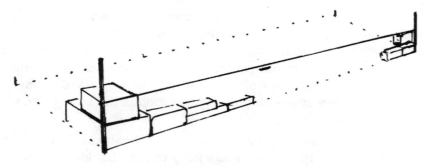

The dotted line shows the layout of the raised bed, which is marked with pegs and string.

The two bold stakes have a level line running between them. This line is corrected using a line-level (center) which ensures that each course of stone is laid level, in a straight line with no odd looking bulges.

Once the line is level, methodically choose stones that fit easily under the taut line. Pay particular attention to bridging all gaps between the lower stones as each new course is set into place. There is an old stonemason saying, "one stone on two, two stones on one" regarding bridging. Bridging not only makes the wall look sharp, it adds strength. Study well-built masonry walls to see how the bridging has been done.

Left, good bridging of the joints guarantees a solid, strong wall. Right, poor bridging allows unsupported joints that lead to weakness in the wall.

If confronted with building a raised bed on a sloping site, even a gentle slope, bear in mind that the top of the raised bed has to be perfectly level, or near enough to level that the eye will not notice a small discrepancy.

It is all too easy to lay out the stakes and strings and just start laying the first course of stones, following the natural slope of the land. If we lay the subsequent courses on top of the lower courses in this manner, the finished walls of the raised bed will follow the slope of the ground, rather than be level.

On a gentle slope, the simplest way to solve the problem is to excavate the foundation of your raised bed until it is level. To do this, place two stakes at each end where the wall will be located and run a string tightly between them. At this point the string need only be a few inches high on the stake at the high end of the slope. Level the string by adjusting it with the aid of a line level. This operation requires the help of another person. Once the line is dead level it is a simple matter to measure from the string to the soil and determine the difference in inches between the top and bottom of the slope. This enables you to excavate a level foundation and then build the wall, confident that the top of the wall will be level.

Dealing with a larger slope requires more engineering. Use the same procedure to establish the level between the top and bottom of the slope. Once the initial measurement has been made it will be obvious that the difference between top and bottom is too great to create a level foundation without a great deal of unnecessary digging. The solution to this problem is to make a stepped foundation. Under many garden conditions this is easily achieved by dividing the length of the wall in half. Set one end of the set of stakes and strings at the low end, the other end at the halfway point, which will be higher up the slope. Then level the line as before and excavate a level foundation from the halfway point upward

The next step requires that the whole operation be repeated. Place one stake on the excavated, now level foundation, and the other at the top of the remaining slope. Again, level the string and dig out the rest of the foundation. You will have created a stepped and level foundation which will save on the stone supply and produce a pleasing run of walling.

On very gentle slopes the situation is more easily solved. After the stakes and string are set and leveled, start placing stones at the low end with large rocks and slowly decrease their size as they creep up the slope. Tie the string to the lower end stake just high enough that your stones fit comfortably beneath it, then level the string. Working just beneath the level string guarantees a perfectly level first course.

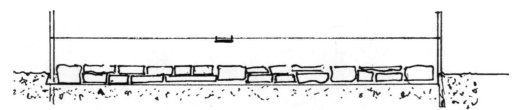

It is relatively easy to build a raised bed on a perfectly level surface. Simply keep the guide line level with the line level and raise it between successive courses of stone.

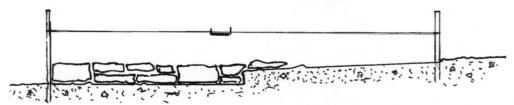

A moderate slope can be corrected by digging the foundation to create a level area for placement of the first (partial) course of the wall. Below, the second course of stones is set into place. Successive courses follow the line level.

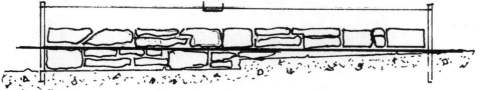

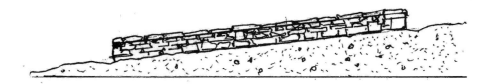

Above, on a sloping site the raised bed follows the slope of the site. While this will be hardly noticeable on a gentle grade, on a steeper grade like this one it will look unstable. One you become aware of it, it will be an irritant forever. Below, the same slope was excavated and terraced in order to have the tops of the bed made level. Two or three stepped, terraced beds make an excellent garden feature.

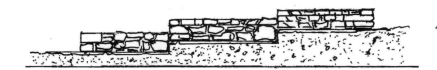

This technique is much less demanding on the builder, and produces a wall that will be pleasing to the eye. There is a series of quite well-built raised beds not far from my home, but unfortunately the gardener followed the gently sloping contours of the garden with the walls. The eye, instead of following level tops, follows the ups and the downs of the walls as they parallel the contours. The whole experience is disconcerting instead of reassuring. As I pass by, I find myself rebuilding the walls, mentally. It is a good thing I do not live there or I would never know peace again.

Raised Beds On Pavement

Building a raised bed on a paved surface is complex, so unless you have experience with masonry work, you should use a contractor. Since the bed will be on a paved area, it will most likely be in a frequently seen, often-used area, where the casual, free style of dry stone walls may not fit with the architectural features of the house. Therefore it may be necessary to choose brick, cut stone, or another manufactured product, such as those described on page 52. Be sure to include weep holes (page 58) in the bottom course of the design, for drainage.

You will have to lay out the approximate position of the new bed, first for your own approval and perhaps that of others. You will need something to mark the site when you have a contractor come to estimate the cost. You cannot drive stakes into a hard surface the way you can into a lawn. It takes a while trying different configurations as you design your new bed, so if your lines are easily relocated it makes the planning job a lot easier. The simplest method is to tie strings to bricks. Then pull them tight enough to be straight, and they will remain in place well enough for your experiments.

Once the plan is finalized, it's a good idea to check the height of the new bed. Pile up a few bricks and run a string between them, which will quickly give you an approximation of the final appearance of the bed.

Once its design has been determined, you'll need a more stable foundation line before work on the bed can proceed. Spray paint is too permanent and chalk can be lost in a thunderstorm. Heavy crayons used in the building trade will serve well and can be removed with little trouble if the bed is not built after all.

Raised beds with mortared walls. If you are planning to build a raised bed using mortar to hold the walls together, a concrete footing will be required. This prevents damage to the walls when frost causes expansion and heaves the soil beneath the wall. The footing is standard practice in masonry work and most contractors are familiar with local requirements. If you have any concerns in this matter, your local building authority will be able to advise you.

Weep holes. A masonry wall demands that weep holes be included every few feet so that any surplus water is quickly drained away. Failure to rapidly get rid of excess water will exert a lot of outward pressure on the walls of the bed. Walls have fallen down as a result of pressure from trapped water coupled with expansion from heavy freezing. Where a bed is built on a solid surface, weep holes should be installed in the first course of brickwork, where the wall contacts the paved surface. This will prevent any standing water in the lower level of the soil.

Filling the Bed

I have read on several occasions that ten inches of prepared soil is sufficient for growing alpines. This is true under some circumstances but I would prefer to a add a few more inches. A lot depends on what conditions are like beneath: would ten inches of soil be enough if the bed were built on a sunny concrete patio? A bed built with walls 18 to 24 inches high would provide sufficient space for plenty of drainage material and a good depth of prepared soil.

Soil medium and rough fill. A three or four-foot high bed has to be handled differently. This depth of soil is prone to compaction. Since it is unlikely that the roots of your plants will occupy the whole depth of the soil, the unused soil just sits idle and begins to sour and compact. I have seen many planters that failed for this reason, even when planted with trees. I realize that a tree will need more soil than alpine plants, but even trees can have too much extra soil.

To avoid these problems, first put in a 12-inch layer of rough fill material such as rocks, concrete lumps, and bricks, often referred to as builder's rubble. But do not use wood waste, paint cans, insulation, or similar junk that can either rot or add damaging chemicals.

After installing the rough fill material, level it off and add a layer of coarse sand or gravel to take up air space between chunks of rough fill. It is not critical which is used, as long as the sand or gravel drains freely. Fill the bed with this material until you reach two feet or so from the rim. Level it off again and compact it to minimize its excessive settling later. It would be a wise move at this point to turn the hose on it to settle it and also to check its drainage.

Then install the soil (see Chapter 5) in layers of 12 inches or so. Level off each layer and compact it by treading on it. Treading is done by systematically covering the surface with shuffling steps and with your weight on your heels. When adding the final layer use plenty of soil. Mound up some extra soil to allow for settling. When large quantities of soil and fill are used, settling is inevitable. If the planting can be delayed long enough to allow the settling to occur naturally, the planting process will be much simpler. Making up soil levels around the plants later is difficult.

Excessive settling is a problem, but measures taken to prevent it can also cause soil problems. It is not difficult to manually compact the rough bottom drainage material or the sand and gravel layer. No matter how much it is packed down it should still drain rapidly. However, the 18 or more inches of soil on top of the drainage material can be ruined by heavy compacting, particularly if water is used in the process, so do not overwork or overcompact the top layer.

As gardeners we have learned that working with wet soil breaks down the soil structure by compressing and breaking soil aggregates. This leads to poor air circulation, poor drainage, and poor root growth. Even though we have created a well drained soil with the addition of extra sand and grit, watering and physically packing the soil down too vigorously will still damage our soil mix. That is why I suggest compacting the raised bed in layers of 12 inches. I suggest that you avoid using the hose or packing the soil if it is very wet.

Above, saxifrages grow best with a top dressing of chipped stone or gravel. Below, a washtub is a handy container for mixing up small batches of potting soil for diverse purposes. Assorted planting media "recipes" are found here in Chapter 5.

5. Soil and Topdressing

Gardeners often ask which soil mix to use in an alpine garden. Soil composition is a confusing issue because so much conflicting advice is written about it.

Many descriptions start out with the pronouncement, 'the soil should drain rapidly, yet be water retentive.' This statement, a bit confusing in itself, is correct. Good drainage and water retention are the most important qualities a rock garden soil can possess. Rapid drainage is an attribute we can readily understand, knowing that overly damp conditions lead to leaf and root rot. Surface water, whether from rain, melting snow, or irrigation, must quickly soak into the soil, leaving the surface free of standing water.

As water passes down through soil, vital oxygen particles needed for plant respiration are drawn in behind it, filling the pore spaces within the soil. At the same time, organic matter within the soil absorbs moisture, which is then stored and slowly released as the plant roots demand it.

Existing garden soil in a rock garden is rarely usable in its natural state. In all probability, it is either heavy clay, or it is so sandy that it is impoverished and always dry. Even the best garden soils, so perfect for perennials and vegetables, are too rich for alpine plants. Rich soil encourages alpines to grow fast, ruining their diminutive qualities and stimulating foliage production at the cost of flowers.

Often, commercially produced soils are also too rich for our purpose. Among other things, they may contain animal manures, bark chips, and sawdust.

So what is the alpine gardener to do? Sandy soils can be improved by adding organic matter to aid in retention of moisture. The drainage in heavy soils can be improved by the addition of coarse sand and gravel, and lots of organic matter.

If you need to import soil for your alpine garden, approach commercial soil producers to see if they will provide a special order devoid of manure. See if they will substitute some other organic component and add extra sand and gravel for you. If this fails, buy whatever basic topsoil is available and add the appropriate amendments yourself (see pages 66 to 72). An alternative is to skim the top few inches of soil from the flower border or vegetable garden, if it's available. To this rich soil, add equal parts peat and coarse grit, which is a coarse grade of sand.

Planting Media

As I explain the terms I use when discussing soil and soil mixtures, I will try to avoid overly technical details. There are excellent books on the study of soil, a fascinating subject, if one wishes to pursue it further. Here are the basic soil types and their components:

Soil Types

Loam. Loam is the name of a textural class of soil, one that contains a moderate amount of sand, silt, and clay. We usually think of loam as topsoil. When the percentage of sand increases, the soil is considered to be a **sandy loam.** A **clay loam** is one with a greater percent of clay particles.

Organic matter. The term organic matter, when applied to rock garden soils, describes the formerly living materials (humus) the gardener traditionally uses to improve the soil. These are leaf mold, compost and peat moss. There are others, but these three are the major ones, each with its own particular role.

Leaf mold, or leaf soil, sometimes spelled leafmould, is the soil-like layer beneath a layer of decomposing leaves. However, partially decomposed leaves are commonly used before they fully reach the leaf soil stage. They last longer and are of greater value if they are not yet totally decomposed.

Soil Components

Compost, whether from the garden composting area or purchased from a garden supplier, is an excellent source of humus for the soil. It provides nutrients and can be a bit too rich at times. It is just right for the regular garden, but the rock garden does not need much of it. Once incorporated into the soil it rapidly decomposes. It is short-lived, so it has to be added on a regular basis. Just to confuse things, compost is also the British term for potting soil, a term widely used in alpine gardening literature.

Peat, also known as peat moss or even moss-peat, is partially decomposed sphagnum moss. The large cell structure of the sphagnum moss allows it to absorb air and water like a sponge. It also is able to store nutrients and fertilizers that have been added to the soil, which normally would be leached away. Peat moss loosens clay soils and binds sandy soils.

Peat is sold in compacted bales of various sizes and is very convenient. The quality of peat that is typically available tends to be on the finer side, rather than containing coarse pieces, and there seem to be many dustlike particles. A few years ago it was possible to get a much coarser quality, which is preferable for rock garden soil mixtures.

In Europe, there is a movement that strongly discourages the use of peat in gardening, because of the damage that the harvesting of it is doing to wetlands and bogs. The Canadian Peat Moss Association assures us that there is no shortage of peat as a raw material, or danger to the environment in North America. This is not the place to debate this issue, but we might eventually have to face up to the loss of our bales of peat.

Coir is an alternative we may have to use instead of peat. It is the outside layer of husk that surrounds the shell of the coconut. It consists mainly of fibers which are used to make rope, doormats and brushes. Between these fibers is the corky substance called coir pith, coir dust, and coir peat. Once the fibers have been removed at the factory the coir pith is unused. It was considered a waste product until recently, when it was found to have values equal to peat moss as a soil amendment. It is available in compressed bales as well as other configurations. Needless to say, producers of peat and those of coir both maintain that their product is superior, but as we gain experience with coir we will draw our own conclusions.

Sand and Gravel. The names and terms used to describe these products are as confusing as the different types of material they describe. The Europeans speak of grit, chips, or chippings. Here in North America, we have a range of names as varied as the localities where the materials are found. We speak of pea gravel, blue stone, crushed rock and coarse sand, to name a few.

H. Lincoln Foster, in his book, *Rock Gardening* (Houghton Mifflin Company, 1968, written by an American for American gardeners), observed, "Sand and gravel in themselves do not vary a great deal, no matter where they are procured."

This is true as long as the particles in the gravel are sharp and angular, and do not contain a high percentage of dust, clay or silt particles, referred to as fines. The size of the stones can range from an eighth to half an inch; a little bit of variance one way or the other will not ruin the soil. But let me add a word of warning: limestone gravel is alkaline and can change the pH of nearby soil.

Lime. Lime or no lime? Sooner or later rock gardeners will need to consider the presence or absence of lime in the soil. It need not be a problem to anyone, as scores of rock garden plants grow healthily and flower well without any concern about whether the soil has lime in it or not, that is, the acidity or alkalinity of the soil. Natural soil varies widely and is influenced by many factors, including the nature of the underlying rock from which the soil has developed.

If the garden is located in an area where limestone rock preponderates, local soil will contain lots of lime and be alkaline (limy). Where other rock predominates, the soil may be either acidic or neutral, depending on the nature of the rock. There are many degrees of acidity and alkalinity in soils and they are referred to as the soil reaction. This is usually expressed as the pH value.

acidic pH			** neutral pH*		*alkaline pH*
4	*5*	*6*	**7 **	*8*	

As shown in the table, pH 7.0 is the point of neutrality. Below 7.0 the soil is acidic, and at any number above 7.0 the soil is alkaline. The optimum range for many crops falls between 6.0 and 7.0. Lots of alpines enjoy a pH between 5.5 to 6.5.

There are plants that are called lime lovers and other species are lime haters. Lime haters will not tolerate any lime in their soil. If lime is present, these plants can turn yellow and sickly. Eventually they can die. These lime haters are said to be calcifuges. This group includes the Asian gentian, *Gentiana sino-ornata*, and its many hybrids which flower with those lovely trumpets of such wonderful shades of blue. Calcifuges also include the dwarf broadleaved evergreen shrublets, *Gaultheria* and *Cassiope*.

Plants that occur naturally on alkaline soils are said to be calcicoles or lime lovers. Since many of these are valuable genera for the rock garden, we are fortunate that they are also happy to grow in soils that contain no lime at all.

Since we are hoping to plant a wide range of plants in our small alpine gardens, we would prefer that our soil not be overly alkaline.

That way, we can plant a number of lime haters as well as the lime lovers. So do not hasten to add lime to your soil mix, for it is very difficult to counteract.

If you do not know the soil reaction in your garden, it is well worth getting the soil tested. A simple pH test is all that is required; ask your local garden center or nurseryman where you can get one done. Regional agricultural extension offices, often at the county level, provide this service in the United States. When you receive the results you will know exactly what kind of soil you have, and can proceed with confidence.

Should you live with an extremely alkaline soil and be tempted to specialize in lime haters, you can create a lime-free soil mix. Once the soil mix is prepared it must be contained in a raised bed well above the natural drainage water, or in a container. Otherwise, you know what will happen! The alkaline water will drain into the bed and contaminate it. Bear in mind that the local leaf mold can contain lime and all irrigation will have to be done with collected rainwater.

Soil for Small Rock Gardens

Recommended proportions for soil-improving amendments for rock garden plants have, over the years, become traditional. They are usually given in percentages or by bulk. As a nursery apprentice many years ago I became so accustomed to soil mixtures or composts that they are second nature to me.

Of course this is not the case for all readers. As I was skimming through Volume 54 (1996), Number 3 of the 'Quarterly,' the *Bulletin of the North American Rock Garden Society*, I spotted something Gwen Kelaidis had written in her excellent feature article "A New Garden: Starting From Scratch" that summed things up very nicely, for experienced gardeners. "I still consider soils a mystery. Who really measures out one third of this, one third of that? I add sand, gravel, manure, leaf-mold, whatever I can get my hands on, whatever looks "right," until I have a loose, good-looking texture."

Until you gain enough experience to know what looks and feels "right," you can use the formulas provided in the next few pages. These recommendations are helpful guidelines. Minor inexactness will not ruin the soil mixture. As Gwen says, if it looks and feels right, it is right.

You should test the soil by giving it a good watering and studying the drainage performance. If drainage is too slow, add more sand or gravel. In good soil for rock gardens, the water should start draining away immediately. Then give the soil plenty of time to drain before you begin to work with it, for nothing ruins soil structure faster than working with wet soil.

Basic soil recipe. We do not need complex soil mixtures for our small rock garden or raised bed, for the majority of plants we are likely to select will grow in the simplest mixture. The following recipe is a proven standard rock garden mixture, based upon using a medium textured topsoil, with quantities given by proportion.

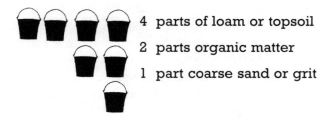

4 parts of loam or topsoil

2 parts organic matter

1 part coarse sand or grit

To get an idea about this before doing a lot of work, just mix up a small batch using a bucket as the unit of measure.

To mix a moderate amount of soil for a small garden, your wheelbarrow makes an excellent and practical unit of measure. Fill a wheelbarrow four times with loamy topsoil and spread it several inches deep on a hard surface where the garden will be. Then get two wheelbarrow loads of peat and spread them over the topsoil. Finally, add one barrow load of the sand and gravel. Mix thoroughly.

What about larger areas? The best way to deal with them is to apply the soil amendments by a measured depth. First, define the area of soil to be improved. The depth of the soil to be improved is 12 inches deep. This now becomes the four parts of loam or topsoil. Now spread six inches of organic matter over the entire defined area (two parts). The one part coarse sand or grit is achieved by adding a three-inch layer over the same area.

Mixing and blending a six-inch layer of sand and peat into a 12-inch layer of soil is no easy job, so it will be somewhat easier to do it in several stages. First, apply the organic matter and mix it in. Then add the sand and gravel and mix again. The mixing operation will take less effort if the amendments are dry.

It is easier to use a large rototiller, if the area can be accessed by the machine, but even a small home garden rototiller will help. With the small machine, it would be a wise move to do the job in two operations instead of trying to deal with the whole 12 inches in one pass. Instead of 12 inches, you can consider a six-inch layer of soil as the four parts loam or topsoil, also cutting the quantities of peat and coarse sand by half. The organic two parts would only need to be three inches deep, and the sand and gravel layer would be only one and a half inches deep.

Once the top layer is well mixed it can be removed and stored near the construction area. Depending upon the season it is a wise move to cover the mixed soil pile with a tarp to keep it dry.

This basic soil mixture with the four to two to one ratio is adequate for growing a wide range of plants in rock gardens and raised beds. The important thing to keep in mind is that these recommended proportions are based upon the topsoil or loam being of medium texture, not a heavy soil or a light, sandy one.

Soil for Raised or Terraced Beds

There are differences between a conventional rock garden and a raised bed or terrace. A rock garden has the advantage of drawing upon the cooling effect of the mass of earth beneath the topsoil. Roots can penetrate deeply to find moisture during prolonged dry spells. In a raised bed, on the other hand, there is nothing more than a column of soil retained between four narrow walls. It has little or no connection with the underlying soil. In warm, dry climates the prepared soil soon dries out, so it may be necessary to increase its water holding capacity with more peat and leafmold.

But wait! What sort of plants are you planning to grow? Maybe you have not decided yet. Then one choice is to use plants that thrive under your local conditions. There are fascinating planting schemes for hot, sunny climates and dry soils. Ask yourself, will the raised bed be in full sun or in full or part shade? This will have an enormous influence on your choice of plants and soil.

Is your primary soil naturally limey? If it is, the die is cast and you will be limited to growing lime tolerant plants (calcicoles). If it is a neutral soil, do not rush to change it, at least not until you are sure you want to grow only lime-loving plants. Lime or no lime, a sunny raised bed full of thriving, colorful, trouble-free plants selected to take advantage of the local conditions is the ideal way to go. But in cool, dry, shady woodland conditions, the soil will require more organic matter to help compensate for the lack of moisture. Chopped leaves are an excellent woodland soil amendment.

Soil for Pots, Troughs, and Containers

Preparing a soil mixture (compost) for growing alpine plants in pots and containers is more exacting than working with large volumes in the rock garden. Plants growing in the open garden require less care and attention than those imprisoned in pots. Their roots are free to wander in search of moisture, nutrients, or to find a cooler root run if their present location is not to their liking. Soil temperatures will fluctuate rapidly in flower pots since they do not have the moisture retaining capacity of a large volume of soil.

The term, 'good fibrous loam,' sometimes opens a paragraph on soil mixtures for containers. That is another frustrating term from the 'good old days,' when good fibrous loam was obtained by digging turf from a field or meadow. Four and a half inches was the ideal thickness for the average turf cut. The turves were stacked upside down in neat squared piles and left to break down into rich fibrous loam. There are not many gardens today that can indulge in this luxury and it is increasingly difficult to buy decent loam. The small garden owner would find it hard to obtain small quantities of this commodity. Many of the proprietary blends of potting soil are too rich for alpine plants because they are designed to grow such crops as flowering plants, bedding plants, and vegetables.

It is possible to take one of these prepared potting soils and use it as a substitute for loam, adjusting it by adding quantities of peat , sand, and gravel. There are lots of tolerant rock plants that will be quite happy with this soil. This practice can have drawbacks. One is uniformity: there can be no guarantee that the supplier will use the same raw materials each time a new batch of product is made. Unless you find a reliable source for loam, you may need to take a few bucketfuls of topsoil from your own garden (provided that pest problems are negligible) and amend them as required.

Loam or topsoil usually contains nutrients and alpine plants require only small amounts of them, so it is not necessary to add fertilizer to the initial potting soils. Peat is a better source of organic matter for pot growing than leaf mold since it is slower to break down. The role of organic matter is more to assist with moisture retention and distribution than it is to supply the nutrients.

Different plants and garden types require different soils, so here are basic soil mixtures for specific purposes.

Loam-Based Potting Soil

This general mixture is excellent for undemanding rock plants, bulbs, and dwarf conifers.

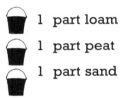

1 part loam

1 part peat

1 part sand

Lean Potting Mixture

This mix is for tricky high alpines and dryland species. This is a very austere compost. This recipe can only be used as a general guide because individual garden conditions will vary.

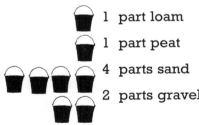

1 part loam

1 part peat

4 parts sand

2 parts gravel

Rich or *Ericaceae* Mixture

This mix is designed for those plants that require a richer, cooler, moister soil, with no lime present in any of the ingredients. This mixture benefits from leaf mold as part of the organic matter quotient. Be sure not to stint on the coarse sand and gravel as the drainage must still be rapid.

69

1 part loam

2 parts peat and leaf mold mixed

1 part coarse sand

Soils for Seed Germination

Each type of plant has its own requirements and soil preferences for germination. The alpine gardener deciding to do some research into what constitutes the right soil mixture for germinating rock garden plant seeds, will need access to a top-notch library. Of course, searching the world wide web can save a lot of running around but will consume time nonetheless. Below is a standard mix for alpines, but many variations exist.

Basic Seed Sowing Mixture

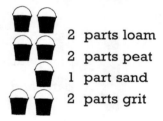

2 parts loam

2 parts peat

1 part sand

2 parts grit

John Innes (J. I.) Seed Starter Mixtures

Much writing on alpine gardening refers to John Innes potting soils, or composts, as they are called in England. The original J. I. seed-starter mixture is excellent for a great many rock plant seeds. Just bear in mind that it was originally designed for seeds that germinate in a relatively short time. Any soil mixture that has a loam, peat, and sand base can be mis-identified as a J. I. Compost, even if it bears no resemblance to the genuine product.

Rock plants and alpine seeds usually take several months or more to germinate. It is advisable to keep pots of valuable or rare seed for several years, as some species take that long to germinate. Therefore, the seed compost must be able to remain effective and not break down for at least two years.

A soil mix containing loam relies on the loam to supply the small amount of fundamental nutrients that young seedlings require to grow into healthy plants. They merely need enough to facilitate germination and primary healthy growth, because the plants will soon be transplanted into pots of new soil.

The sand is critical. It should be coarse, to the point of being grit. The particle sizes ranging from an eighth of an inch down to a sixteenth of an inch, with little or no fines or dust (clay and silt particles). Once the seeds are sown they are stored outside exposed to all weather, so the drainage must be superb.

The John Innes Story

John Innes was a London businessman who, upon his death in 1904, left his estate to be used to establish a horticultural research establishment. Six years after his death, the John Innes Horticultural Institution* was founded at Merton Park in England. Among the many research projects was one being studied in the 1930's by two scientists, William Lawrence and John Newell. They worked on the problem of poor quality soil composts then prevalent, setting out to standardize composts that offered ideal physical and nutritional qualities and would guarantee consistently good results. They established methods of heat sterilization and developed two standard composts, one for seed sowing and the other for potting. The John Innes Centre, although it developed formulations for composts, never was a commercial producer of these composts.

Composition of J. I. Composts. These composts are composed of a blend of loam, sphagnum peat moss, coarse sand or grit, and fertilizers.

Loam clearly is the main ingredient, forming the base of the compost. It performs vital functions in the availability and management of plant nutrients and the presence of micro elements.

Peat increases the porosity of the soil and improves both its aeration and its water retaining capacity. Because of its important role, the Institute recommends that the best quality sphagnum peat moss be used in the compost.

Coarse sand (grit) is added to obtain the correct physical condition and good drainage. It should be clean and sharp, free from clay, silt, lime, and organic matter. In an ideal sand, 60 to 70 percent of the particles are between 1/8 inch and 1/16 inch in size. The traditional ratio is:

7 parts loam
3 parts peat
2 parts grit

* Now the John Innes Centre, Norwich Research Park, Colney, Norwich, NR4 7UH, UK

71

The pH is adjusted using ground limestone and fertilizer is added to produce the level of nutrient desired in the formulation.

J. I. Seed Compost

J. I. Seed Compost has the low nutrient level required by germinating seeds and for rooting cuttings. Alpine gardeners have been conditioned to avoid any fertilizer in their seed composts, as were gardeners and nurserymen many years ago.

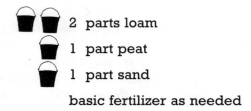

2 parts loam

1 part peat

1 part sand

basic fertilizer as needed

J. I. Potting Compost

J. I. Potting Compost has higher levels of nutrients to sustain larger plants over longer periods. In fact there are three formulas for the potting mix, each with a higher level of fertilizer.

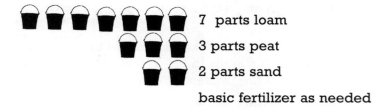

7 parts loam

3 parts peat

2 parts sand

basic fertilizer as needed

Drainage Considerations

Whether you are building a rock garden, making a raised bed, creating a rock garden in a greenhouse, or just planting a trough or pot, it is necessary to rapidly rid the soil of excess water. Earlier, I warned of the dangers of poorly drained sites and trust that you have been able to avoid them.

The successful cultivation of rock plants depends on the rapid removal of surplus water from the soil. Rock plants will not tolerate having their roots remain in poorly drained, soggy soil.

Rock Gardens

There are gardeners who are fortunate enough to garden on a site that has naturally free-draining soil. For instance, a slightly sloping hillside with a light, sandy subsoil will never have a drainage problem since the water will find its own way down hill. On the other hand, a slope consisting of heavy clay soil offers no way for the water to move through the soil, so drainage can be a problem.

Luckily there are ways to assure good drainage. One is to build the new garden directly on top of the soil surface and not disturb the existing surface. This lets the water move unimpeded as did before you came along.

Be certain that the new garden itself is not constructed in a way that blocks downhill drainage. If it does, the lovely alpine soil mixture you have so carefully prepared will act as a dam and block the movement of the water, forcing it to back up behind the new soil. With no other choice, the water will eventually flow into the new soil. Regardless of how much sand and gravel you have incorporated into the new soil, this will make it far too wet for alpines.

An alternative is to divert the unwanted water before it reaches the rock garden site. Lead the water away from the garden area by digging small drainage channels higher up the slope that will intercept and redirect the water.

A common error is to excavate and remove heavy, poorly draining soil and replace it with a prepared rock garden soil mixture. This creates the ideal makings of a pond, as the water quickly finds its way into the space with the new soil. It matters little whether the site slopes or is flat. If the drainage water has no way of escaping, it will fill the hole with water and saturate whatever soil mixture is present.

Sometimes a good, thick layer of gravel or similar free-draining substance is recommended to underlie the prepared soil. This sounds like the ideal solution but unfortunately the downward-draining flow of water does not penetrate the interface between the gravel and the garden soil. This situation is referred to as a perched water table, which simply means that there will be a layer of water where the garden soil meets the drainage gravel. This can be avoided by blending several inches of the soil with the top few inches of the gravel. This creates a smooth transition zone between the two materials and lets the water drain away.

These situations are extreme and suggest torrents of water pouring downhill onto the rock garden site, which, fortunately, is seldom the case. Impervious subsoils are fairly uncommon and the majority of sites do not require such radical treatment. One of the simplest and most effective solutions is to dig and loosen the subsoil

73

to a depth of ten to 12 inches and mix in lots of drainage gravel with the loosened subsoil. When you add the prepared soil mix to the surface, again blend several inches of the two materials together in order to create a gradual transition zone, for better drainage.

Drainage in Rock Gardens and Raised Beds
Built On Solid Surfaces

Rock gardens or raised beds built on top of a solid, impermeable surface such as a concrete patio or flat natural rock will have drainage issues. Often, after the project is completed, the natural movement of water through the soil carries fine particles of sand, silt or clay along with it. They flow out with the water and leave deposits on the hard surface after the water has dried.

The best way to control this is by placing several inches of drainage material right on the hard surface, below the garden soil of the raised bed, before the new soil is introduced.

Rock gardens. Building a rock garden with an informal design on a solid surface, unlike a conventional rock garden on a soil surface, demands a series of rocks to define and outline it and to retain the soil and drainage material.

Once these stones have been arranged more or less to your satisfaction, go ahead and place six inches or so of gravel within the circle of rocks and level it off. Six inches is a safe depth for achieving better drainage. Then cover the whole surface of the gravel with several inches of prepared soil, remembering to integrate the interface between them.

Once this is complete, shovel in several more inches of the new soil to protect the drainage layer, and then continue building the rock garden.As you continue to build, you may find that the original outlining stones are not working out as you planned, so it may be necessary to rearrange one or two, taking care to reinstall the drainage layer.

Raised bed. Similarly, a raised bed on a solid surface is treated in the same manner except, of course, the walls will keep gravel and soil contained. Be certain that the drainage holes in the lowest courses of the wall are adequate. These weep holes are usually covered with wire screens to keep the gravel in place until things settle down.

Mulch and Topdressing

In rock gardening circles, mulches are usually called topdressings. They are widely accepted as beneficial and can be applied to the rock garden, to raised beds, troughs, and pots, and to containers. They prevent and discourage weeds, slow the drying of the soil, and, at the same time, keep the soil cool. A few inches of gravel spread over the rock garden or site provides a soil-free layer of open material, thus severing any contact between the plants and soil-borne fungi. Another value, not so obvious, is that the layer of topdressing keeps soil from being splashed onto short-stemmed, early alpine flowers by spring rains. The materials used will depend on the design of the garden and to some extent on esthetics. By no means least, the inspiration and common sense of the gardener.

The consensus is that a gravel mulch should be sized at about a quarter to three-eighths of an inch in diameter and be laid about an inch and a half deep. This is only a guide, since spreading chippings is an inaccurate operation. Whether they be larger or smaller, thicker or shallower, is not overly significant. Concentrate on getting the chips under branches and stems, and on spreading a good, thick collar around the neck of choice cushion plants.

The materials used for mulching depend on the design of the garden and to some extent on esthetics. By no means least, selection depends on the inspiration and common sense of the gardener.

Since you are adding a layer of insulation, the logical time to apply mulch or topdressing is in mid spring. By then the soil will be warmed up but not overheated. The moisture level of the soil is usually optimum. With a new planting, it pays to delay topdressing until the plants have settled in and any settling of the topsoil has ceased. It is very inconvenient to do much planting or replanting once the mulch is in place. Furthermore, the mulch makes it more difficult to determine if the soil needs watering, and the newly planted plants must not be allowed to get too dry.

A carefully chosen topdressing will enhance the garden picture. Many alpine places feature numerous rock fragments that have fallen from surrounding rocks as they weather. The color and composition of these chips and fragments is usually the same as the neighboring rock. When we obtain them from a gravel pit, they seldom are of a uniform size, although I have seen some that are pretty close.

When it comes to topdressing your project, by all means purchase the greater portion of the washed gravel or chippings in a uniform size. Once the topdressing has been spread, add some random larger sizes to give it a natural look.

Topdressing alone will not stop those perennial weeds already established in the newly added rock garden soil, or those in the native soil below. The plants we introduce can also be a source of pernicious weeds which hitch a ride to your site in the pot in which they are growing. It pays to check new plants over carefully, root and top, before planting. Hand weeding will keep weeds under control.

When it comes to mulching the flat surface of a raised bed, there are several choices. You do not aim to duplicate a natural feature, so go ahead and use a uniformly sized topdressing. Select a size and color that you find pleasing and harmonious.

You may wish to build a rock garden on the raised bed. Formally landscaped areas might not be compatible, which is why a raised bed was chosen in preference to a rock garden. The height of the walls of the bed will have a bearing on how the top is landscaped. If the bed is three feet tall, a rock garden that high in the air will not have much credibility. But in other cases, a few carefully grouped rocks just peeping through the surface of a raised bed will provide interest by breaking up the otherwise flat surface. If arranged carefully, they will provide some excellent crevices for choice plants.

Shady gardens. Mulches serve the same purpose in the shade garden as in any other garden. However, gravel or stone chippings may not be in keeping with shade-loving plants.

There are organic materials that can be used instead. Avoid those that are too suggestive of the formal mulches used in city and commercial landscapes. Uniformly sized and colored bark mulches come to mind immediately. Smaller sizes of finely ground bark products are more in keeping, but be sure they do not contain any natural chemicals injurious to some plants.

It is always possible to create a mulch to conform to your ideals by mixing and blending bark with other materials. The same can be said for peat moss, which is uniform in texture and color.

If the garden is in an area where pine needles are available, they make an excellent mulch and they are unobtrusive. They do not break down or compact readily.

Coarsely textured compost makes a lot of sense. It will be in keeping with the compost used in the bed, and it will gradually return to the soil. It will also help to provide the casual air of the natural woodland scene.

There are diverse mulching materials available from east to west. Some are local products, not widely available or understood. By all means check them out. If they look good in your garden, use them.

6. Alpine Plants in Containers

Some dealers carry hand-carved stone troughs.

A rock garden and container-grown plants work well together, offering a gardener with little space some interesting opportunities. Perhaps you have room for only a very small rock garden, too small to accommodate the number of plants you wish to grow. Containers, large or small, can be the answer since they can be housed on practically any hard surface.

Where actual floor space is minimal, containers may be displayed on racks or even shelving. I was visiting alpine gardeners in Holland recently, where garden space is very limited. In the garden of Harry Jans, a prominent rock gardener in Holland, I was amazed to see several trough gardens actually set into the brick garden walls and cantilevered like shelving.

His garden walls are made of brick and are at least ten feet high. He removed a large section and replaced it with a wall of lumps of tufa stacked one upon the other, right to the top of the wall. Both sides were planted with the choicest of alpines. His neighbor, needless to say, was in complete agreement with this arrangement. He had no objection to visitors crossing into his garden to photograph the plants Harry had planted on his side of the wall.

Containers give you many alternatives. Take, for example, a rare alpine plant you have acquired at no small effort. After you plant it, at first all goes well, until the plant begins to show signs of distress. It

In Holland, Harry Jans makes space for his alpine plants by embedding a tufa growing site into the brick wall. It can be seen from both sides and the neighbors do not mind at all.

obviously is not happy in the exposed rock garden. So you remedy this by digging it up and putting it into a pot so you can give it individual attention. This works in reverse, too. After a spell in a pot, a plant can become seriously root bound and will die if not dealt with. There are two options: either put it into a larger container or plant it in the rock garden.

The Container Option

If your property offers no likely place for a conventional rock garden or a raised bed, you can still grow alpine plants because many will thrive in containers. For rock gardeners, there are any number of different ways to go about it. Plants can be grown outdoors year round, or under various kinds of shelter. Growing conditions can be matched to the fussiest of plants.

When there is precious little space, container gardening may be your only choice. A small garden, even when surrounded by buildings and pavements, will house a large number of plants in a variety of containers, particularly if you select the smallest species. You will need at least a few hours of sunlight, some basic supplies, and your favorite alpine plants.

Although I have a rock garden, I also grow many alpine plants in containers. Pots allow me to grow plants that are not happy in the open rock garden. They allow me to cultivate plants that need protection of some kind, either from winter cold or summer heat. Plants in pots are portable, and that allows me to work under shelter, even under lights if I feel like it. I can garden in the rain, the wind, or summer's heat. I can extend my gardening season simply by carrying my plants to a comfortable (for me, that is!) shelter, and there is always something to do. I do not have to work all the time—just enjoying the plants is enough. I am an incurable collector and enjoy working with my pots of plants, and in this I am not alone.

I have plants in several different styles of containers and troughs. This adds diversity to the conditions I can provide to plants with varying needs. There are many plants that are excellent subjects for a collector. Dwarf conifers are a case in point. In some regions they are less difficult in pots than in the garden. In my region they do not need to be grown in pots, but what appealing container specimens they make! (See Chapter 8 for more on particular plants.)

Dwarf cushion saxifrages, with their mounds of silvery leaves, are perfect for many types of containers. You can even grow them in lumps of tufa, directly in the rock itself, with no soil required (page 26 and the end of this chapter). Furthermore, delicate early spring flowers last longer when a pot-grown specimen is protected from gales and frosts.

There is responsibility that goes along with having a collection of plants in containers, indoors or out. They are like pets—totally dependent upon the gardener for their survival. So they will tend to tie you down. You must make arrangements for their welfare during your absences. Finding someone who understands their needs can be a problem.

Selecting containers. Today, dealers offer an increasingly wide range of handsome containers. They offer such an array of sizes, shapes and materials it is difficult to decide which to buy. It is possible to choose from rectangular, vase-shaped, urn-shaped, and oval shaped. There are planters designed to hang on walls.

I recently made a visit to the local garden center to study the options. After looking through many rows of planters it was obvious to me that the majority were not suitable for growing alpines. Many of the popular planters of today are far too deep, requiring a large amount of soil, much too much for the comfort of austere, slow-growing alpines. Moreover, I realized that there is very little space at the surface of an urn-shaped pot when it is filled with soil, certainly not enough to create a meaningful rock garden theme.

I noticed the range of bright and shiny stoneware containers, ranging from neat, one-gallon sizes up to huge, 20-gallon ones. I enjoyed the bright blues and greens mixed with the reds and some other darker shades. But for the most part they were rounded, urn-shaped pots, and quite deep. There were a few oval bowls reminiscent of a baby's bathtub and one or two square designs.

The use of bright colors, fancy shapes, and decorative patterns is a personal thing and has little bearing on the cultivation of the plants within. To me, the unglazed stoneware pots look at home in the garden setting. The brightly colored ones certainly have a place in the scheme of things, when used by a skilled designer, even in the tradition-bound alpine world..

Italian terra cotta was well represented in both traditional rounded pots of all sizes plus a range of different sizes in squared planters. The squared planters carried fairly simple designs in relief. They have a beautiful smooth finish and excellent proportions for alpine growing.

Container gardening presents the same challenges as interior design. There are planters decorated in classic European or Asian motifs, and there are plain, unadorned designs too. You will have a bewildering choice of finishes, textures, and colors. Any kind of container can be used to grow alpines.

Pots and planters made from concrete are weather-resistant and popular, and are available in endless patterns, from huge classic urns to shallow dishes. Square and oblong planters are also available in a range of sizes and materials. Some are decorated with ornate patterns in relief, but there are unadorned models too. The choice is personal, although unadorned ones are appropriate to the natural alpine theme.

Smooth-finished concrete in its natural color makes excellent planters. I was impressed by a several planters of a plain, lightweight concrete mixture with no decoration, especially the square and oblong ones with well balanced lines and a depth of soil of six to eight inches. They are available in window box shapes up to 18 inches long.

The issue of classic design and decoration in pots and urns need not be a problem: it is all a question of what plans the gardener has in mind. A case in point, I was examining an nice-looking urn decorated with a baroque design and thinking I could not put alpines in this, until it dawned on me how great it would look overflowing with the bright reds and purples of sempervivums.

Wooden half barrels are relatively trouble free once established, but I am hard pressed to suggest a purely alpine planting scheme for a half barrel. If you added plenty of drainage fill to the bottom and the appropriate soil mixture it would make an impact when planted with dwarf rhododendrons. Or, while on the shady theme, how about a grouping of gaultherias and vacciniums? In a sunny site, one or two of the larger daphnes would be fitting

Be sure that any container you purchase is manufactured expressly for garden use and will withstand the rigors of both winter and summer. It is reassuring to see that some makers identify their products as frost resistant.

Primula minima, only an inch or so tall in flower, is perfectly framed by this antique concrete square pot, which was made during the Depression by Ed Lohbrunner and his brother, of Victoria, British Columbia.

Rock plants for containers. There are lots of rock plants that will produce a bright floral extravaganza in containers, and they do not have to be replaced every year, like annuals must be. They will go through the winter and flower the next season without replanting, and go on year after year with nothing but a bit of clipping and trimming. True, the soil might have to be renewed once in a while if the vessel holds only a small amount. The time to do this is in spring, at the time when it is safe to start normal transplanting in your area.

Soil renewal is straightforward. Remove the plants from the planter and replace the old soil with new. Cut back any old growth on the plants and divide large clumps and replant them, and off you go for another couple of years.

In my garden, in early June there is a lovely, billowing mass of color composed of pale-pink, lilac-blue, and deep pink. Some might describe the latter as rose-purple. The pale pink flower is *Aethionema grandiflora*, a shrubby bush (technically a woody-based perennial) some 12 inches high, covered with silvery needle-like foliage and masses of terminal racemes of light pink flowers. It hails from the sunny, rocky dry slopes of Turkey, Iraq and Iran. The lilac-blue is a bell flower from Dalmatia called *Campanula portenschlagiana*, too lovely a plant to have such an unwieldy name. It was originally named

Campanula muralis, which is easier to remember. Its bright green, leafy cushions of small ivy-shaped, crinkly leaves are all but obscured by masses of deep-blue, bell-shaped flowers. This species enjoys a bit of shade, which makes it useful for gardeners with a shady exposure for plants.

The deeper pink color is supplied by a small plant that I regard as a bonus. It self-sows in the pots and garden, so all you have to do, once you have it, is dig up a few seedlings in the early spring and plant them wherever you wish. It is a biennial, semi-dwarf form of the European plant, *Lychnis flos-jovis*. It romps and sprawls about, and heads of flowers pop up above the rosettes of grayish leaves. They are easy to pull out when they turn up where they are not welcome. It is an easy and prolific plant from warm, dry climates. Give it some water during hot, dry spells, and it will show its appreciation by giving you masses of flowers. Never a collector's item, it is well worth growing for its carefree nature.

For ease of cultivation and bountiful flowers, many of the so-called ordinary rock plants should not be overlooked for pots. The once-popular *Aubrieta* species make excellent, undemanding container plants. Easily raised from seed, they give a generous display in a wide range of great colors. They love sun. Many years ago there were dozens of named varieties and clones in pure colors, but over the years many have been lost. However, today a single packet of quality seed will provide plenty of variety in the white through pink, rose, and lavender color range.

They are all lovers of sun and enjoy lime soil. Flowering starts early in spring and they will flower again if cut back right after the flowers fade. The name was given in honor of Claude Aubriet 1668-1743. The genus seems to have suffered from misspelling ever since, often listed as *Aubrietia* or *Aubretia*.

For shades of yellow, little can rival *Alyssum saxatile*, which is now correctly listed as *Aurinia saxatile*. It is a woody-based perennial that will grow to a foot or more with gray leaves and heads of bright yellow flowers. There is also a form with lemon-yellow flowers as its name *A. s.* 'Citrinum' suggests. Another named variety, *A. s.* 'Dudley Neville', offers orange-buff flowers to add to the medley of yellows.

Among silvery leaved *Dianthus* species there are larger varieties that make excellent container plants. They start to flower in early June, love the sun, and do not mind lean living conditions. The smaller alpine plants have a quieter appeal. Certainly the floral display is very generous in relation to their size. Maybe a planter with a suggestion of age about it would be appropriate for these. Perhaps an urn or pot with a solid, rustic, hand-hewn look would suit the timeless quality of these alpine flowers.

When the flowering season is over, the containers of alpine plants do not look dull and forlorn like those of annual summer flowers. Many rock plants are evergreen perennials, so the foliage persists throughout the year. In many cases the texture and color of foliage are just as effective as the flowers. Wonderful planting schemes are made by blending and combining foliage shapes and colors, using the same principles in these miniature landscapes as those employed in the fashionable perennial borders so popular today.

With care, several different varieties of plants will live in the same container for many years. Each year the plants increase in size, further enhancing the display. Once planted, the container is left to fill out and grow. Much of the enjoyment comes from watching the development of the plants to their full potential.

Pots for Alpine Plants

Good alpine plants start small. We normally obtain our plants from nurseries where they start very young plants in small pots and gradually move them, step by step, into slightly larger sizes as they grow. The pot, the roots, and the soil are all in balance. The roots get enough moisture, the vital air exchanges take place in the soil, and the soil remains fresh. This has long been good horticultural practice, and applies to the development of any plant whether it is an alpine, a rare tropical specimen, or a prize chrysanthemum.

A young alpine seedling or cutting thrust into too large a pot will be in trouble right from the start. It will not be able to utilize all the

soil around it, so the surplus will sit there until it becomes sour, and that is the end of the plant.

An ideal alpine plant should develop as slowly and naturally as possible. It is this tight, compact mounding habit that is its primary appeal. Our object is not to produce a big plant in a hurry. We are aiming for a solid plant with a sound root system and sturdy top growth, stems, branches, and leaves, all in harmony and balance with one another. Forcing growth too quickly gives us long, out-of-character stems and soft, floppy foliage.

All plants do not have the same rate of growth and this is very significant when it comes to many alpine plants. Slower growing alpine varieties have to stay in the same small pots in the nursery for several years before they reach a salable size. Other alpines grow much faster.

Provided a plant is well rooted in its pot, it will transplant equally well directly into the rock garden or, along with others, into a large trough or container.

Examine your plant. Here is a typical situation. Say you have just acquired a very choice little plant in one of those two-inch square plastic pots the nurseries use. You have decided to grow it as a potted specimen. Take it out of the nursery pot and look at the roots. Are they plentiful and active? Is the foliage healthy and growing? If the answer is yes, the active, healthily growing plant can safely be moved from the two-inch to a four-inch pot.

What if, on the other hand, the plant in question is not so vigorous. Its roots are weak and few, and there is not much activity with the foliage. To be cautious, leave it in the same pot until it brightens up and shows some activity.

More often than not, the less active plant is unhappy after being transported, perhaps as a mail order plant. Give it a few days of rest and recovery in a cool place with no stressful wind or hot sun.

Once the plants have settled down, you will be able assess their growth speed and make a better judgment on the pot sizes required. As alpines are relatively slow growing plants, they usually can remain in the same pot for the entire growing season.

Clay Flower Pots

Everyone is familiar with the clay garden pot and the jumble of shapes and sizes in which it appears. For the straightforward job of growing alpines, the standard clay flower pot is one of the best.

Clay is the traditional material for flowerpots. The classic terra cotta (baked earth) reddish orange clay flowerpot, plain or decorated, looks suitable everywhere. Shapes can be boxy or round, low or tall, and small or large. Pots come with or without pot feet or pot liners. Plants tend to do well in terra cotta pots because the thick sides provide plant roots a buffer from excess heat. They wick out excess water, making a healthy environment that is neither too wet nor too dry. Glazed pots are not absorbent, so they hold water in the pot longer, as do plastic pots.

As a rule, clay pots of all sorts need to be brought indoors for winter, for the water in the soil expands when it freezes. The slight enlargement of the contents of the clay pot is forceful enough to crack them.

The majority of sizes are convenient to handle and they will hold enough soil to sustain plants for a surprising length of time. Standard sizes are deep enough to offer an attractive depth of soil for a solidly supported root system. If it is used with a well designed potting soil it is able to retain enough moisture.

When shopping for pots, be sure ask whether they are intended for outdoor use, and can withstand frost. Look for the heavier make of pot, rather than the delicate, artistically formed ones. They usually look and feel solid and have a broad band around the rim. They are not elegant but are extremely practical. They will be heavy and costly if bought new.

Preferred sizes. Many of the plants we are likely to grow in pots will live happily in a six- or seven-inch standard sized flower pot. A typical pot with a six-inch diameter, measured from the inside just below the rim, will have an inside depth of close to six inches. Both larger and smaller sizes will have the same ratio of depth to width.

Most of my specimens, a wide selection of disparate species, are housed in six-inch standard pots. There are a few larger plants in seven- and eight-inch pots.

It is difficult to manage large potted plants, for, not only are they are they heavy to lug about, they require a lot of space and any benching or staging has to be build strongly enough to support this much weight.

⋙ Creating and Planting Alpine Gardens

Over time I have found it very convenient to standardize the type of pots I use, mainly limiting it to a single brand and model. A wide selection of sizes is not warranted and can become an annoying storage problem. Limit the number of small sizes at all costs. Two- to three-inch clay pots are too small for most purposes and I find it difficult to keep plants in them uniformly watered. It is better to use plastic pots for very small plants.

Minimize the number of larger sizes you stock to perhaps three or four. Select pots in the five, six, and seven-inch range and you won't go far wrong. If there is a sudden requirement for a larger pot, that is the time to acquire it.

Clay pans for alpines. As well as the full-depth standard flower pot, it is possible to use clay 'half-pots' or bulb pans. They are the same diameter as regular pots but only half the height. They are an appealing and useful range of pots, particularly the larger diameters. The three- to four-inch sizes can be a problem as they do not hold a lot of soil, but larger ones are fine. Small alpine species not needing much soil depth are great in these pots. They are unbeatable for growing the rare and choice small spring bulbs.

Wonderful spring displays can be produces by planting a pan of dwarf crocus, or even snowdrops. You can use sunny yellow aconites, Eranthis, or blue *Iris reticulata*. The bulbs do not have to be rare or difficult. In the early days of spring they will be a huge success.

Drainage holes. When viewing potential planters it is vital to check the drainage holes. I found many that were woefully inadequate. It is not difficult to upturn the planter and carefully enlarge the small holes. In many pots, despite seemingly adequate holes, there was an inch of water remaining from a summer shower because the holes were not made in the lowest point.

Watering is a regular task, and summer downpours can be torrential. During hot weather, gallons of water will pass through the planting, so ensure that the soil can drain rapidly.

In some cases irrigation water draining from a pot causes unsightly residues on the surface where the pot rests. Where this is an annoyance, use saucers. This is fine as long as the water evaporates before long. Otherwise, the water stored in the saucer will wick its way back into the roots.

A similar situation can arise on an uneven surface where the surface water drains back to the base of the pot and will be drawn back into the container's soil. All that it takes to stop this is a couple of thin shims under the pot, just enough to break the flow of water.

A newly planted trough with thin, linear slabs of tufa and complementary topdressing.

Troughs and Sinks

Old pig troughs and kitchen sinks may sound strange as garden containers. However, they are used for making some of the most attractive and successful alpine gardens. In Europe, the troughs and sinks are handmade stone artifacts from the distant agrarian past. Extremely heavy, they are attractively weathered and covered with lichens and mosses. Each one shows the individual chisel marks of the mason who made it.

Owing to their popularity, genuine troughs command very high prices where they are obtainable. In North America it is possible to see a few of them in botanic gardens and private rock gardens. There are also excellent reproductions chiseled from real stone. Originals can sometimes still be seen in the villages of Europe, where a hand-hewn public horse trough may be in use on the village green.

These sinks and troughs were made from blocks of local stone, first roughly squared and then hollowed out, no easy feat. Smaller troughs were made for feeding and watering smaller animals. Dyers, blacksmiths, and housewives all had their custom made troughs and sinks with the proportions they needed. In England, Saxon kings were

87

buried in hand-hewn stone coffins, similar to troughs. Yes, gardeners have been known to grow alpines in them, too!

Trough garden history. Where or when the cultivation of alpines in stone troughs actually began, whether in Europe or England, may never be known for certain. Reliable writers in England give most of the credit for originating the practice to Mistress Mary Saunders, a skilled alpine plant grower. In her Yorkshire garden, she used old discarded stone troughs and sinks as hospitals for sickly alpine plants in about 1920. She filled the troughs with river sand, and carefully planted and nursed the plants back to health.

Encouraged by the lovely results she achieved, she began to fill more troughs with healthy plants, sometimes filling one trough with a single species, each with its own special soil mixture.

A prominent nurseryman, Mr. Clarence Elliott of the Six Hills Alpine Plant Nursery, was impressed with her ideas He took the concept to his own garden and enlarged upon it, building miniature rock gardens in his own troughs. He planted a full range of plants in troughs in a way that extended the time that the plants could be seen in flower. Many people believe that he initiated this style of gardening. His son, Joe Elliott, who managed his own Broadwell Nursery in the English Cotswolds, wrote in his popular handbook, *Alpines in Sinks And Troughs,* written in 1974 for the Alpine Garden Society,

Container gardening at Wave Hill.

England, that his father had never claimed to be the originator of trough gardening.

That may well be the truth, but he certainly did more than anyone else to popularize the art of growing alpine plants in troughs. He regularly displayed his planted troughs at the prestigious Chelsea Flower Show in London, and as an outstanding garden writer, he wrote about them often. As their popularity grew, genuine troughs and sinks became hard to find as gardeners snapped them up.

Rural people had no use for them except as foundations for walls and buildings. Some were smashed and used as roadbed material. But as soon as they were found to be valuable, the price soared. Local quarries at the time made excellent copies to sell to gardeners, but even they proved to cost more than many were prepared to pay.

Faced with these problems, gardeners began to experiment with ways to make their own troughs, using various mixtures of concrete from which they cast, in wooden molds, troughs to suit their requirements. Today, many gardeners use foam insulation board for the molds because it is easier to cut the pieces and nail them together.

Tufa and hypertufa. 80 or so years ago, tufa rock was discovered and popularized as an excellent medium for growing rare and difficult alpines. It was sometimes ground into small pieces and mixed in with potting soil. Excellent rock gardens were built using tufa as the stone. Gardeners discovered that small alpine plants would thrive if planted directly into small holes drilled a block of tufa, with no soil added; every need came from the rock itself.

Clarence Elliott, as far back as 1929, planted a piece of tufa measuring about 18 by 12 inches with a dozen or so saxifrages, some sempervivums, several *Draba* species, *Polygala calcarea*, and a small edrianthus. All it required was moisture, which was supplied by sinking the block to half its depth in the rock garden.

These successes drew attention to tufa, creating demand and driving up the price, a situation that prompted thrifty alpine gardeners to find a substitute. Hypertufa was invented to serve as a substitute for real tufa. It is a porous, rocky substance with enough plant food to sustain alpines, and a root run for the small, tough fibers of the plants.

One of Clarence Elliott's early recipes for hypertufa consists of:

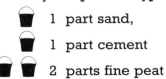

1 part sand,

1 part cement

2 parts fine peat

Measurements were by ratio or proportion by volume, not weight. The ingredients were thoroughly mixed in the dry state, and then water was stirred in until the mix had the consistency of thick cream. It was then poured into a sand mold that helped give it the impression or shape of an attractive rock.

Modifications and shortcuts were not long in coming. One involved inserting half-inch round wooden pegs into the sand mold at spots where plants would later be inserted in the hypertufa. Eventually the hypertufa was poured into the mold but stopped half an inch from the top. A day later the top half inch was topped off with a stronger mixture of concrete without any peat moss. This gave extra strength to the casting.

It was not long before the inspiration to make replicas of troughs from the same material (but with less water) came along and opened endless possibilities to imaginative gardeners, as it does to this day.

Making troughs today. Modern recipes for hypertufa are more scientific than the original mixes of Portland cement, sand, and peat. They are much lighter in weight because they use airy perlite or vermiculite in place of the heavy sand. A popular combination is :

3 parts Portland cement (Type I)

4 parts sifted peat

4 parts perlite or vermiculite

Reinforcing fibers, bonding agents, and cement coloring compounds can also be included. Water is carefully added to the mixed dry ingredients, but only the minimum amount is used: just enough to wet all the particles. This makes a stiff mixture that can be pressed firmly into place on or in a mold. Drainage holes can be formed as the troughs are molded, incorporating mesh or screen to prevent entry of bugs and pests.

The weight of the finished trough is of great concern to many gardeners, so lightweight hypertufa mixtures are in demand. They can be used for smaller editions of the classic trough which can be hauled around with no difficulty. Miniature rock gardens can be created in shallow, dish-like containers and then landscaped and planted with rock plants.

Large but relatively lightweight troughs can be fashioned by covering Styrofoam™ boxes with a modified hypertufa containing a bonding agent. It requires lots of work and planning and a skill that comes from practice, but great troughs are the reward.

Making troughs is a popular group project with garden clubs. The work and some of the costs can be shared and experts can be on hand to advise.

Where weight is not a problem, the old mixtures are still just as effective. I still use a simple mix of one part Portland cement to four parts coarse sand, and do not move the heavy trough very far. This way, I produce a trough that can withstand freezing without chipping and flaking.

Others have made small but heavy troughs using ordinary concrete mixes, packaged as "sand mix" or "mortar mix." These are off-the-shelf mixes of cement and sand, often sold at hardware stores in easily managed 25-pound bags. This is just enough to go with a makeshift rectangular mold such as a dishpan with the corners cut from rim to base and then taped. Since the concrete is larger when dry than when wet, make sure that the mold can be untaped or taken apart to release the trough when it has cured.

By carefully sculpting and distressing the hardening concrete 24 to 36 hours after molding it (the longer time is best in summer), it is not difficult to scratch in some strata lines to suggest stone. An old wire brush works wonders for this. Add some marks resembling the mason's hand chisel marks, round off the corners to suggest the hard use of the ages, and you will have an authentic looking trough that can pass for 200 years old—once it starts to show some weathering!

This relatively new hypertufa trough looks ancient because it has been distressed.

Trough design. Trough gardens catch the spirit of the high mountains when they contain several pieces of rock, placed using the same principles used in a large rock garden. This creates the impression of a miniature landscape. It is your choice whether or not to include rock and which sizes and types to use. Stones with interesting features, a rough or fissured surface, or prominent strata lines work well. When it is available, use pieces of real tufa. Brightly colored rocks can be used if you wish, bearing in mind that the overall effect is better if the rock color is in harmony with the color and texture of the hypertufa trough.

Arrange the rocks to provide crevices for choice plants and add interesting contours to otherwise flat surfaces. Like rocks in the rock garden, they should be partly submerged. Parallel lines of rocks can make a pleasing design.

Above, trough feet lend to the charm of this small trough by the doorway. Below, freeform hypertufa can look uncannily like real tufa, if well done. This is the author's trough planted with sempervivums.

92

During the planting and landscaping operation, do not bring the soil too close to the top of the trough. Leave half an inch or so of space below the rim. This will contain the topdressing as well as the irrigation water, giving it time to soak into the soil.

Topdressing. Now comes the finishing touch, the topdressing of gravel or stone chips. (See page 73.) Generously fill the space with the topdressing, allowing it to completely obscure the rim of the trough. It looks more natural if the inner sides of the trough are not visible. Don't be concerned—the topdressing will not hinder the watering. A topdressing not only adds that authentic touch, it also helps with water retention and keeps the soil temperature down in summer. It is reputed to keep weeds under control, but I have not found weeds a problem in my troughs.

The size and color of the gravel contribute to the look of the trough. Selection is a personal choice. The size of each particle is a matter of the scale. A large trough with good sized rocks will carry larger sizes of topdressing than a small one with small rocks. I think range of sizes looks more natural than a uniform size. One of my troughs has a topdressing that ranges in size from 1/4 to 1 inch. A less mountainous one has bits with a range of 1/4 to 1/2 inch.

Trough feet. Once planted, troughs are sometimes raised off the ground on sturdy stone bases, called feet. As far as I can see there is no essential horticultural reason for this, but it certainly adds to their visual impact.

There are several points to debate. A trough raised above the soil level will dry out faster. However, in most summers it will eventually dry out whether elevated or not. The same trough will freeze sooner because frost can assault it from all sides. The trough in contact with the soil will gain a small reprieve, but in any decent winter total freezing is inevitable.

It could be that raising a trough on feet improves drainage and keeps out sowbugs and other undesirable pests. It would be easier for them to enter a trough that is in direct contact with the soil or pavement, despite the fact that the drainage hole should be protected with a mesh screen. A trough raised above the soil will not be in danger of having the drainage hole become blocked by the surrounding soil.

A trough displayed on an impermeable surface is unlikely to have a drainage problem. Regardless of the surface texture, there is bound to be space between the two for the water to escape. The mesh screen will prevent unwanted creepy crawlies but the space beneath the trough and the ground may provide a haven other pests.

The answer belongs once again with the individual. It is traditional for troughs to be elevated at various heights, depending upon the landscape and the number of troughs involved. Where a number of troughs are involved, variety can become an important esthetic factor. When personal convenience is a factor, simply do what suits you. After all, it is your garden!

On a visit to Sissinghurst Castle I noticed that there were several troughs spaced along the building, and they were raised quite high on brick and mortar stands. I found them a little too high for me, until I remembered that Vita Sackville West was taller than I.

Slab Gardens

A slab garden is an alternative to the conventional trough, and offers opportunity for different designs. Many years ago I saw a wonderful rock garden built on a huge piece of flat Welsh slate. It must have been at least eight feet long, and it was set up on stone blocks, raising it off the ground maybe two feet or so. A border of small stones was artistically placed around the edges and cemented in place, making a low, irregular wall to help retain some soil. The rock garden was built within the walls. Soil was added and then planted with small alpines. The whole thing was magnificent. It had a timeless look and the patina of age. Mosses and lichens were established on the rocks. It had a glorious quality that has kept it fresh in my mind for many years. Someday I will have such a slab garden; unfortunately, I know it will not be made of Welsh slate.

It is possible, with effort and some skill, to make a similar garden using a concrete slab. I recently saw a couple of these modified slab gardens at Siskiyou Rare Plant Nursery, in Central Point, Oregon. A circular concrete slab several inches thick was poured. I am sure there would be some reinforcing steel within. The slab may have been four or five feet across and was raised on concrete blocks. I saw no retaining wall of stones around the edges. The slab may have been slightly dished but I could not see whether that was so. It was then landscaped by artfully stacking pieces of tufa rock in a tapering pattern. Plants were growing between the tufa chunks, and several saxifrages were thriving naturally in the rock itself.

This two-foot tufa rock was planted with succulents by Carl Greishaber.

Growing Plants on Tufa

One of the most natural as well as most space saving ways to grow alpines is to plant them directly in a handsome piece of tufa rock. It need not be a huge boulder, but the bigger the piece, the more you can do. On a large chunk, there is space for more and larger plants. One can create a whole rock garden on one stone.

The nature of tufa was explained earlier (page 26), noting its variable quality. In order to be able to plant living plants into the rock itself, it must be high quality tufa. The iron-hard kind will not do. Neither will soft, crumbly pieces.

Some pieces of tufa show patterns of a hard shiny substance running through them. These are best avoided. Sometimes hard, unattractive looking pieces are softer on the inside, and therefore usable. Test the surface by tapping a big nail into it. If the nail penetrates readily, this may be the piece that you are after.

Finding a piece with the right texture will not be easy. When shopping for tufa, check each stone carefully, looking for lots of small tunnels and spaces within. This is where the roots will live and where the moisture will be stored.

Once a piece has been selected, study it as you would a landscape to decide where the plants will be located, and roughly

95

mark the spots. Much will depend on the shape of the rock and any other features it may possess. Take advantage of depressions, bumps or cracks. Try to plant as naturally as possible,

The spacing of individual plants will be influenced by their ultimate size. A certain amount of guesswork will be involved because we will not be able to predict exactly how much growth each species may make.

Space larger growing varieties six inches apart and smaller ones as close as three inches to one another. Do not limit planting to the upper surfaces; feel free to use the vertical planes as well.

Making holes for plants. All it takes to make the holes is an electric drill with a 3/8-inch drill bit, or something similar. Drill slowly, aiming the drill toward the center of the stone, where the reserve of moisture is held.

The diameter of the hole does not have to be more than half an inch or so. A wider hole is not a better hole. The object is to get the roots to establish as quickly as possible into the solid tufa. I have found that a hole three inches deep works for most plants.

As the work progresses save all the tufa dust, then wash out the holes with water. At the same time, test them for drainage. I allow pressure from the hose to really clean the holes. I am always a little concerned that the rotary action of the drilling could seal the sides of the holes with compacted dust particles.

Planting. Plants in large holes usually fail because they are planted in soil-like composts within the holes. Once they have rooted in soil they are not going to adjust to living in bare tufa. They usually die of drought or starvation.

Always select a small rooted cutting or seedling and gently take away the soil from the roots. Resting the roots in a shallow dish of water will speed up this operation. After you wash off most of the soil, carefully remove the plant from the dish and allow the roots to drain. You will see how they form a neat tidy, tapering bundle, ideal for lowering them straight into the awaiting hole.

A drinking straw is a good tool for coaxing the roots into the bottom of the hole. Insert it gently, holding the plant so that its base just above the roots is exactly in line with the top of the hole. Think of the top of the hole as the soil level, so planting it in rock is like doing the same thing in a pot or the rock garden.

Now it is time to fill in the hole, but first here is a word about the planting medium. It must be virtually pure tufa dust saved from the hole-drilling operation. Since you are unlikely to have enough dust, you should make more by smashing a few small lumps of tufa and screening out the larger granules. Do not add any loam or peat to the dust, but a few particles of dustless sand can be used in desperate circumstances.

Keep the mixture dry so that it will flow easily into the depths of the planting hole. It may be necessary to gently assist it to settle around the roots using the rubber end of a pencil. Some gardeners top of the hole with a few pieces tufa wedged under the plant's leaves.

Watering and Care. Then the important step, watering, begins, requiring great care. Use a small eye dropper to water each hole slowly and repeatedly, allowing a few seconds for the water to thoroughly soak in.

Not every plant will grow. Those that fail will do so within the first couple of weeks. Hopefully you will have a few spares.

After planting and watering, find a cool, protected place for the planted tufa for the next couple of weeks and keep it moist. Once the plantings have settled down it is quite safe to water the tufa from overhead with a fine, gentle watering can.

A more reliable system of watering is to set the piece of tufa in a shallow vessel of water until it has absorbed enough to guarantee that it is thoroughly moist. It is not wise to leave it soaking for days at a time, as it encourages mosses.

Planted tufa rocks on display can be rather large boulders planted with a dozen or more plants. Not everyone is fortunate enough to own such prize pieces. I have several lumps the size of a small loaf of bread. One is planted with a silver saxifrage, another with a dianthus. Some of the smaller species of European primulas would be great in these modest pieces. My little tufa gardens are set in a flower pot filled with sand to keep them moist, and they make great displays.

Once the plants are well established, the pieces of planted tufa may be placed in their permanent homes. A particularly handsome piece of tufa makes great statement as a solitary feature in an intimate patio setting. The surface of a raised bed is also a natural setting for one or more. Do not overlook the rock garden itself. Where else would it look so natural?

I keep several planted tufa rocks of various sizes in my alpine house in shallow trays. There, they are always admired.

Above, Mike Lambert's 'wok' garden. Simultaneously a joke and a feat of horticulture, sedums and succulents grow beautifully in an alpine house, potted in a discarded metal wok. Below, an alpine house with the sashes up. Note the two gardeners on the left, who can work with the plants at a comfortable waist-high level.

7. Rock Gardens Under Glass

There are many ways to grow alpines, even in regions where they do not normally grow with ease. Among the best is certainly the type of greenhouse known as an alpine house, which has less heat than a traditional greenhouse. Coldframes and indoor growing arrangements are other rewarding possibilities. Inside protective structures, you can control moisture, pests, light, and temperature.

The Alpine House

You may be wondering, exactly what is an alpine house? Why would a rock gardener want a greenhouse? Rock plants are supposed to be hardy, and a greenhouse is extra work.

For many gardeners this is perfectly true, and a greenhouse or alpine house is not necessary for success with rock plants. The rarest and choicest alpine plants will grow in the outdoor rock garden, but the climate must be just right.

We know it is not possible to control the weather, so possession of a small greenhouse will add a great deal to an absorbing pastime. For example, a gardening friend recently stopped by for a visit. It was a warm afternoon and I was working in my greenhouse enjoying the cool, shaded interior, and planting rooted cuttings of silver saxifrages into a lump of tufa.

Within the protection of a greenhouse like mine, plants or cuttings have a greater chance of succeeding. These new plants are handy for creating a pan garden or planting a new trough garden at any time. They provide insurance, too. A newly purchased plant could die, so taking a few cuttings is always a wise move, particularly if the plant was hard to come by. Young cuttings in pots make excellent gifts and exchange material. Lots of my plants are obtained by exchange with other growers.

During my friend's visit, we looked at other projects in the greenhouse. He admired the piece of tufa planted with clumps of *Draba*, *Petrophytum*, and *Saxifaga*, tiny compact mounds of plants from the Big Horn Mountains in Wyoming. We examined the lump of Nevada pumice with a dozen or so thriving young seedlings of the challenging and fascinating native plant, *Kelseya uniflora*, from the mountains of Wyoming, Montana, and Idaho. Then we admired my favorite tufa planting, a stone planted with the almost legendary

⇾≫ Creating and Planting Alpine Gardens

Saxifraga valdensis and *Saxifraga caesia* from the rock crevices and fissures of the mountains of Europe. These plants are generous gifts from overseas friends. It was a pleasant garden visit for us both.

My small collection of *Primula allionii* pales in comparison to the incredible collections I have seen in Europe. Nevertheless, it gives me satisfaction to watch these plants slowly fill their four-inch pots in the alpine house. Early spring will see them covered with almost stemless flowers in a range bright pinks, regardless of the weather outside.

As the end of the summer approaches, it is time to start planning which dwarf bulbs to order for fall planting, for they should be potted as early in the fall as possible for early spring flower. Several pots of dwarf crocus, snowdrops, tiny narcissus, and wild tulips will brighten the dark days of late winter. These bulbs do not demand the fuss of the traditional methods of forcing into flower. In the alpine house, you just pot them up and keep them moist, but not wet, through the winter, and in early spring you will be rewarded.

The history of alpine houses. Having a greenhouse can add to your enjoyment of growing rock plants. The original idea of growing alpine plants in a greenhouse was established in Europe, most likely in England, where the damp and rainy winter weather is too wet for plants from drier climates, and for plants that spend their winter deep under a blanket of insulating snow. Eventually the greenhouses became known as alpine houses.

Kabschia saxifrages in the author's alpine house.

Originally the plants were grown in pots and pans of various sizes placed on waist-high benches covered with a layer of stone chippings, which assisted with rapid drainage. Some growers plunged their potted plants into several inches of sand to slow the drying of the soil and to add a measure of insulation from both heat and cold.

It was not long before those gardeners who disliked growing plants in any kind of pot decided to create small rock gardens within their greenhouses. Some people chose to build them directly on the soil floor and fill much of the greenhouse this way. Others built small, naturalistic rock gardens on top of strengthened benches.

The advantage of a bench is that it does away with bending. With all the plants at a convenient height, it is easier to work on the plants, to groom them, to spot potential troubles, and, last but not least, to enjoy them.

Heating and ventilation. Greenhouses normally contain tender plants that require cosseting and do not like being exposed to rapid or extreme temperature changes, nor do they relish frigid drafts. Alpines and rock plants, on the other hand, demand as much fresh air as they can get when housed in greenhouses or cold frames.

Regular greenhouses are normally equipped with one or two windows along the side walls and along the ridge. These windows, called ventilators, may be opened partially or fully open, depending on the inside temperature and the amount of outside air required to cool the inside.

These few ventilators are not enough to supply the constant flow of cool air which the alpine plants demand. Therefore, rows of ventilators are added, one row along the vertical sidewalls, plus two more on each side of the ridge. All of them run the full length of the house. They are usually joined together as one.

Windows along the entire side of the alpine house open for the good ventilation preferred by alpine plants.

101

⇛ Creating and Planting Alpine Gardens

In smaller greenhouses it is convenient to manipulate them by hand. In larger structures it may be necessary to install mechanical or geared opening devices operated by the turning a wheel. The ultimate ventilators are operated automatically by thermostats that respond to preset temperatures.

There are other sophisticated options available, including a device that senses rain and automatically closes the ventilators.

Several years ago in Great Britain we had sliding shutters installed in the walls, beneath the inside benches. By manipulating them, ventilation was possible during heavy wet fog or wet and strong winds. These were designed prevent moisture from entering and wetting the leaves, which could encourage decay.

In the beginning, the British alpine house was unheated, and any form of heating was looked upon with disdain. Over the years, attitudes have changed with the widening scope of alpine species which have become available from new places far and wide. To succeed with the challenging new species, modern greenhouse devices are used. Heating, cooling, and air flow can be controlled. It is feasible now to have an automated greenhouse—costly perhaps, but a boon to the absent gardener.

The prime consideration is fresh air at all times, summer and winter. In winter, the plants are kept barely moist. Just enough moisture is applied to keep them from drought damage. Watering should always be done on a bright sunny morning, particularly in wintertime. Wait until it is no longer freezing. This way, the plants have all day to rid themselves of surplus moisture before night brings freezing temperatures once more.

There were six alpine houses at the alpine nursery where I was trained, and none had any artificial heat. On cold winter mornings when pots were partially frozen, the ventilators were gradually opened as the outside temperature began to rise. This permitted the plants and pots to slowly thaw, minimizing root and foliage damage. Under bright sunny conditions, sheets of newspaper were used to cover susceptible species to shade them. This kept them from suffering from leaf-burn from the sun.

The British method of keeping an alpine house sounds so simple, but will it work here in North America with our long, cold winters and hot summers? In a few mild regions we can employ unheated greenhouses, but in most, we must add heat to maintain a temperature at or just above the freezing point. We need a method of shading and cooling the greenhouse to combat the heat of spring and summer. In some regions we must use fans to combat excess humidity.

Sunrooms

Existing sunrooms attached to buildings can sometimes be used to grow alpines. There may be space for informal pools and waterfalls, a raised bed, or benches of potted alpines. It is conceivable that propagation facilities could be incorporated. But don't go rushing in. There are important environmental conditions plants must have, and, alas, not all sunrooms provide them.

First and foremost is light. What is the sunroom roof made of? Is it clear or colored glass? Or is it a conventional roof? The room is attached to a house, so consider the direction from which light comes. What route does the sun take?

Is the atmosphere warm and dry, or is there a comfortable degree of humidity? Most plants must have humidity. Without it you will be restricted to cacti and succulents. There is nothing wrong with that plan if it appeals to you, and many of these dryland plants grow in the mountains anyway.

Can a cool temperature be maintained throughout winter and summer, without opposition from family members? Then there is the ever-present demand for good ventilation for the plants.

All these are important factors that will influence the types of plants you will be able to grow in a sunroom.

Are there plants growing there now? If so, what are they? Are they low light varieties? The condition of existing plants will indicate the adequacy of the environment. Unhappy plants never look attractive. Without sufficient light, your lovely dwarf alpines will be reaching for it, either leaning toward the windows or reaching toward the non-existent sky. Furthermore, any foliage produced will be a sorry looking sight and be at the cost of flowers.

If your sunroom is not suitable for alpines, you can grow the plants somewhere else and bring them into the sunroom to be displayed, then return them outdoors or to an alpine house when they begin to show their displeasure.

Consider Adding a Greenhouse

Does a greenhouse have a place in your alpine garden? Perhaps it does, if there is room for it. Before making any serious decisions, ask yourself whether you are you prepared to accept the demands of the totally dependent plants within. It is the same as having pets. Obviously this not for everyone. On the other hand, if you like to be at home, love dabbling with rock plants, and enjoy making your own gadgets, then an alpine house is a must. There are endless things to make that will improve and simplify the daily operations.

My ideal alpine house would be large enough to house an indoor rock garden on the ground with a circular path all around it. Plus I would have a small seating area where I could sit and enjoy the surroundings regardless of the weather outside. Finally, it would offer the luxury of space for a bench where I could do a bit of plant propagation and also grow some choice plants in pots.

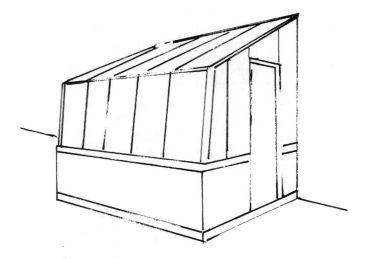

Styles of Greenhouses

Greenhouses are available in many shapes and sizes, from very basic structures to top-of-the-line Victorian classic styles with curved eaves and architectural embellishments, including lots of finials. Virtually any model of greenhouse can be modified for use as an alpine house. A free-standing greenhouse with low-pitched roof is a good choice. The lean-to style built against the wall of a building is a convenient alternative, if it receives plenty of light. Greenhouse frames may be manufactured of wood or aluminum, with a wide range of finishes.

Where site conditions permit, install a second door, so there is one at each end. This is a great convenience during daily operations, and helps you capture free ventilation from summer breezes.

Glazing. Greenhouses may be fully glazed. That is, the glass or plastic used to enclose the greenhouse can extend from ground level to the apex of the roof. This may cause heat loss but allows maximum sunlight to enter. Greenhouses may be partially glazed, instead. There are designs utilizing a low, solid side wall of brick, concrete blocks, stone, or wooden boards. Partial glazing is generally used where plants will be grown on benches, and having light under the bench is not so important.

Some free-standing greenhouses have vertical side walls while others, for crops grown at ground level, have inwardly sloping side walls. Roof shapes vary and include simple span roofs, angled hip roofs, and simple hoop-shaped structures, which are very popular.

How the alpine house will be used affects the choice of vertical or sloping side walls. A rock garden built at ground level within the house requires that light reach the plants at ground level. This is where the fully glazed model is ideal. Where you plan to grow plants on benches, the sides can be made of boards or other kinds of low walls, since light is not normally required under the benches. As you can imagine, heat loss can be minimized with solid side walls, even though a lot of heat loss still occurs through the roof.

Consider the options as you select the type of greenhouse that meets your requirements. The right choice is a matter of personal opinion. Esthetics can be important. Not every site is enhanced by a greenhouse, nor does everyone see beauty in one.

Headroom. Where a rock garden is to be built in the center of the greenhouse floor, and paths are planned to circulate around it, headroom is important. Consider the height of the side walls and the roof shape. Free access all around is vital. This situation requires that the walls be straight. A simple span roof is best. As an alternative design, the rock garden can be constructed around the outside walls with a single central path. In this design all viewing will be done from the central path, where headroom is plentiful.

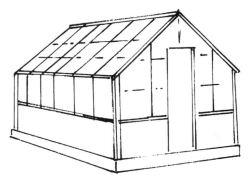

Headroom is greatest in the center of the hipped-roof alpine house. The lower portion of the sides is solid, which minimizes heat loss but admits less light than totally glazed sides.

When benches will be used in the alpine house, sloping walls are not so problematic although they do tend to take up valuable floor space owing to the slope of the side wall. Since plants will occupy the benches, headroom presents no problem. The space beneath benches can be valuable space for storing dormant or resting plants, and in summer the shade is an asset. These are points to consider when planning whether to select fully glazed side walls or solid ones.

Exposure. As part of your planning, it is wise to study the environmental requirements of the greenhouse. A greenhouse is much like a plant. It requires plenty of light and air, so try to locate it with this in mind. On a small site there may not be a lot of choice in finding a spot for the greenhouse, but avoid dark corners and the close proximity of trees.

Study the direction of the prevailing winter winds, particularly those that bring icy gales. Where there are alternatives, choose a place where the structure will receive some degree of protection. When this is just not possible, there are a few things that can be done to lessen heat loss.

Plant a hedge if space permits. Hedging is a long-term project, so an open fence, set up on the snow-fencing principle, will help enormously in cutting the icy blast. It can be removed in the spring. The windbreak fence can be designed as a garden feature in its own right using decorative trellis work.

To me the alpine house is a haven where I can go and work with my plants on those wet, windy days. Even in the dead of winter there is always something you can do, even if it is removing the odd dead leaf or two. It always pays just to pick up a pot and examine the plant; you can spot early signs of disease or insects. You may find that the plant is dangerously in need of water. Even in sunny, freezing weather, plants will use moisture.

About Heating

Gardeners who dwell in places where winter is long and bitter will have to introduce heat into the alpine house if they want to grow alpine plants. It is true that alpine plants are tough, adept at surviving cold. Most of the plants spend their winter under a blanket of snow. Once this insulating blanket arrives in fall, it remains until spring.

Plants that live on hard, windswept, snowless ridges and crags survive by developing an extremely low, ground-hugging profile with compact, tight, wooly foliage.

These little gems are designed to survive the cold, dry weather of their native habitat, but not a warm spell in mid-winter, winter rain, or alternate freezing and thawing. We come along and stick them into a flowerpot with no other insulation than a thin layer of terra cotta, then set them up, exposed, on raised staging in a house made of glass, and expect them to thrive. No wonder they have trouble surviving!

All gardeners know the value of a good snowfall and are familiar with the damage a cold, snowless winter can do.

How much heat is needed inside the alpine house? Just enough to prevent heavy freezing. Ideally, we should maintain a temperature at the freezing point or just above it, but this is hard to do. Our object is to approximate conditions below the snow, where alpine plants remain dormant, unaffected by weather conditions at the soil surface.

In an alpine house, the major problem is repeated freezing and thawing. A sunny day will send the temperature up high enough to thaw foliage. The leaves then start to transpire. Normally this moisture would be replaced by the roots. Since the roots are still encased in frozen soil, they are unable to function, so the leaves are damaged by the lack of moisture.

If pots and plants once frozen would remain so, all would be a lot simpler. The soil within the pot expands upward as it freezes, which is the only direction it is free to go, unless it bursts the sides of the pot. As the soil expands, the roots are strained and torn. Eventually parts of the roots will sit naked and exposed to the next cycle of freezing and thawing. When the next sunny day arrives, the cruel cycle starts again. Damage to the roots is repeated and the drying effect of sunshine further weakens the plants until they finally die.

Winter Management

It would be ideal if there were an overall formula for the winter management of an alpine house. There are so many variables due to geographic differences. Additionally, winters are seldom the same from year to year. A constant minimal winter temperature of 33 to 35 would be ideal. If only it were humanly possible to maintain it! But of course it is not easily accomplished when the temperature outside fluctuates from warm to cold, and the weather from sunny to cloudy.

The first challenge begins early on a winter's day. The morning sun soon raises the daytime temperature within the greenhouse by several degrees, eventually reaching a point when some ventilation is required to bring the temperature down. On such occasions it may be necessary to shade a few of the plants that are susceptible to sun damage. Often this is only a matter of covering them with a few sheets of newspaper. It is a simple matter to raise the roof ventilators to cool things down, but what if you are at work or otherwise absent? Then you need a good and trusted friend who will do it for you. Or you can install an automatic system. There are uncomplicated systems that will either open the vents when instructed by a thermostat or a heat-sensitive wire device, or introduce cool air and circulate it using fans. As sunset draws near the temperature starts to drop, the ventilators will have to be closed. The thermostats will shut down any cool air systems that are operating.

Do not be tempted to build up a little free heat by shutting the house down while the sun still has some strength in it. The temperature will rise, but so will the humidity. As the air starts to cool, moisture held in the warm air will condense. Everything you touch will be beaded with moisture including the foliage and all parts of the sleeping plants. This is the perfect condition for the spread and establishment of all manner of decay fungi.

As freezing weather penetrates the walls and glass, it will first freeze those pots closest to the glass, the doors, and the walls, particularly at ground level and near the exposed gable ends. Icy winds will find weak spots in an apparently snug house. Little piles of driven snow will appear in the strangest places, indicating that there are leaks. It is a simple matter to rearrange the plants once these cold pockets are known. Alpines are not tropical plants, and a few degrees of frost are not necessarily fatal.

This is a good time to remember that there can be no half measures. Temperatures must be kept low, even at the risk of some freezing. The alpine greenhouse is not the place to store those pesky geraniums, fuchsias, and dahlias. It will be far cheaper to buy fresh stock in the spring than jeopardize the whole alpine collection by raising temperatures to accommodate tender plants. Later on, when spring rolls around, it will be possible to start a few seeds of early vegetables and herbs in the alpine house. Do not let a few dollars worth of bedding plants ruin your alpines.

Minimizing frost exposure. There are several ways to take some of the edge off the penetrating frost. The greenhouse has been situated where it will be somewhat protected from cold wind, and this is a great help. Fences, temporary or permanent, should be in place if the site permits.

Next there is double glazing, a large, heavy item. For the greenhouse to carry the extra weight, it must be engineered into the original structure of the house, so it is a cost factor. Double glazing cuts down considerably on light penetration. Once the growing season starts, this can be a problem with some plants.

Lining the inside walls with a blanket of thin plastic sheeting for the winter months is an excellent way of insulating, although I find it a challenging operation. It calls for a great deal of ingenuity and patience.

Specially-made insulating panels attached to the vertical walls will make a difference in how much heat is lost. There are many efficient fiberglass products available for this purpose. This is a good project for the home handyman. He can devise a method of attaching the insulating material to a series of lightweight wooden panels to keep the material dry and protected from wear.

Where benches are arranged along outside walls, be sure to distance them from the walls by about six inches to allow free air circulation between them and the wall.

Heating Equipment

I have been emphasizing the need to preserve low temperatures, but sometimes temperatures can suddenly become too low. Although a sharp temperature drop overnight may not be fatal, it is better to avoid it, since under some conditions it can cause damage to the greenhouse structure and susceptible items within, such as water pipes. Therefore, purchase an effective heating unit that it large enough to supply the demand for heat without having to strain.

The popular methods of heating are with oil, natural gas, electricity, and kerosene. Your choice may be dictated by the method used to heat your home. It may be possible to extend the house heating to the greenhouse, providing the distance is not too great. It is worth investigation.

Heating systems are complicated and expensive, and it is wise to consult a specialist before making a decision. There are several excellent books on the subject that will give an overall introduction to greenhouses. One is *Growing under Glass** by Kenneth A. Beckett. The content is valuable and presented in a straightforward manner; the illustrations and diagrams are excellent.

My preference is for thermostatically controlled electric fan heaters that are able to control temperatures to within a degree or two, quickly, with no waste. The fans circulate the warmed air, keeping the atmosphere buoyant, and thereby combatting fungal diseases.

One drawback with electrical heating is that there can be a power failure. This always happens on the coldest night of the year. Nine times out of ten there is a cold wind blowing, which cools the greenhouse down very fast. Without electrical power, the choice of heating becomes limited. Look at emergency heaters that were designed for the smaller greenhouse which are safe and trouble free. The larger models use propane cylinders, to which they are connected in various ways. When considering a propane heater, discuss the options with a qualified supplier. Be sure to ask about the fresh air supply each model requires and what type of venting should be provided.

* Published in cooperation with the Royal Horticultural Society, Mitchell Beazley Publishers, 1981.

The alpine house at Wave Hill in New York features tiny cylamen. The glazing is removed for temperature control during warm months.

Similar advice applies to kerosene heaters. Again, go after models made for greenhouse work. Kerosene heaters can be dangerous. They give off fumes that are harmful to plants and humans. These heaters produce water vapor as they burn. After prolonged use, they create sufficient humidity to be quite harmful to dormant foliage.

Spring and Summer Management

No sooner do we relax after winter and its problems are over, and enjoy the early spring sunshine, than we suddenly find that the temperature in the greenhouse begins to soar. The plants enjoy it for a while, but soon start to grow fast and demand more water. Unfortunately, some of the tender foliage, unaccustomed to the strong sunlight magnified through the glass, will be damaged.

Temperature can be lowered by opening doors and all the ventilators during the bright daytime. Close them again at night, for spring frost still has a bite. Do not rush to close the greenhouse—remember that the condensation of moisture is a problem.

Before long, the sun will become so strong that the greenhouse will have to remain fully open night and day to maintain a cool temperature. The winter problem of maintaining a minimum temperature is replaced by the panic of trying to cool things down.

Left unresolved, the alpine house will soon assume a desert-like climate where alpine plants cannot survive.

There are alternatives. If space permits, remove the plants from the alpine house and install them in outside cold frames (page 114) or plunge beds (beds in which the pots are mostly submerged in the soil). Sometimes these amenities can be incorporated adjacent to the greenhouse. They can be made into an added attraction, particularly if the pots of plants are staged to show the plants to their best advantage. Bear in mind that you should not place them too close to the greenhouse because rainwater from summer storms pours off the roof. It is hardly necessary to mention what heavy snowfalls will do when they slide off a pitched roof.

Whatever action is taken, the greenhouse itself will have to be shaded and cooled. This is normally done by installing some form of shading to the glass. It is generally accepted that shading materials applied to the exterior are more effective than interior installations since they prevent the full force of the sun from hitting the glass, which does not heat up and transmit the heat inside.

One of the quickest and easiest methods of shading is to whitewash the glass. Today there are products prepared solely for this purpose; they are usually tinted green. I recall that back when I was an apprentice it was my job to do this in the early days of spring. We used hydrated lime mixed with water and sprayed it onto the glass. It worked well and was easily washed off by the next spring rain, which was the plan, so as not to deprive the plants of light during cloudy days.

Whitewash has several drawbacks for the home gardener. It is a messy procedure, and it gets on the greenhouse structure. It can stain aluminum sash bars, it makes a mess of paintwork, and it splashes onto the ground and anything nearby, such as the garden furniture and the patio. Commercial shading compounds have a bonding agent that ensures that they stick to the glass. This works all too well, as you will learn when removing them in the fall.

Slatted roller blinds of wood or metal, attached to the central ridge are the ideal solution, for it is a simple matter to raise and lower them by manipulating the strings. Then there is the ultimate but more expensive solution: automatic blinds that are operated electronic ally. The roller blinds are best. Less costly ones can be made from the many shade cloths available.

It is not difficult for the owner of a modest sized greenhouse to fabricate a method of shading using one of the several cloth-like shading materials available today. Much depends on the model of house. For example, my alpine house is ten feet wide and 18 feet long. I have made eight light, wooden frames, four feet by four feet, to which I have nailed strips of one-inch wooden lath, spaced about one and half inches apart. Since I have a simple span roof on my alpine house it is a simple matter to lay them on the roof. I screwed small wooden stops to the eaves of the house to prevent them from sliding off the roof. So far I have not had to secure them down, and, so far, the wind has not blown then off. However, in some parts of the country where winds are not so gentle it would be wise to secure them with stronger fasteners.

While my wooden screens are not particularly heavy, they are not that easy to handle alone. Lighter screens can be made by substituting shade cloth for wooden lath strips.

While exterior shading is very effective, some gardeners might find it difficult to install single-handed, as some ladder work may be required. Employing a contractor to install it might be just too much for the budget. Shading can be applied to the inside where it is simpler and more affordable than installing outdoor shading.

A good method is similar to household curtain systems; the shade cloth is attached by curtain rings to wires running the length of the top and bottom rafters. When shading is needed all one has to do is draw the curtains.

Summer. Realistically, there is little that can be done to really cool the house down in the heat of a North American summer. A lot can be accomplished to combat summer heat in the initial planning stage. Many greenhouse suppliers will provide continuous ventilators along the ridge and the sidewalls of their greenhouses. Full-length

continuous ventilators permit the house to be fully opened all along the length. The open doors at each end and the shading system go a long way to alleviate heat from the sun.

Many alpine house owners have electric fans running constantly. On still, muggy days, they help to circulate the heavy, damp air. Any movement of air around a plant on such days is better than none. At least it helps to prevent attack by decay fungi. With all the doors and windows open, all the fans can do is stir the ambient air.

Large commercial greenhouses use a cooling method where air is drawn through a moist pad mounted on the side or end of a greenhouse. As the moisture evaporates it cools the air. This cool air is drawn through the greenhouse and extracted by means of large fans in the side opposite the pads.

This method is a bit complicated for a home greenhouse but many greenhouse owners do install extractor fans without the moist pads to provide the cooling. I would recommend having a shaded and well-ventilated structure with a fan or two to stir the air rather than an air-cooling system.

Size and Style

When selecting your greenhouse, consider buying the largest model that will fit in the space you have available. A small greenhouse may sound attractive and even manageable, but the small ones are inefficient. They heat up rapidly and cool down just as fast, which contributes to various difficulties. The small volume does not provide the reserve or buffer that a larger structure offers. The extra volume slows down rapid temperature change.

You will have no trouble utilizing the space, and the cost factor in operating a larger greenhouse will not be that significant. The main difference will be the initial cost.

If you plan to build a rock garden within the structure, then you have to decide on the form it will take, as this will have a direct bearing on the style of house you choose. Draw a rough sketch of how you imagine the rock garden will look when completed. Naturally you will have to set some limits on its width. The height of your rocky structure is not such a consideration under glass, since all irrigation will have to be supplied anyway. Then think about access to the garden—in other words, the placement of the path or paths. Convenience is paramount, not only for visitors who come to enjoy the garden, but also for the gardener who has to do the maintenance. Don't forget that everything has to be hauled in and out. Perhaps you can consider double doors.

When it comes to deciding the width of your greenhouse, the usual home garden choices are six feet, eight feet, ten feet, and 12 feet. Wider houses are available in commercial sizes.

Where you are thinking about an indoor garden, a square greenhouse makes it easier to design a plan that includes paths. A 12 by 12 foot format provides better options than the long narrow shape of a 10 by12 foot model.

Where space is not a problem, an added six feet of length for a working area will be extremely convenient and you will appreciate it. A bench for potting, perhaps a small propagating area, and some extra storage space are always valuable. A stool tucked under the bench is very handy for all kinds of purposes, including just sitting on it to enjoy your surroundings.

Cold Frames

The cold frame was originally a simple, bottomless wooden box covered with a removable pane of glass as a lid, and many gardeners still use this basic design. Today, cold frames can be purchased in a wide range of sizes, models, and materials. The units are much lighter and easier to handle. Glass is still popular and is used along with fiberglass, polycarbonate, and other similar films. Before selecting any type of frame, thoroughly think through what you intend to grow in it, for this will influence your choice.

The simple oblong box idea takes a lot of beating. It is easy to make, relatively inexpensive, very versatile, and convenient to work in. Select some wooden boards and arrange them so those that make up the rear walls will be higher than the front walls. Make the side walls with angled boards cut to four feet long (or the length of the sashes). The angle corresponds to the difference in height from rear to front walls.

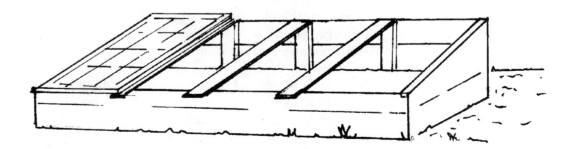

Sash bars are placed at intervals spaced to receive and support the covering glass or poly film sashes. Three feet by four feet is a convenient size. The length is optional, depending on the length of frame that is required. A solidly built frame will have sashbars running from front to back, not only bracing the walls of the frame but giving the sashes themselves support.

These sash bars normally are grooved on each side providing a channel to drain rainwater or melting snow that finds its way between the sashes. The sash bars should protrude slightly at the lower end, or front of the frame, to make sure the water drains away from the frame. The same applies the sashes themselves. Let them protrude a few inches, allowing water to drip outside the frame. There is little point in putting a rainproof cover over the frame if water drips back into it.

Where solid structures are required the wood can be replaced with bricks, masonry or poured concrete. Glass-walled models where the glass is set in metal frames may be purchased in several sizes.

Several patterns of very attractive span roofed frames of glass and aluminumare available; they look like very low greenhouses. These are excellent for the summer culture of bulbs.

Hot beds

If there are cold frames then it stands to reason that there are hot frames too, except they are called hot beds. These were traditionally heated by layers of manure buried beneath the surface soil mixture. It was part of the gardeners' skill to know exactly what thickness of manure would produce the right amount of heat and the length of time it would last. Today, methods are more precise and the heat is controlled by thermostats. Instead of manure, the heat comes from piped steam, hot water, or electric heating cables.

Originally, in all likelihood, no artificial heat was used in cold frames, hence the name. They acquire their heat from the sun and their cold protection from the thickness of the glazing material. The temperature within was controlled by opening or closing the glass covering. Additional frost protection was provided by covering the glass with insulating straw mats. Frames were located in an open, sunny place where drainage was perfect.

The purpose was to extend the growing season, getting a jump on spring and gaining a longer frost-free period in the fall. Seedlings from the greenhouse were housed in the frame to harden them off prior to planting in the garden. Often cucumbers, melons, and tomatoes were grown right in the frame.

Uses of a cold frame. Alpine gardeners use frames to harden off seedlings both ornamental and edible, prior to planting in the garden, as a place for bulbs in their resting period during summer, and to house hardy alpine plants during winter or for cool summer quarters.

115

A cold frame is ideal for propagating and protecting plants. For instance, I visited a friend recently and came home with a few cuttings and a couple of tiny, rooted pieces teased from the parent plant. What was I to do with them? The temperature outside was warm, above 80. I suppose it might be possible to root the cuttings in a window, but what of the delicate rooted pieces? They wouldn't last five minutes planted outside in the sunny rock garden, but a cool, shaded frame would be ideal for them. The cuttings could be rooted in a pot of sand and the division potted in a light compost.

A parcel of plants arrived this morning right in the middle of a warm dry spell. They arrived in good shape, but to go and plant them outside, straight from the box— I think not! They have been potted in a light mix and have enjoyed a cool respite in an inch or so of water. Now the foliage looks great and a few flowers have appeared. You know where they are!

Do you have a few choice specimens grown in a pot? When they are out of flower, where are they? Sitting around the patio or the service area, (we all have one), perhaps suffering from heat. They would do better inside a cool, shaded frame.

If you grow dwarf bulbs in pots, you may already know the value of the cold frame. Where else can they go in the summer but the cold frame, with its cover preventing summer rains from disturbing the dormant bulbs.

Do you have a greenhouse that you use as an alpine house? Do you think the plants therein would be happier in the cooler environment of a cold frame for the summer? They will require less attention there and it will be simpler for the lucky person who will have to care for them when you go on that trip to the mountains.

That makes a pretty convincing case for a cold frame for summer use and I trust the references to the frame being a cool place were not

missed. As a summer resting place for alpines, the frame is more effective if can be located in a spot protected from full sun. A partially shaded spot will do fine and if more protection is required, the glass or plastic sashes can be replaced with sashes covered with a lightweight shading cloth. Be sure to permit free air movement by raising the sashes several inches above the top of the frame.

Having been trained in England I was raised to refer to the glass that covered cold frames as a 'light.' In the U.S. I learned to call it a 'sash.' There are several variations. During my early years I encountered French lights, Dutch lights, and a couple of others. The only significant difference among them was their size, so now when discussing frames, I call them sashes.

It is not difficult to make a case for the value of investing in a frame for the summer months, but for the dead of winter it is not so easy. However, if the plants are dormant and quite hardy, a frame is very useful. It is far better than nothing at all.

At Stonecrop Nurseries, near Cold Spring on Hudson, N.Y., we overwintered most of the saleable three-inch potted plants in very traditional cold frames. They were built of wood and sloped from back to front in the approved manner. The frames were covered with glazed sashes once the plants had a layer salt hay. The sashes were partially open to allow a flow of air to keep the salt hay dry so it would not decay. They were firmly closed and anchored down once winter's grip was firmly established.

Any plants grown in a frame will have to be pretty hardy. Despite the insulation a frame provides, it is not enough protect borderline plants. Plants housed in a frame over winter have to be checked regularly for mildew, other fungi, and pests. Do not forget the little vermin that think they have found paradise. A frame is not so easy to manage through the winter. The vagaries of winter cause fluctuations within the frame that have to be regularly monitored. Opening and closing the frames is not the most pleasant task, particularly after a heavy snowfall.

The Bulb Frame

My earlier reference to growing bulbs in a cold frame warrants further discussion because bulb growing can be a rewarding aspect of alpine gardening. It is popular with many skilled gardeners, and over time they have developed the art of managing the bulb frame.

117

In its most rudimentary form, a bulb frame is nothing more than a raised bed with a cold frame set on top of it. The main objective is to control rain falling on the bulbs at a time in their life cycle when they are resting and moisture is not welcome.

The raised part of the bulb frame is built in the same manner as a raised bed, with two exceptions. One, the walls are made of concrete blocks, bricks, or railway ties; and are strong and stable enough to bear the weight of the frame that will be securely anchored to the top of the walls.

Two, the four walls should be rodent proof, which is not possible with natural stone. There must be no convenient gaps for them to wriggle through. It is wise to lay wire netting over the base of the bed to prevent underground entry. Purchase extra width and length so that there is enough to bend it part way up the inside walls, forming a basket. This will prevent burrowing creatures from gaining access through the sides or beneath the foundation of the frame.

The raised bed can be between 18 and 24 inches high. Bearing in mind that good drainage is the object, the raised bed may have to be higher on a damp site. A four foot wide bed is convenient, allowing access from both sides without your having to reach and strain. The length is up to the gardener. Decide on the dimensions of the frame, then build the raised bed wide enough to allow enough space for the frame to be solidly anchored, Plan it so that the sashes overhang the wall slightly, to shed rainwater. That way it does not drip into the soil, so defeating the whole purpose of the bulb frame.

Choosing a top for the bulb frame. There are models of aluminum and glass which look like a small greenhouse, with a span roof. Some have glass-sided walls which may or not be designed to open for extra ventilation. I find the design attractive, but side walls make it difficult to reach inside. The glass windows are usually hinged at the ridge, but some slide up and down. This makes them vulnerable to sudden gusts of wind.

I prefer the conventional cold frame to a span roof type. It is easier to work with because you can remove the window sashes and climb right in to the frame. If the structure is strong enough, it is convenient to sit on it as you work with the plants.

Sashes covered with glass are heavy, due to the weight of the glass and the sturdy lumber required to support it. A sash measuring three feet by four feet is awkward for one person to handle. With today's plastics it is possible to make far lighter sashes. Be sure they are well anchored, or they will end up in the neighbor's garden.

A solidly built frame must have sashbars running from front to back, not only to brace the sides but to give the sashes themselves support. The sashbars normally are grooved to channel the rainwater the gets in between the sash. There is little point in putting a rainproof cover over the frame if the rain pours off the end of the frame, right into the soil.

Growing the bulbs. The bulbs may be grown in pots, or they may be planted directly into a prepared bed in the bulb frame or alpine house. Pot-grown bulbs may be plunged into sand, pot and all, inside the bulb frame.

Winter temperatures will influence which species can be grown outside of an alpine house. Within an alpine house, the bulbs have protection from extreme cold. The bulbs will be grown in pots unless the greenhouse is operated solely for them. If it is, you can grow them in raised beds or in pots, or both.

The objective is not to force the bulbs into early flower by manipulating light, darkness, or temperature. Many choice dwarf species would not cooperate. There will be plenty of enjoyable early flowers on some of the bulbs, without having to force them.

Bulbs planted directly in the bulb frame certainly grow well, for they have plenty of root run and sufficient nutrients. The large volume of soil is less inclined to fluctuate in temperature and moisture content than the small volume inside a pot. The taller species must be planted toward the back of the frame where there is more headroom. Early flowering and fall-blooming types are managed more easily when they are grouped together.

Once planted, the frame requires a minimum of attention, some weeding perhaps. The second season, make a topdressing with a low analysis organic fertilizer. Do not be in a hurry to cut the old foliage off, for the plants need to return the nutrients to the bulbs as the old tops die down. Once they are dried sufficiently the tops should be cut and removed entirely from the garden to remove disease spores.

Eventually, the difficult time comes when the bed needs renovation, for the soil will have become exhausted and the plants crowded. Renovate in summer just as the foliage is just about dried off. It can be a tricky operation, since some of the bulbs will have spread and may have grown together. There will be lots of small bulbs that have to be found and removed since they will not be welcome in the new display.

Above, a trough made by Gwen Kelaidis, with draba, saxifrage, dianthus, and eritrichium. Below, the 2004 exhibit of the Delaware Valley Rock Garden Society, made by volunteers, at the Philadelphia Flower Show.

8. Plant Talk

Sempervivum ciliosum nestles in a trough, among rocks.

The plants described here are suitable for small alpine gardens and can be used without any danger of their inundating other plants. I offer suggestions on how to grow them and how to use them. This directory has been divided into three sections: *Herbaceous and Semi-Woody Plants for Alpine Gardens* (p. 135); *Small Bulbs* (p. 224); and *Woody Dwarf Trees and Shrubs* (p. 242).

These selections are not fussy plants when it comes to soil requirements. The presence or absence of lime is not critical except in those cases where I have specifically mentioned it. As a rule, these are plants that grow in a sunny rock or alpine garden and also do well in light shade. Any other requirement for a given species is explained in the discussion.

Hardiness is a priority for many readers, so plants of dubious hardiness have been excluded, for the most part. This provides a straightforward choice of plants. Realizing that not all readers garden in the colder zones, I have included a few species for gentler climates along with warnings that apply to them. For those readers who may want a greater challenge, I have included a few treasures to whet their appetites for more advanced garden selections.

The plants listed are mainly perennial and will not normally need annual replacement. Deaths among newly purchased and planted material can occur, although not on a regular basis, I hope. Some of

121

the plants are evergreen and retain their green or silvery gray foliage all winter, though it may get a little disheveled from winter abuse.

I have selected varieties that are readily available from nurseries in many parts of the country. There is nothing more frustrating than reading about great plants, only to find that no one sells them.

If possible, buy from a nearby supplier if you are lucky enough to have one. Otherwise, buy from reputable mail order nurseries that can be found across the nation. They provide catalogs full of valuable information and are remarkably efficient at packing and shipping.

Winter Hardiness

Is this plant hardy? Will it survive my cold winter? These questions are heard when a new plant comes along. If it is from a local plant sale, go ahead and chance its survival. If it is a hard won rarity that cannot be put at risk, carefully consider plant hardiness.

Most gardeners are familiar with hardiness zone maps. In the Plant Hardiness Zone Map develped by the U. S. Department of Agriculture, there are ten zones based on ten degree F. differences in average annual minimum temperature. This map was made up from data from numerous stations in Mexico, the United States, and Canada. While helpful, it cannot cover every corner of every county or state. How much winter cold a plant can survive before it dies is only one factor involved in plant hardiness, which involves a complex set of circumstances such as heat, wind, and moisture. Most of the current plant hardiness information given in books, plant lists, and nursery catalogs uses the USDA Plant Hardiness Zone Map, which concentrates on the cold tolerance of plants rather than their heat tolerance.

The American Horticultural Society (AHS) has developed and copyrighted the AHS Heat Zone Map. The 12 zones on the map indicate the average number of days each year that a given region experiences "heat days"—temperatures over 86 degrees F (30 degrees Celsius). Zone 1 has less than one heat day while Zone 12 has more than 210 heat days. This system, once it becomes universal and more plants are rated, will be used along with the cold rating systems. In the meantime it will guide gardeners who live in warmer climates.

Determine which map to use, and use the latest revision to find your garden's zone. Some nurseries list the hardiness ratings of their plants, first showing which map they use. Each plant is given a zone range of two numbers. The first represents the coldest zone the plant is expected to tolerate. The second, a higher number, indicates the warmest zone in which the plant can be expected to flourish.

Snow cover. Gardeners appreciate a winter-long covering of snow and recognize the damage that occurs when snow does not fall or a good snow cover disappears in mid-winter. There is nothing you can do to influence winter snows, but you can lessen the damage by covering the alpine garden with evergreen branches. With small gardens this is not an unreasonable task. It helps enormously by giving the plants relief from cold, drying winds as well as minimizing the rapid freezing and thawing of the soil. It protects frozen plants from cell damage caused by rapid thawing and subsequent desiccation from winter sun.

It is difficult to understand why rugged plants from the frozen heights of the mountains can fail in our lowland gardens, until we realize that these plants are accustomed to plentiful snow cover. The insulating quality of the snow protects them from widely fluctuating temperatures. Robbed of this insulating blanket the plants become vulnerable to harsh conditions.

Not all alpine plants enjoy snow protection, for there are species that dwell on ridges, cliffs, and bare rock where no snow ever sticks. They survive because they have adapted to these conditions, mainly by growing very close to the ground, thereby offering as little surface to the wind as possible. The foliage is narrow and held tightly in hard mounds. It is often covered in masses of silky, insulating hairs.

Winter wetness is another hardiness factor. A plant from a snow covered Alp or from a dry steppe or high, cold desert is fully equipped to survive a cold but dry winter. However, planted in my garden in Zone 8 with its mild, wet winter, where Pacific storms alternate with freezing spells and the soil is always moist, the plant will have a difficult time.

Dormancy is another element in winter hardiness. To prepare for winter, a plant ceases to make new growth. Dry fall weather gradually hardens the tissues, preparing them for winter. If fall weather is mild and wet, the plant continues to grow slowly and the tissues remain green and soft.

A great deal can be done to protect our plants. By studying the natural habitat of a plant, we learn about its native climate, elevation, soil type, aspect (sun or shade), and summer and winter conditions.

It may be that a plant requires conditions we cannot provide. I have had to accept that I cannot successfully grow meconopsis or certain primulas and mossy saxifrages. Should I give up and try something else? There are many gardeners who will go to great lengths to succeed, including building all manner of structures equipped with climate control devices. It is easy to understand why

123

gardeners resort to using cold frames and alpine houses. It all boils down to what the challenge of growing these plants means to you.

Tony Avent, a well known horticulturalist, lecturer, writer, nurseryman, and owner of Plant Delights Nursery in North Carolina, has his answer. He has said on many occasions, "I never say I cannot grow a plant until I have killed it at least three times."

Heat Tolerance

It is a fact that some alpine plants will die in the heat of summer. They cannot survive for long under hot and dry or hot and humid conditions. Plants from northern climates cannot take long hot summers. Gardeners who have experienced these circumstances have tailored their choice of plants by using those that can adapt, and there are plenty of them.

Plant explorers are constantly introducing new plants that are adaptable to climates that are too warm for the cool-weather loving species. Let us refer to them as rock plants rather than alpine plants. In the plant entries I will differentiate between those that are truly alpine, originating in the mountains of Europe and other alpine regions, and those that are not.

Rock plants, if they are meant to harmonize with alpine plants, should at least resemble alpines. They should be dwarf, compact, and small-leaved. It helps if they have lots of flowers on short stems. Using these plants need not alter European classic rock garden design, but may lead to the creation of a local design that is more in keeping with regional conditions and a lot less troublesome to maintain.

Acclimatization

Spring deliveries are popular because plants become acclimated very well in this season. You should give a nursery-grown plant an acclimatization period, not necessarily a long one, early in the garden season while it is actively growing. Later in the summer and fall, provide newly acquired plants with a longer acclimatization period to give them time to get a good foothold before winter. Plants grown in warmer zones and shipped to colder zones will tend to be less cold resistant than locally grown ones.

To avoid first winter losses, overwinter recent purchases in an alpine house or a cold frame. If you do not have either of these facilities, the newly arrived plants can be left in the pots and plunged into the ground in a protected area of the garden. Here, watering and shading can be monitored. When winter arrives, cover them with evergreen branches.

Mail order nurseries have to consider shipping weight when they create their soil mixtures. Some of the ingredients used are lightweight and sterile, so the necessary nutrients are supplied by fertilizers. Once the plant leaves the nursery, the flow of nutrients depends on how the nursery applied the fertilizer and which product was employed.

A major consideration is that the soil mixture the nursery used will be different from the soil in your garden, so it is important to make the transition to a different soil type while the plants' roots are still growing.

Here is a good method to use if plants are to remain in pots during the transition period:

1. Prepare a planting mix similar to that of the site where the plant will eventually be planted.

2. Lighten your mixture further by adding extra sand and gravel.

3. Remove plants from the pots, allowing all loose potting soil to fall away from the roots. Do not deliberately shake any soil from the roots.

4. Repot the plant using your new mix. Use a slightly larger pot if the plant has lots of roots, but re-use the original pot if roots are totally bare or not particularly plentiful.

5. There is no need to add fertilizer because your new soil mixture will provide enough nutrients to see the plant through until it has adjusted.

Planting Time

When is the best time to plant perennials and small shrubs in a rock garden, raised bed, terrace, or retaining wall? This is a difficult question, for weather has as strong an effect as the part of the world where the garden is located. In most regions, there are two prime planting opportunities for planting alpine gardens, spring and fall. If you are making a major planting of a new rock garden involving valuable plants, it is wise to select one of these two main planting periods, preferably springtime.

Planting in spring is good, but do not rush into it. Wait until the soil drains away spring's excess water and has a chance to warm up in the sun. It is best to plant in well drained soil. The structure of the soil will be damaged if you handle it while it is too wet, for the soil particles join together when compressed, forming lumps that are hard to reclaim. Simply walking on wet soil is harmful. With this in mind, avoid too much firming of soil around the roots of newly planted plants.

Time a major planting program between the initial draining of wet soil and the arrival of hot dry spring weather. This is not easy, for often a new planting must be watered to get it through an early warm spell. You can set out a few potted plants, particularly if they are well rooted, at virtually any time by providing water and a few days' light shading when the weather is sunny and warm.

Fall is another popular time for planting, but rock garden plants need several weeks to get their roots firmly established before winter arrives. Frost will push poorly rooted plants out of the soil. Plants need time for the foliage and stems to adjust to their new environment. This period allows them to prepare for winter and return nutrients to the root system. Woody stems have a chance to harden before frost. Some species form next spring's flower buds in this period.

The exact timing for fall planting of a rock garden will depend on your geographic location. In some places, autumn is a gradual time of cooling nights and sunny days, which is ideal. Other areas experience a long period of rain. Some gardeners have no fall at all and go straight into winter. If you plant in autumn, plan your project for that period when the summer sun is starting to cool and the evening and nights are cool. August often turns out to be a good time to start.

126   Choices at the Beth Chatto nursery in Colchester, England.

Saponaria olivana blooms in June on radiating stems.

Preplanting

Alpine plants are usually supplied to us in small plastic pots grown in widely differing soil mixtures, some good other not so good. They should have a solid and active root system, the rootball. When removed from the pot the rootball should remain intact and not disintegrate. The first task is to 'top and tail' the rootball.

Topping can be done with the fingers. All it requires is the removal of the top inch or so of soil from around the neck of the plant. This removes old stale soil, mosses, algae, liverworts, some pests and diseases, and weeds and dormant weed seeds. If the soil comes away easily, let it.

Tailing demands a certain amount of ruthlessness. The object is to release the roots from the circular pattern they formed within the confines of the pot, so they are free to spread into the garden soil. Hold the rootball in one hand and with your fingers tease the soil from the lower couple of inches of the mass of roots at the base of the ball. A well rooted plant withstands a fair amount of tailing without damage.

Normally these two operations are enough but occasionally a rootball will be such a solid mass of roots that you must loosen and free the roots around the sides of the ball. Maybe a few pulls with your fingers or a pointed dibber will be enough to free the roots. I have seen drastic cases where the roots required a few vertical slashes from top to bottom with a knife. A vigorous plant can survive and prosper this drastic but sometimes necessary treatment.

127

Before proceeding, check the soil of the root ball. If it is at all dry, thoroughly soak it in a few inches of water, let it drain, and then plant. Where the soil is peat based, be doubly sure it is thoroughly moist. A dry peat rootball seldom can absorb sufficient moisture when planted in garden soil, even with careful hand watering. Try to free the roots and remove some of the peaty potting mix.

Making the planting hole. Prepare the soil according to the advice in Chapter 5, for this is all that is needed. We all know the old saying "a two dollar hole for a one dollar plant." It applies to alpine plants except that the hole only has to be deep enough to comfortably hold the root ball. The hole should be a least twice as wide as the width of the root ball to allow you plenty of room to spread out the roots. Arrange the plant in the hole so that the neck of the plant is at or just above the soil level. Do not bury the neck of the plant deeply because it may rot off. If the hole is too deep, correct it by lifting the root ball and popping in a layer of soil underneath. Adjust as required and then fill in the rest of the soil.

Firm or tamp the soil lightly after planting. Firm it just enough to ensure that the roots make good contact with the soil, with no large airspaces. I use my knuckles because I can feel the soil and recognize the right amount of pressure. The handle of the trowel makes a handy firming tool also.

Now apply the topdressing of gravel by working it around the neck of the plant and under the branches or creeping stems. Water well but gently with a watering can with a fine rose.

Design Factors

Perhaps you have the planting plan all figured out by this stage. If not, one method of developing a plan would be to list the plants you have on hand and those you intend to purchase. Identify their potential growth patterns and habitat requirements. Are they fast or slow growing? What is their ultimate height or spread? Are they low, spreading mats, cushion or carpet-forming plants, or upright and spreading? Which are sun lovers, and which prefer shade or partial shade? Which are evergreen and which are deciduous.

Select and identify any special places in your rock garden first, particularly those premium vertical and horizontal crevices, for they are often in short supply and are quickly used up. Also look for choice pockets or rock arrangements where smaller plants will be safe. Take a few days to study and define where shade, if you have any, may be found. Try to find the right spot for each plant with its special needs. This will prevent that frustrating experience of walking around with a plant in one hand and a trowel in the other, looking for a planting spot.

The final arrangement of the plants is a personal thing; nevertheless preplan the plants' placement to avoid a haphazard approach and allow for a well-balanced design.

Here is an interesting design idea to consider. The higher on the mountain you go, the smaller the plants become. Why not reserve the higher elevations of your rock garden for the small, low growing species suggestive of the alpine landscape above the timberline? Plant the larger varieties at lower elevations, closer to the paths and traffic. Take great care locating the trees and shrubs, especially the evergreens, because they that will become the frame and backbone of the garden during the bare winter months. Avoid the temptation to plant an upright conifer on the highest peak!

Care and Maintenance

Care and maintenance responsibilities begin immediately after planting your rock garden. First, ensure that each plant's needs are met. Check carefully to see that each plant has moisture at the roots. Dig down close to the roots and probe with your finger to be sure. Where a plant shows flagging or wilting, check the root ball closely. The culprit could be one of those peat mixtures drying out.

If the weather is bright and sunny, stick a few leafy twigs into the soil to shade individual plants until the roots take hold.

Once the initial watering begins to dry up, start watering on a regular basis until the plants are well established.

Weeds will inevitably appear despite all efforts to prepare a sterile soil mixture, so keep pulling the weed seedlings. Weeding is not all bad for it keeps you in close contact with your plants, enabling quick detection of problems.

Spring-planted varieties will flower. By all means enjoy the flowers, but then as they fade, deadhead the plant and give it a light trim. This will save the plant from expending energy setting seed and will promote good, strong growth.

Plant management. Even in their first year, one or two species will romp ahead, spreading rapidly. This will be the first test of your planting plan and you will see whether the plants have the space they clearly require. If it is obvious that they are going to crowd their neighbors, take action. Dig up the plant, trim it back, and relocate it to a spot where it will have more space.

Grooming. Grooming will be an ongoing job and pleasurable pursuit as long as you have a rock garden. Trim off any untidy growth and cut back dead flower heads. I have no problem taking the hedge shears to my plants. By all means, clip the shoots back to form a tidy carpet, cushion, or mound. It is all right to clip around the perimeter of the plant, but guard against creating a series of round, uniform dinner plates.

Rock garden management is where the fun begins as you develop your creation. If you are imitating a wild mountainscape, feel free to let it develop naturalistically. Let some plants run together; no one clips and prunes on the mountainsides. There are plants with their own particular character and qualities, and you may prefer to see them in a degree of isolation. Trim and space them so they do not run together.

As the garden develops, things will change, including your own ideas. A few plants will have to be removed and others will become more interesting to you. Those that are removed can be potted up and given away or traded. Those you wish to propagate may be divided and planted right back into the garden. Do this during a cool spell. Replant them firmly and keep the divisions moist.

When the plant you wish to increase has not made a lot of growth, which is often the case, it can be divided into tiny pieces with or

Groomed for show, these sempervivums in elegant troughs are on display at the Hampton Court Flower Show in London.

without roots and the stronger pieces replanted and given care and attention. The remaining pieces will grow if potted into small pots and grown in a protected cold frame. This operation is very rewarding but it is habit forming.

Fertilizing. When the soil for a new rock garden has been properly prepared, there are enough nutrients in it to last a long time. Alpine and rock plants do not need high nutrient content, in fact it would be detrimental to them. Instead of developing into dwarf mats with attractive, low-growing foliage and flowers, they would produce overabundant foliage and floppy growth, losing their main appeal. Soft plant tissues are more vulnerable to disease and frost damage.

After a year or so, established plants will appreciate some fertilizer, particularly if they have been groomed and cut back regularly to force them to produce a continuing mass of flowers. Even some classic alpines such as *Gentian acaulis* respond to gentle feeding after flowering. Rock gardens do not need as much fertilizer as lawns and flower gardens.

Apply fertilizer in late spring, after flowers begin to fade and growth commences, or whenever you become aware that the flower crop is dwindling and the fresh green foliage of new growth is slowing down. Give the whole rock garden, raised bed, or terraced garden an overall application of a low-analysis fertilizer which is low in nitrogen, 6-8-6, for example. It is manufactured for general use and formulated to be accident proof. Cut the recommended application rates in half. For sheer speed and convenience it is hard to beat a balanced chemical fertilizer. It can be spread by hand from a bucket and forked into the soil.

Before buying a bag of chemical fertilizer, however, consider that many alpine and rock plants are more than satisfied with an annual dressing of a few inches of a good compost, instead, especially if it can be worked into the soil. This will maintain an adequate level of soil fertility. If you do not have access to compost, use peat moss. Although it is a fine source for organic matter, it has little or no nutrient value, so add fertilizer along with the peat and work them into the soil together.

Many gardeners choose organic fertilizers, for they are considered safe and environmentally friendly. They cannot damage foliage or roots as some chemical products will, if incorrectly applied. A disadvantage is that the nutrient levels of most organic products are very low and they are slow acting, having to break down before the nutrients are available to the plants. Some of them are derived from animals and may be smelly, attracting garden pests of the four legged-variety.

131

Making Compost

Small rock projects, including raised or terraced beds, do not require large amounts of compost. You can concentrate on making the finest compost by using high quality ingredients.

Compost for the rock garden must be free of weed seed and plants or plant parts with live roots that are capable of regenerating: such horrors as couch grass, ground elder, etc. You can use garden waste such as leaves, grass clippings, plants and weeds, and soft plant stems. By all means add any used potting soil. Also use vegetable waste from the kitchen such as fruit and vegetable trimmings. Shred the ingredients to hasten the process.

If you must locate the composter where it is visible to others, consider purchasing a manufactured model. Your skill in making one is another consideration. If the composter is out of sight then very basic do-it-yourself construction is adequate. The simplest unit can be made with wire mesh (chicken wire) or snow fencing supported by a few metal fence posts.

A 15- to 20-foot length of 36-inch chicken wire or other fencing produces a good sized bin. To determine diameter, divide the length (circumference) by 3.14 (pi).

On a flat area, roll out the required length of chicken wire. Then fold back the first three of four inches of wire at each end. With pliers, fold back any protruding ends to provide two good clean edges. Form a circle with the wire and close and secure the ends with wire ties. Drive some sturdy posts around the inside perimeter and attach the chicken wire firmly to them. Steel fence posts are convenient. Note that you can place the supporting posts to make the composter either round or square.

Annuals in the Alpine Garden

Purist alpine gardeners shudder at the suggestion of using annuals in a rock garden. Those bright colored summer annuals used for bedding would soon chase away any suggestion of pristine mountainsides. Summer color is important, but, even so, why duplicate what everyone else is doing by creating a nonstop riot of color?

When a rock garden lacks summer flowers it is time to revisit the planting plan and incorporate more of the perennial or shrubby varieties that flower in summer. However, certain annuals can also find a niche. It is not true that all annuals are too bright and not in keeping with an alpine garden. Annuals can be used to fill in in a newly planted rock garden where the permanent residents have not covered sufficient ground. They can make a temporary planting in a space opened by the failure of a permanent planting, and can clothe barren areas left by ambitious plantings of spring bulbs.

However, certain annuals have a tendency to seed freely, and once allowed in the rock garden, they may be very difficult to eradicate. Another danger is that fast-growing annuals may encroach on smaller alpine plants and rob them of soil and moisture, or even suffocate them.

Garden centers today offer and interesting range of new and unusual summer annuals that are excellent for the rock garden. Offered in containers containing four or six plants, they make it convenient to try several small groups of different kinds. At the point of sale, the plants are advanced enough to make it easy to evaluate the flowers and growth habit.

Seed catalogs are fun to study and I always buy more seeds than I can manage. Some annuals must be seeded where they are to flower and the packets say so. Sow the seed in small patches where you want them. In most regions, do this when spring planting weather arrives. Growing annuals by directly sowing them is an age-old garden practice. Whole borders are still created in this way.

The varieties listed in popular seed catalogs are displayed differently from the plant nurseries who list genus and a species, in some cases followed by a variety or cultivar name.

Seed catalogs often list the genus name in capitals followed by a list of variety names which are selections or hybrids, often with complicated parentage; they are no longer true species. Study the listings and pick those dwarf kinds which appeal to you. Where the genus and species names are listed then you have a true species or a special selection thereof.

With these points and warnings in mind, here is a short list of small annuals to consider:

133

⇛ Creating and Planting Alpine Gardens

⇛ **Ageratum varieties.** Seek out the smallest varieties. Plants are available in blue, pink, and white.

⇛ **Alyssum varieties.** Use the low, spreading white carpets.

⇛ **Anagallis varieties.** The rock pimpernel provides masses of spreading stems bearing gentian-blue flowers.

⇛ **Antirrinum varieties.** Before you scream there are some dainty, very dwarf mini-snapdragons out there.

⇛ **Gypsophila muralis.** While light and airy and covered with tiny, pale pink baby's breath flowers, this plant is capable of attaining three feet in height, so use it with caution.

⇛ **Limnanthes douglasii.** a hardy native of California and Southern Oregon forms mounds of fernlike foliage covered with masses of white yellow centered fragrant flowers from June to September.

⇛ **Linaria maroccana.** The tiny, violet-purple flowers with yellow markings are often described as snapdragon-like. This grows to around 9 to 12 inches. Avoid taller forms.

⇛ **Lobelia varieties.** Trailing varieties are suitable for planting among rocks, but watch out for your smaller plant treasures.

⇛ **Nemophila varieties.** The well-liked baby blue eyes is very useful. It enjoys some light shade and cooler conditions.

⇛ **Thymophylla tenuifolia.** The Dahlberg daisy has been a favorite of mine for years, perfect for the lower reaches of the sunny rock garden. The seed is usually sown where it is to flower, and soon forms a mat of miniature golden daisies. Native to Texas and Mexico.

⇛ **Verbena hybrids.** The modern, colorful verbena hybrids offer a good choice of colors. It is a sprawling, trailing plant, great for tumbling over rocks.

134

Verbena hybrids trail gracefully and withstand hot, sunny exposures.

9. Herbaceous and Semi-Woody Plants

Here, under the herbaceous and semi-woody plant heading, in alphabetical order by genus, are specialized plants that serve well in the alpine garden, filling the crevices, slopes and rocks appropriately. They include desirable low, flat, creeping plants to flow over the rocks, and tight little mounds to fill the cracks and crevices. The taller species provide masses of flowers, creating colorful carpets to clothe the miniature open meadows of the alpine landscape.

Many of the plants are herbaceous perennials which die back every winter to an underground rootstock, springing into life with the advent of spring. Note well where you plant them! It is all too easy to plant on top of them, particularly when they are dormant. A few are used as annuals although they can be perennial in certain conditions.

Semi-woody plants are discussed in this section, too. These fall between being true shrubs and evergreen perennials. The branches and twigs assume a woody texture, which permits them to withstand winter. They are an important group because they are usually covered with flowers in spring and summer and grow into featured plants that add substance and permanence to the landscape.

Acantholimon

It can be as easy to remember a Latin name as an obscure common name. Take lead wort, which seems to be the current common name for ***Acantholimon* species.** The older common name, prickly thrift, is more descriptive. The growth habit and foliage are similar in appearance to the thrifts (*Armeria* species) but touch the foliage and you will soon see why it is called prickly.

Acantholimons originate from the high semi-arid regions of the Eastern Mediterranean including parts of Greece and Yugoslavia. They are prevalent in Turkey and move into Syria. In Central Asia they are found from Russian Armenia and Afghanistan to the Western Himalayas. The genus has received a lot of attention in recent years because more seed collectors were able to enter places along the Turkish and Iranian borders. This rich alpine country gave us a surprising number of new species of plants to try. The acantholimons are fascinating plants to collect and cultivate, but only a larger rock garden benefits from use of these prickly mounds.

These appealing plants range from sub-shrubby types to mounds and mat-forming species. They have densely tufted growth and needle-like foliage which often ends in sharp points. The foliage color varies from gray- green to silvery gray. Plants bloom in late spring or early summer, and are valuable for extending color in a rock garden. The flowers are found in varied shades of pink depending on the species. Some flower on arching spikes, others in closely packed heads, and others on very short stems.

Cold does not seem to bother them, and they are grown from Zone 5 to 9, but they do have a problem with excessive winter wetness. They love the sun and do well in deep, gravelly, fast draining soil where roots penetrate. Once established, some species will spread to 18 inches across. They are not normally recommended as a trough plant but the restricted size of the trough will keep them neat and compact. A plant in full flower in a good-sized trough makes a magnificent sight.

A. acerosum makes a blue-gray mound of dense foliage and branching stems of pink flowers. It is worth mentioning that there is a subspecies *A. a.* ssp. *brachystachyum* with larger flowers that are closer to red.

A. bracteatum and subspecies *A. b.* ssp. *capitatum* are silver mounds of spiky foliage with heads of pink flowers on leafless stems.

A. glumaceum is recognized as having been in cultivation longest. My plant has been with me for many years despite wet winters and has developed into an undulating mound some four inches high and over 24 inches wide. It is a pleasant plant of green needle-like leaves with rose-pink flowers in short, dense sprays, almost covering the plant.

A. ulicinum is an excellent plant, formerly listed as *A. androsaceum*, which comes to us from the Eastern Mediterranean and the Balkans. It is a variable plant in the wild, and as a result there are several named forms offered. Nurseries usually offer the choicest and dwarfer forms, those with compact foliage of blue-gray leaves. Flowers are pink and carried on short spikes with the characteristic papery calyx that sets them off. The flower stems range from almost stemless to a few inches high. This is normal in such a variable species, so check with your nurseryman if this is an important issue. I would feel safe in planting the smaller forms in a decent sized trough.

136

Acantholimon ulicinum

Achillea

One or two of these small alpine yarrows (*Achillea* species) are
excellent for those sunny, well-drained spots in the rock garden. I
think they are a bit too large for most troughs. They are mat-forming
plants about six inches tall with long, narrow, gray, woolly, pinnately
dissected leaves, which means two ranks of smaller leaves. Under
well-drained, sunny conditions they are hardy.

A. ageratifolia comes from Greece. It has a subspecies named *A.
ageratifolia* ssp. *aizoon* that is sometimes found in the trade as *A.
aizoon.* It has long, narrow, silver leaves that are deeply toothed and
very aromatic. The large white daisies are carried one to a stem, about
three-fourths of an inch across. Plants grow six inches tall and the
flower stems are a few inches taller, appearing in July and August.

A. x jaborneggii is an excellent plant. Its foliage is a silvery light
green and grows into a mound six or so inches tall and spreads about
12 inches. The flowers are small and white, carried in loose heads on
short stems.

A. x *lewisii* 'King Edward' is a
manmade hybrid with heads of sulfur-
yellow flowers. This variety looks better if it
gets a light clipping after the first flush of
bloom, otherwise it looks untidy. It will
flower into September. Two people
introduced this hybrid almost simultaneously, one calling it 'King Edward' and
the other calling it *A.* x *Lewisii.* 'King
Edward' it remains.

Achillea ageratifolia

137

Aethionema

Aethionema species are a group of sub shrubs and woody-based perennials which grow from Turkey down into Iran and Iraq. Also known as stonecress, they are excellent subjects for sunny rock gardens, walls, and raised beds. They make good pot plants if the potting medium is well drained. They are surprisingly hardy, often found in Zone 5 and even Zone 4 where they will occasionally be frozen back, usually regrowing in the spring. They must have an open, sunny exposure and freely draining soil. They are for the most part hummocks of twiggy growth with gray or blue-gray needle-like leaves. The small flowers are carried in terminal heads.

A. armenum will vary in height between four inches to six or eight inches. It forms a typical cushion of twisted branches covered with tiny, needle-like blue leaves. This plant has pink heads of flowers.

A. caespitosum grows to about two inches tall and eventually will make a tight hummock up to eight inches wide. The flowers are rose colored or tinged with varying shades of lavender.

A. 'Warley Rose' is the classic aethionema and has been popular since the early 1900's. It does a little too well with me but I feel it warrants space in the small garden. As soon as the main crop of flowers begins to fade I shear and trim the plants to keep them compact. This cultivar is typical of the genus with its blue-green foliage with a stronger touch of dark green. It is very free flowering in a good shade of pink, very reminiscent of *Daphne cneorum*. *A.* 'Warley Ruber' is a similar cultivar with much darker flowers.

There are several other species available that look promising, but, for small spaces, check their credentials carefully.

Alyssum

The smaller species of *Alyssum* are great plants. They do an excellent job when planted in a light soil in a sunny rock garden, for they are most generous with sheets of bright yellow flowers. They make great, trouble-free mats of gray twigs and leaves, sprawling over rocks or planted at the edge of a trough where they are free to hang over the edge. I have found that giving the plants a light clipping with shears right after flowering is a wise move as it keeps the plant low and compact, rather than allowing them to develop into leggy, open mats.

A. montanum is a shrubby plant about three inches tall. Its prostrate branches are covered with narrow, gray, hairy leaves that become obscured by the racemes of golden-yellow scented flowers. A native of the mountains of Europe, it flowers during April and May.

A. propinquum is another small spreader, this time from Turkey. Again, the plant with its gray foliage and pale yellow flowers is small enough to include in a trough garden.

A. ptilotrichum (syn. *Ptilotrichum spinosum*) is a pleasant little bushy plant with wiry stems and small gray leaves from the Mediterranean mountains. It has proven to be hardy and is rated to Zone 4. It is capable of growing into a mounding mat up to two feet wide in some situations. Planting it in a trough will restrict it considerably. I shamelessly prune my trough plant to keep it in scale. It flowers in my garden in May and June, so wait till it has finished flowering. It can have white or rose-purple flowers; there is a superior form named *A. p.* 'Roseum' which is worth searching for. There are several recent introductions of low, flat types from Turkey and nearby places. All are hardy sun lovers. Check any descriptions you see and select those which appeal to you.

A. serpyllifolium has been around for a long time. It forms a spreading mat of gray foliage and golden-yellow flowers.

I notice that there are a few new introductions that have become available, mostly from Turkey. They are yellow flowered in spring and gray-leaved, with a neat, small habit. Check the catalogs and see if any of them appeal to you.

Androsace

The genus *Androsace* contains plants that embody everything we find so appealing in alpine flowers. They dwell in the high mountains amid the rocks. Many of them are iron-hard buns of silvery foliage that are both dwarf and floriferous. When they flower the foliage can be buried beneath the mound of white or pink stemless flowers. Down from the austere heights, other androsaces can be seen sprinkled across the alpine fells. Little tufted clumps of dark green leaves send up short stems that culminate in attractive heads of white or pink golden-eyed flowers.

There are androsaces in the high Himalayas that are very appealing with their woolly rosettes and stemless, primula-like flowers. Others with small umbels of flowers provide silvery-haired cascades of verbena-like flowers.

At these higher elevations come the true gems of the genus. The trouble is that many gardeners will find them almost impossible to keep alive for long in cultivation. Either winter's lack of snow cover and icy blasts will kill them, or summer humidity will decay them before your eyes. If this is the case, why do I mention them at all? I do so, first, for those who have a climate where it is possible to take up the challenge, and, second, for those enthusiasts who will resort to any means to succeed with plants.

Androsace vandellii, with sparkling white flowers.

Many years ago the desire to collect and grow these tiny cushion-forming species was a major factor in the popularity and development of the art of alpine plant culture. Named the Aretian Androsaces, many belong to the Section Aretia of the genus *Androsace*, a section in which the flowers are carried singly rather than in umbels.

The determination to master their culture led to many original gardening ideas. Perhaps the first was the construction of moraine gardens designed to approximate the wild alpine sites where cool moving water from the melting snows ran beneath the surface of the specially prepared, gritty, gravelly soil mixture.

Subsequently, elaborately designed scree gardens were constructed copying the debris slopes of pure rock fragments through which melt water ran—slopes that hosted hundreds of plants. These gardens reached an extreme where slopes were coated with concrete to direct the introduced water to the roots. Efficient systems were developed to provide water in even flows, with drainage systems to collect it and remove it after it had filtered through the plants.

If this system did not work they grew them in clay flower pots filled with special , sometimes secret, soil mixtures. The need to protect these valuable plants from winter wetness led to the use of cold frames and alpine houses.

There are several nurseries that supply these plants. Mail order is successful when plants are shipped rapidly, just when they are beginning to recover from winter dormancy. Growing them from seed is practical, and seed is available from the specialist seed lists. Sow the seed as early as possible since they need all the stratification time they can get before spring germination. Never throw a seed pot away because the seed can germinate at any time and in any year.

If you become serious about this section, I advocate lots of advance research reading on soil mixtures, germination tactics, and subsequent management requirements; then there are the growing facilities to consider. Here are names for you to look for: *Androsace alpina, ciliata, cylindrica, hedraeantha, helvetica, hirtella, pyrenaica,* and *vandellii.*

Fortunately not all androsaces are tricky little cushions. There are some species from Europe that do well in a gritty rock garden soil.

A. carnea is typical and best described as a small mound of loose rosettes composed of dark green spiky-looking leaves. The wide distribution of this species contributes to its variability, so plants will vary in the length of the individual leaves and compactness of the rosettes. The delightful cup-shaped flowers are borne in umbels and are a lovely shade of pink with a yellow eye. The height ranges from half an inch to three inches when in bloom. Plants of this species, when raised from seed, may well produce white flowers.

A. carnea varieties take sun in rock garden soil, but the soil must be deep enough to keep the roots cool and moist. A little extra gravel added to the soil never hurts, as they like good drainage also. Those who garden where summer humidity reigns will probably have difficulty with these plants in the open rock garden. As a rule they are not difficult plants. They are fine in troughs, but do not let them roast in the sun.

A. carnea subsp. *brigantiaca,* from the Cottian Alps on the boundary between France and Italy, has narrow spreading leaves that recurve at the tips and are somewhat toothed at the edges, and bears soft pink flowers.

A. carnea var. *halleri* is the robust member of the group with strong, broad leaves that have an outwardly curving habit. It, too, has rose-colored flowers.

141

A. carnea subsp. *laggeri* is from the Pyrenees and is a compact, refined edition of the species. Each cup-shaped flower of glowing pink has a beautiful golden eye.

Reading plant lists, you may find a confusing array of *A. carnea* varieties. Owing to wide distribution, the species is variable and the pink flowered plants will sometimes produce white flowers and the white ones will sometimes be pink. Interestingly enough, as a collection of these plants grows, these and other differences become part of the fun. Perhaps you'll raise your own plants from wild-collected seed.

There are several excellent hybrids between *A. carnea* and some of the Aretian Androsaces. Some are named, but others are just listed under the names of the parents.

A. x 'Millstream' is an introduction by the great gardener, H. Lincoln Foster; unfortunately the history of this hybrid is already becoming cloudy. The plant resembles *A. pyrenaica* by its domed shape and narrow foliage, and has the pink stemless flowers of *A. carnea*. Luckily, it prospers in the USA. I have seen it in gardens on both coasts, in troughs and rock gardens. It requires the same conditions as the others in this group.

A. lanuginosa (see gallery page f) is one of the more accommo-dating Himalayan androsaces, and a particular favorite of mine. In my garden it thrives on the sunny west-facing slope, and seems always to have a few heads of flowers. It favors planting where it can trail or cascade, so raised beds and walls are ideal. The roots seek the cool depths. Although it is a bit large for small troughs, what a display it makes in a deep trough! The long, red, wiry, trailing stems are clothed with gray-green silky leaves. The normal flowering period is late summer but it always carries some flowers well into the fall. The flower heads are often compared to verbenas. *A. lanuginosa* is soft lilac pink with a darker eye. There is a lovely white variety named *A. l.* var. *leichtlinii* with a prominent yellow eye that turns red as the flower ages. It is common to see red and yellow eyes on the same umbel.

A. sarmentosa (see gallery page f), an agreeable and popular Himalayan species, finds our gardens acceptable. Given several inches of well-drained soil, it will withstand sun and a small degree of dryness. It is a low clump of silky-haired leaves in rosettes and a tangle of scarlet runners that quickly become part of the clump. In full

142

growth the rosettes are open and leafy. *A. sarmentosa* flowers generously in May and June, sending up stalks from two to four inches tall, covered with bright pink, primula-like, yellow-eyed flowers.

There are several different varieties available with names originally given to wild collected forms such as *A. studiosorum* 'Chumbyi', *A. sarmentosa var. watkinsii* and sometimes 'Salmon's Variety'. These names no longer have botanical standing, yet the plants so labeled are excellent varieties with rose-pink, soft-pink, carmine, or even mauve-red flowers (to list colors garnered from nursery lists). It is not a lover of long wet winters, but somehow survives in its winter mode as tight sempervivum-shaped rosettes of dense white, wooly foliage. Occasionally this species will be listed as *A. studiosorum*.

A. sempervivoides is the choice where space is limited, as it is a neat, compact plant. It spreads by way of short stolons. The tiny spoon-shaped leaves are dark green with slight marginal hairs, and crowded into rosettes that average less than an inch across. With generous cultivation the rosettes and runners become larger and lax, so the plant is far more attractive when kept on a lean diet. Umbels of pink flowers in varying shades have an attractive yellow dot in the center of each bloom.

When grown in truly gritty alpine soil, the plant will become even smaller and more compact, and is sometimes listed as *A. mucronifolia*, a rare and difficult gem from Kashmir. The *A. mucronifolia* of horticulture is almost always *A. sempervivoides*.

A. villosa is choice and not so easy to grow, but many gardeners do succeed with it, so it is worth trying. It is an excellent selection to include in a trough planted with other choice, non-invasive plants, and is a good candidate for a collection of potted alpines as well. There are the lucky few who can grow it in the open rock garden.

It is a variable little species that originates from the high mountains of Europe and Asia, usually in areas of limestone rock. I find the species particularly attractive. It is composed of thin red stolons, small tufts of gray-green, silky-haired foliage forming tiny rosettes in a close clump or low two-inch mound. Flowers in small heads are white with the yellow eye that matures to red.

A. villosa var. *jacquemontii*, another Himalayan well worth a try, reminds me of a refined *A. sarmentosa*. A good sized specimen would be about two inches high and spread into a six-inch low mat of gray leaves and tight little rosettes. The flower color is hard to describe from memory. Some say it is rose-pink but I recall it closer to the lavender shades. Regardless of color, the flower heads are supported by reddish, one- to two-inch stems.

Antennaria

Antennaria is the genus name of a popular low carpeting plant usually called pussytoes a name which, a friend tells me, refers to the clusters of unopened flower buds that arise from basal rosettes. They resemble a cat's paw with the toes withdrawn or curled up. Flowers range from white through several shades of pink. It is a hardy perennial plant that prefers light soils and full sun. It is a good subject for planting on paths as an addition to or a substitute for thyme.

Antennaria neglecta

A. dioica is the species offered in most lists. It is a carpeting plant for sun and light soils, quite hardy, which remains a scant few inches tall. It is quite capable of spreading widely, so be careful where you plant it. Flower stems will grow from two to four inches tall, depending on the soil and light, bearing heads of tiny, papery flowers.

A. parvifolia 'McClintock' is completely new to me, having only recently made its acquaintance in the gardens of Denver, Colorado. It was introduced to gardens from Wyoming and it, too, is a hardy, sun-loving, drought-tolerant species. I am told that it can be used as ground cover under trees and it does well in dry shade. The fact that it does not produce many of the pearly-white flowers and the resulting spent flower heads contributes a lot to the year-long neatness of the plant. This is known as an evergreen carpeting plant and a spreader, so plant it with caution.

Aquilegia

The smaller columbines (*Aquilegia* species), when they are correctly named and truly dwarf, are among the most ideal plants for the small garden. Their delightful diminutive perfection makes them welcome in the smallest scheme. They are immoral, hybridizing with any other aquilegia within range. The only way to be sure of getting the species you are after is to get wild-collected seed from a responsible collector or buy plants from a good nursery. Some nurseries indicate in their lists that the plants are grown from wild seed. Once you have decided on the limit of the height you will allow

144

your plants to achieve, it is time to start checking the lists. The range of choices for plants six inches tall or under is not bad. Species 12 inches tall and higher are more plentiful. I will limit my selections to the former.

Regrettably these little gems do not normally live for that many years, a great shame because they are perfect miniatures. No small rock garden could have too many. Their foliage is low and condensed. One or two species are worth growing for the foliage alone. The flowering stems on some species are a bit tall for troughs, but since they are light and airy with few leaves, they do not overshadow smaller neighbors. If their appearance is a problem, cut the stems back after they flower, if you don't need the seeds.

Give columbines a sunny or partly shaded place that is not roasted all day long. After all, they are alpines from the cool climate of higher elevations. They don't like winter wetness, so give them a well-drained spot and an alpine soil mixture. A couple of the species are found on limestone and these may need additional ground limestone or limestone chips in the soil.

A. bertolonii is an excellent plant, the classic columbine in miniature, with rich, blue, large flowers. It is rated as growing from four to six inches and for me it certainly makes the six inches. Perhaps in leaner climes it will be shorter. Be sure you get a dwarf *A. bertolonii* as there is some confusion over the status of the name. You could end up with **A. pyrenaica**, also a wonderful plant from the alpine meadows, which is better for larger projects because it can grow to up to 12 inches tall.

A. jonesii will probably be the end of me: if I do not include it I will be censured, but when I do describe it I may well frustrate every gardener who tries to grow it. If you can grow and flower it success-fully I know you will be thrilled. It is an exquisite alpine columbine from Wyoming, Montana, and a bit of Canada at the Montana border. Picture low, densely packed clumps of blue-gray leaves, reminiscent of curly parsley, with countless, almost stemless, long spurred,

145

up-facing, huge flowers. It has an astonishing number of these exquisite, cerulean blue flowers, for the size of the plant.

A. jonesii is frustrating to grow even in favored gardens and alpine houses. It does well from seed and loves lots of dolomitic lime and sun. The problem seems to be in overwintering it. I winter it in the alpine house but the flowers never are a patch on those wildlings in the Big Horn Mountains.

A. pyrenaica ssp. **discolor** is a Spanish alpine rated at six inches with soft powder-blue and creamy-white flowers. Discolor means two colors; in this case the two colors are on the same flower. It flowers in late spring.

A. saximontana, the Rocky Mountain columbine, has blue sepals with yellowy petals. The short, slightly hooked spurs are very appealing. The plant is usually around the six inch mark in open slopes, but with part shade it produces taller, deep green foliage and longer flower stems.

A. scopulorum. As lovely as *A. jonesii* is, if I had to make a choice, I would take this little species from the Great Basin in Nevada and Utah, where it lives in high, sunny limestone screes at altitudes from 6000 to 11000 feet. Usually it is a dwarf a few inches tall with blue-gray, finely cut foliage. The long-spurred, upfacing flowers can be up to two inches long. The flowers are usually lavender-blue with pale yellow or white centers. However, the species varies, with many shades of blue to violet blue, and an incredible pink form. It grows well from fresh seed and is well worth growing regularly. The plant does not stay with me for many years, but it is a great adventure to see what colors you get from seed.

There are many more wonderful native columbines out there that are worth growing, but they are not all dwarfs. Remember my warning that they hybridize freely, so be prepared for disappointments and surprises among the volunteer seedlings.

Arabis

Arabis, or rock cress, is a species comprising extremes ranging from the vigorous *A. alpina* ssp. *caucasica* (still listed as *A. albida* in some catalogs) to the petite Greek species from the high mountains.

A. androsacea is a tiny alpine gem from Turkey, safe to use in troughs, pots, and small rock gardens. It is a low mounding plant comprised of rosettes of leaves covered with fine silky hairs. The white flowers are on two-inch stems.

A. bryoides without a doubt belongs to that group of small compact buns from the high mountains that are so challenging and fun to cultivate. We have to resort to pot culture and often the alpine house. This species from the Greek mountains forms a tight bun of softly hairy leaves in closely packed rosettes. Slender flower stems some two inches high carry white flowers.

A. bryoides 'Olympica' is often listed as a more compact form. 'Olympica' may refer to Mt. Olympus. Information on this form is very minimal; one would have to grow both plants to see the difference.

A. alpina ssp. caucasica is included because if you need something to put in a large planter in a sunny spot with minimal care, this is one of the best plants to use. It is on the coarse side with long greeny-gray leaves that form mats that will festoon from a wall or fill a planter and hang over the sides. Do not over-plant with it; leave room for others just as good. It flowers early with the coming of spring. I recommend the excellent double flowered form, *A. alpina* ssp. *caucasica* 'Plena'. I use the variegated form with its white-streaked leaves. The attractive pink form usually goes under the name 'Rosea'. It is always wise to take the shears to arabis after it flowers. Don't be afraid to give it a good haircut.

Arabis alpina ssp. *caucasica*

A. x kellereri is an old hybrid from the famous Sundermann Nursery in Germany, the originator of remarkable plants, many of which are still going strong today. I like this plant for the good quality of the white flowers. It is a dwarf, cushion-forming plant with small lanceolate leaves so covered with appressed hairs that the leaves appear to be ash gray. It is a lime-liking plant although it will survive without it.

147

The North American mountains have a population of dwarf *Arabis* but because I have very little experience with them I cannot give advice, other than to urge that they be considered. I have one plant of *A. parishii* in a four-inch pot. It has nice very gray leaves and the plant is a small tufted thing.

Arenaria

A. balearica is worth mentioning even though it has very limited use because it must have a cool, moist position and its hardiness is not great. Why list it? Simply because it is a lovely plant when grown in association with cool, damp rocks. It grows right on the moist, porous rock surface, appearing as a green film of tiny bright leaves almost covered with one-inch, threadlike dancing stems with white flowers. It is a simple matter to root a few pieces before winter comes and carry them over in a cold frame or alpine house for use the following year.

A. tetraquetra is another of the great mounding plants. It rarely makes a cushion over three inches high and it spreads very slowly. It is a trough plant, a pot plant, and a garden plant. Its does not mind sun in the open garden provided it has a depth of gritty soil beneath it, since it needs a root run to withstand drought. It is pointless to try to describe the leaves as they are imbricated. In other words, they are so tightly overlapped, like tiles on a roof, that you hardly notice the individual leaves. Flowers are stemless and white.

A. t. var. *granatensis* is an even more compacted form from the Spanish mountains. It forms iron-hard buns of grayish green foliage. It is a good candidate for growing on tufa, although I have never tried it myself. I remember I was once told, "it does not spoil its beauty by flowering." It can bear white, stemless flowers in late summer.

Armeria

I have always had mixed feelings about the role of armeria, or thrift, in the rock garden. After a recent visit to the Maritime Alps and seeing *Armeria* species in their natural habitat I am convinced there is a place for them in the small rock garden. They grow wild on sunny rough meadows and among rock outcrops.

A. juniperifolia (syn. *A. caespitosa)* is a popular plant and is readily available. It is a sun lover and does not demand special soil. Its place is on top of outcrops or on open slopes; it loves crevices if you

Armeria juniperifolia

have one to spare. It will grow in a trough where the lean diet will keep it compact. The plant makes a low mat that will spread to well over 12 inches, with prickly looking leaves of dark green and the round papery flowers on short stems. The color can range from soft silvery pink to a lilac-pink. *A. j.* 'Bevan's Variety' is the one to grow if you prefer a deeper pink. I have a bit of a problem being certain I have 'Bevan's Variety'—the only way to distinguish between them is to grow both and wait for them to flower. *A. j.* Alba has papery white flowers that turn a bit brown as they fade. Other than that it makes an agreeable trough plant.

A. maritima 'Victor Reiter' might be a little bigger but it is worth a try. It is named for or by Victor Reiter, a nurseryman from San Francisco, and is a small tight cushion with rich pink flowers.

Artemisia

Artemisia is the genus of sages and wormwoods, and there are a few dwarfs suitable for alpine gardens. The names and descriptions in some lists are confusing and very difficult to sort out. Some species have as many as four different names. The primary value of these plants is the brightness of the silvery-gray foliage. The greenish yellow flowers have less significance.

A. caucasica (syn. A. assoana) is one of the best wormwoods for the small garden. It has silvery, filigreed foliage in light open clumps, with flower stems rising above the four-inch high plant. This is particularly attractive when the pale, silvery buds appear. My plant is no more than two inches tall and has spread eight by 14 inches,

149

covering the top of a rocky outcrop in full sun. The tiny leaves are lobed and very aromatic. They are so densely covered with tiny hairs it is hard to call them gray. They are not really white—aluminum comes to mind. I would use it in a small rock garden. Plant it in the deep soil behind one of the outcrop stones and it will decide where to spread. My plant spread onto the shallow soil covering the rock.

A. schmidtiana **'Nana'** is well known. Be certain that you get the dwarf 'Nana'. It makes a nice, silvery accent in the rock garden or raised bed.

Asperula

The little alpine forms of *Asperula*, or sweet-smelling woodruff, have been around rock gardens for many years now, quietly growing without a great deal of notice. Some are happy in the sunny rock garden and will grow well when closely associated with rocks where they can obtain a cool root run. Others are not so easy going. Heat does not seem to bother them if it is dry, but heat paired with humidity kills them. Unfortunately, in many climates they are better suited to the controlled environment of the alpine house. There are some newer species and geographic variations coming from seed collectors in Turkey that look like they will be fun to grow, but I suspect that most of us will have to try them in pots for a while.

A. gussonii has been with me for many years and remains a neat, tight mound of very dark green curly little leaves. I grow it in association with a rock or two, where it can seek a cool root run. This is mainly a slowly spreading, mat-forming species covered with heads of small pink flowers carried in almost stemless heads. It comes from mountains of Sicily.

A. nitida is a very similar species, also with green foliage and heads of pink flowers. At a quick glance, you get the impression that the flowers are white, for they are pink fading to white when fully open. It comes from the mountains of Greece and Turkey.

A. sintenisii has been around for a while now. It forms a tiny gray-green mound and covers itself with strongly colored, pink, tubular flowers.

150

A. suberosa is a confused little species which flits across the scene for a while and then disappears. It is a pretty plant with thin looking, hairy, gray leaves. It grows quite fast and can cover itself in masses of pink flowers in late spring. It is hard to know whether winter dampness kills it, or frost, or summer's humidity. The *A. suberosa* encountered in horticulture is usually *A. arcadiensis*.

There are several newer species of asperula coming to us from seed collectors working in Turkey, and some of the mail order nurseries offer them periodically.

Aurinia (Formerly *Alyssum*)

A. saxatilis (formerly *Alyssum saxatile*) is included because I recommend it as a container plant, knowing full well that it is a large plant and better suited to old, sun-soaked walls. It is a simple plant with clumps of long, gray-green leaves that spread and form a clump up to 18 inches tall. From April until summer it will be a mass of golden flowers in dense corymbs (flat-topped or convex inflorescences where the outer flowers open first). There are several clones available at garden centers, usually sold as 'Basket of Gold'.

A. s. 'Citrina' is, as the name suggests, lemon colored. *A. s.* 'Dudley Nevill' is described as buff-yellow or orange-buff. However it is described, it is a good color and adds to the palette of yellow and gold shades.

Campanula

Beautiful *Campanula* species are known by many names: bellflowers, harebells, bluebells of Scotland, and nun of the

Campanula cochlearifolia 'Alba'. This white form is known as nun of the meadows.

151

meadows. By whatever name you call them, they are valuable plants in any garden design. Many are rock plants. Campanulas can be found throughout the Northern Hemisphere at virtually any elevation. Nun of the meadows, which grows in screes and rock crevices in the mountains of Central and Southern Europe, is the white form of *C. cochlearifolia* (formerly *C. pusilla*), pictured on page 151.

There are quite a few species ideally suited to the small rock garden since they are small enough to be in scale with the miniature landscape and not, as a rule, invasive. Besides, they flower later than many rock plants so their personalities can be appreciated without the competition from more flamboyant neighbors .

Fortunately, alpine nurseries stock a good selection of smaller varieties, so by all means peruse the lists and select whatever appeals to you, but be sure the description contains the words 'not invasive.' I have severely limited the suggested varieties to non-invasive ones since the rock garden is small and space is at a premium. Not all gardens and climates are acceptable to all species, and even gardeners who are favored with success will find that campanulas are a great delicacy for the slug.

If the rock garden is positioned where it receives some protection from long summer days of sunshine, the easier varieties will do well in the open. The difficult species require extra fussing. Find or make a horizontal crevice and add a soil mix to which sharp chips and humus-rich soil have been added. The safest time to transplant campanulas is in the early spring, just as tiny green shoots are beginning to show. Well established pot-grown specimens can be moved almost any time, but recover faster if planted early.

If your space is very limited, do not succumb to beautiful illustrations of such species as *CC. poscharskyana, portenschlagiana,* or the delicate pendant fairy bells of the harebell, *C. rotundifolia.*

I make room for *C. garganica* 'Dickson's Gold'. A raised bed or terraced wall garden makes an ideal home for this all-year plant. In the dull days of fall the lime-green foliage darkens to gold. It makes a solid clump about four inches high and is capable of spreading to 24 inches. Its flowers are white-eyed lavender stars.

If I were restricted to one double campanula I would choose *C. x haylodgensis* 'Plena' which you can see on gallery page g. The double flowers remind me of a diminutive hybrid tea rose, opened to perfection. It is described as a rich blue, but I see a touch of violet in the flowers. There is also a pure white variety named *C. x h.* 'Warley White' which is equally charming. Both flower from July to September and require about a square foot in which to develop.

Campanula garganica 'Dickson's Gold'

C. carpatica is a grand plant, but many of its forms and varieties grow to well over a foot tall and twice as wide, so they must be excluded. Luckily there are a few varieties that just squeak in under our restrictions. Two excellent examples are *C. c.* 'Blue Clips' and *C. c.* 'White Clips,' since they are in the eight-inch range. Both make leafy clumps of bright green foliage and carry their numerous, widely bell-shaped flowers on erect wiry stems. The flowers are over an inch across and perhaps are better described as saucer-shaped. They are found in many shades of violet, blue, and purple as well as several white varieties listed under the name *carpatica*; just check up on the ultimate height and spread to be sure the plant you select will not swamp its neighbors.

C. carpatica originates in the Carpathian Mountains in Eastern and Central Europe. There is also a much dwarfer form called *C. c.* var. *turbinata*, which carries one violet flower to a stem, grows to about six inches, and has hairy leaves. A really good form of this may take some locating. Then there is *C. c.* var. *turbinata* f. *alba* 'Hannah', dwarf and white-flowered. There is an array of named varieties listed in nursery catalogs, all originating from this species. I have not seen them all, so my advice is to go through the list and select the smallest varieties in the colors you prefer. Bressingham Nursery in the UK is responsible for a few excellent introductions, and several nurseries in Europe are introducing some great new varieties.

Most *carpatica* species are happy in normal rock garden soil usually in full sun or part shade. They require some moisture during the summer dry months. Although they are not suited to trough growing, they are great for walls, raised beds, and terraced beds. For those who are interested, the carpaticas were popular many years ago as pot-grown specimens or in larger containers. They are good for only one season in pots, so enjoy them and then plant them out.

C. cochlearifolia is the correct, if ungainly, name for this truly alpine species (see photo on page 151). It means the foliage is cochleate or spoon-shaped. For ages the plant was known by the much nicer name, *C. pusilla*. It still retains the original popular name, fairies' thimbles.

This species loves to run around in crevices and beds. It will creep into paths and I am sure it would take over any trough planting. To some it can be a problem; in my garden it delights in invading my saxifrages. Flowering from June to August, it is valuable if given a spot away from smaller treasures. It is quite variable, ranging through mid-blue, gray-blue, lavender-blue, and white. A healthy plant will grow into a patch of dense foliage, up to four inches tall. There are a few selections offered from time to time. *C. c.* 'Miranda' is ages old, having been discovered by Reginald Farrer. I like the shape of the flowers because they look like thimbles rather than bells. The true species has fat, dumpy bells of pale lavender.

There is a double form called *C. c.* 'Elizabeth Oliver'. It is a little on the floppy side but is not invasive. It has so many light blue petals that the whole bell is solidly packed with them.

C. formanekiana. For fun, raise a few seedlings of *C. formaneki-ana* and grow them in pots in the alpine house. It is a monocarpic plant originally found in Macedonia. It will die after it flowers but there is no time limit on when it will flower. There can be two or three years to enjoy the magnificent rosette of crinkly, downy gray leaves. With skillful cultivation it can be grown to six, eight, or even more inches across. Usually around May it will flower, sending up a noble stem from the center of the rosette that can ascend one and a half to two feet tall, and this is part of the challenge and interest.

You will lose your plant once it flowers, but it goes out with style. A shapely, well-grown specimen produces symmetrical laterals spreading horizontally from the base, tapering to the top, forming a cone shape. Large tubular bell-shaped white flowers, sometimes tinged with pale blue, are borne on the laterals.

To grow it, keep stepping the seedlings up by gradually potting them into slightly larger pots, using a light, open soil mix. Never let it become seriously pot bound, which will hasten flowering before it reaches full size. Do not force it with heat, fertilizers, or rich soil: these do not work.

The plants do better outside during spring and summer months . Keep a watchful eye on watering and do not let them suffer prolonged drought. Take them into the greenhouse for protection before the cold fall rains begin.

While on the topic of growing campanulas in pots, there are several exquisite dwarf alpine species that are very difficult to cultivate, although it is sometimes possible to succeed inside the alpine house or on a lump of tufa.

C. garganica, the species, is a lovely plant (see photo on page 153) and deserves consideration. It comes from the rocky coasts on both sides of the Adriatic Sea. It chooses shady rocks but we must offer it a sunny, well-drained spot. The true species is a refined plant with decumbent stems that do not grow beyond five or six inches long, making a modest clump of bright green, ivy-shaped but toothed leaves. The flowers are held erect as open faced stars; while variable, they are usually light blue with a small white center.

There are a lot of plants listed as *C. garganica,* and they may be named correctly since it is a capricious, variable species. Many will be coarse and inclined to be greedy. Take care to buy a known small variety. The variety *C. g.* 'W. H. Paine' has been around for many years and I still see it listed once in a while; it has much darker blue flowers. There is another variety named *C. g.* 'Blue Diamond' pictured in a few books. I like the deep, deep blue of the flowers but have not grown it; if it comes my way I will buy one.

There are several choice and difficult campanulas that stand a better chance in a well cared for trough garden. Then there are species rare in cultivation that have to be grown in pots, and often with winter protection.

C. scabrella on the other hand prefers rocky slopes and screes where the running stolons pop up making small tufted colonies of the gray-blue leaves and upturned blue flowers on two inch stems. Do not berate me for introducing a difficult species! I have seen the plant growing in North America, England, and Europe. The more gardeners who try to grow it, the sooner the key to success will be found. Granted, it can be frustrating, but who wants everything to be easy?

C. shetleri favors granite cliffs and huge rock outcrops where it thrives in the shady spots. Filling the fissures in the rock with masses of tightly packed tiny dentate leaves. Flowers are strongly reminiscent of *C. piperi,* although perhaps somewhat smaller but of similar shape and color.

C. zoysii heads my list of desirable species since it has the characteristics of the true alpine; it is a tiny plant with large flowers. But it is so tricky to cultivate! Once you get the plant, which is not easy, you must find the ultimate home for it. I cannot do better than to quote from the master, Mr. H. Clifford Crook. In his book, *Campanulas* (County Life Ltd., London, 1951) he writes of *C. zoysii*, "An Austrian or Northern Italian species whose home is in the almost inaccessible crannies of the Karawanken. It forms tufts of small roundish shiny leaves with short stalks and entire but hairy margins and produces short stalks about three inches high each carrying a few short stalked, obovate lanceolate or linear leaves and terminating in anything up to six pale blue stalked flowers which have been well described as 'soda water bottle' shape."

To cultivate it, Mr. Crook advises a rich limy crevice, a scree watered from below, or potting it in a rich scree mixture and growing it in an alpine house. It has been my experience that it has a nasty habit of dying after flowering; it may lack the strength to live on. The moral is, retain any seed that comes your way and try to take some cuttings in early spring. As with all campanulas, watch for the wily slug and the damage it does.

If the story of *C. zoysii* appeals to you there are several more of these challenging species from the mountains of Europe just waiting to challenge your skills. Here in British Columbia we do not have to go far to find exquisite dwarf mountain campanulas. In the Olympic Mountains of Washington State there lives the endemic *C. piperi*. Although I live within the sight of Mount Angeles where it grows along with the mountain goats, I cannot grow it for long. It is a delightful plant with a completely prostrate habit, spreading stems and open-faced, saucer-shaped blue flowers. Colors range from pale blue to deep blue and some into blue purple. Striking red anthers add emphasis to the brightness of this lovely species.

Several variations in color have been discovered and introduced by local nursery operators and rock garden enthusiasts, including a couple of attractive white forms.

Convolvulus

Many gardeners would wonder why anyone would recommend morning glories (*Convolvulus* species), but *C. boissieri,* formerly called *C. nitidus,* offers possibilities. The present name is firmly established in most nursery lists now. You can be sure this one will never become invasive since it can be a challenge in the garden. I have had to resort to growing it in a pot. A friend who lives a mile or so away grows it quite well in full sun on a very dry spot at the top of his rock garden.

 It hails from the Spanish Sierra where it is found in sunny limestone rocks. In cultivation there is some question of hardiness and an aversion to winter wetness. The raised bed or vertical wall or pocket in the sunny rock garden would be the best bet. I think the trough garden might be a bit too shallow for the roots.

It is a very attractive plant making a cushion no more than an inch high covered with spectacular deeply nerved leaves, essentially green but so heavily covered with silky hairs that they appear silver. The typical morning glory white flowers, heavily tinged with pink, are about an inch across and virtually stemless.

Corydalis

Corydalis is a huge genus containing around 300 species as well as numerous garden hybrids. A few of the species are good rock garden plants but are better grown in partial shade, which limits their value in the sunny garden. As lovely as some of these woodland varieties are, they have a tendency to grow up to 24 inches or more. They are often described as ferny leaved perennials, frequently with gray green foliage. The flowers are borne in racemes and are narrowly tubular with a rear-pointing spur.

C. cashmeriana. "From the flower-filled high valleys of Kashmir grows startlingly lovely *C. cashmeriana*" says Will Ingwersen when describing this little plant in his book *Alpine and Rock Plants* (J.M. Dent, 1983). This little plant is composed of small tufts of finely cut blue-green leaves with six-inch stems bearing glacier-blue flowers. Then he continues, "This capricious plant, succeeding here and failing there for no apparent reason..." It is evident that the plant demands cool, damp, and misty air and does well in Scotland, so if you have a Scottish climate you are in business. Failing that, a cool garden in North Vancouver at the foot of the Coast Mountains will do; I did see two plants growing there. All the rest of us will have to continue to try growing it in an alpine house.

Since I have implied that it is a tricky alpine species, I must mention the other wonderful blue *Corydalis* species to prevent confusion. We see these other blues in garden centers, and seldom if ever find *C. cashmeriana* there.

C. flexuosa. I do not recommend these lovely varieties for a small rock garden for they truly belong in the woodland garden setting. I recall the day I first saw one-gallon pots of *Corydalis flexuosa* 'Blue Panda' for sale. The intensity of the blue flowers was irresistible. A few years later other forms were introduced from China. *C.f.* 'China Blue', *C.f.* 'Père David', and *C.f.* 'Purple Leaf,' (this last one I have seen listed as *C.f.* 'Purple Prince') are equally appealing varieties. For the full story of these introductions read *The Explorer's Garden* by Daniel J. Hinkley (Timber Press, 1999).

C. solida is a popular tuberous species that occurs widely across Europe. It is rated as six inches tall but will reach 12 inches under shady conditions and rich humus soil. The foliage begins to develop early in the spring to form a clump with several stems which carry spikes of purple flowers. The plant does not stay green very long, and by summer the foliage has died down. There are several color variants of this species, so check the listings carefully to see what is available. These examples will give you an idea of the range available.

C. s. 'Blue Pearl' has sky-blue flowers.

C. s. ssp. *solida* 'George Baker' is a superb variety with red flowers. Be prepared to hunt for this plant.

C. s. 'Harkov' is a flourishing Ukrainian selection with large spikes of rich violet-blue flowers.

Cyclamen

Cyclamen species are appealing little plants, so it is a pity they are not always easy to grow. There are a few fortunate locations where it is possible to succeed with several *Cyclamen* species in an open garden, usually in the higher numbered zones. Even there, research is advisable when deciding where and under what conditions they should be planted. Gardeners often resort to growing them in pots and bulb pans with winter or summer protection, becoming very proficient at producing prize-winning specimens. In protected alpine houses or bulb frames, cyclamens make ideal companions for small bulbs.

Cyclamen graecum

Dwarf cyclamen are truly enchanting little plants and it is surprising what tough conditions they thrive under in their native habitat. There are about 20 species in nature—the number fluctuates as botanists rearrange the classification. The epicenter of their native habitat is the Mediterranean region, which features hot, dry summers. Normally, the only rain occurs in spring and fall. Winter temperatures can be low but are not prolonged.

The inability to approximate this climate is the reason many of the species do not survive outdoors in every garden in the USA. Luckily, there are several species that do well in Zone 5 and parts of Zone 4.

C. coum is the smallest of the recommended trio and has long been in cultivation. It is popular in milder winters for its ability to supply a few flowers in early January days. Even if they freeze overnight, there is a new crop of colored buds lying on the soil awaiting their turn to arise and open. The main flowering period is the

159

spring. Flower color is mainly a deep crimson, but seedlings vary from near-white to pink through dark magenta. Flowers have short petals, giving them a slightly dumpy look. The roundish, kidney-shaped leaves are small and neat, and may be a dull and unmarked green; there are others that will be heavily marbled with silvery-white. The underside of each leaf is a deep purple-red.

Since flowering begins so early, it is nice to have them in a spot where they are easily seen and enjoyed. They appreciate protection from cold winds and enjoy association with rocks; they are not so demanding of shade.

C. hederifolium is capable of developing into a substantial plant with spreading leaf-stems, often producing quite large leaves, so it would be safer in a place where it has room to spread. It hails from woodlands, open scrubby areas, and rocky slopes.

Occasionally a flower will appear in summer, without any leaves showing, and there is a rivalry among gardeners to see who has the earliest flower. The main floral display begins in August and can last until October, when the leaves begin to appear. The flowers are borne on stout stems, about five inches tall, making them excellent for use as cut flowers.

The flowers are usually found in pleasing shades of pink, but whites are common in cultivation. The typical cyclamen-shaped flowers are often flushed with deeper shades toward the base of the petals. A closer look reveals the distinct 'ears' or auricles at the base of each petal, a feature of this species. Furthermore, while not considered as a scented flower, there are occasional cyclamen plants that do have fragrance.

Finding the ideal spot for this plant, particularly in a small rock garden, is tricky. It is not a typical alpine plant, but rather a plant of the semi-shaded woodland and scrub areas just below the open alpine areas. If you have such an area, one that suggests the transition between the lower forested slopes and the alpine region, you have the quandary solved. If not, cyclamen will stand sun in a rock garden or raised bed providing the soil is well-drained and the roots can enjoy rambling around among the rocks.

C. purpurascens can be planted as an alternative to the preceding species if the former is too aggressive. It is not as easy to grow and is a more refined species. It is a mountain plant from southern alpine ranges where it inhabits deciduous woods or those woodlands mixed with coniferous species. The soil should be free draining. It helps to add limestone and humus. The plant is difficult to please. Since it does not go dormant in summer it requires cool soil that does not dry out in summer. Hardiness can be a problem. Even though it is grown by many gardeners in Zone 4, the microclimates of the planting sites, even within a single garden, can spell success or failure.

C. purpurascens has roundish, kidney-shaped to broadly heart-shaped leaves. They may be a clear, dull green on the upper surface and virtually unmarked, or they can have beautiful marbling of silvery-white. All leaves are red to purple on the underside. This cyclamen is summer flowering. Flower color varies from nondescript pink to good rose-pinks and a fine carmine; all are sweetly scented.

Dianthus

For such a lovely genus of alpine plants, the *Dianthus* species do not receive the appreciation they deserve—I am not sure why. They are easy to grow and do not require lots of fuss or watering, certainly not rich soil. They are sun lovers that love lime in the soil yet do just as well if it is absent.

I have heard fellow rock gardeners say that if you have seen one dianthus you have seen them all.

There might be a modicum of fact in the statement. Many types have similar silvery, narrow foliage and pinkish flowers with frilled petals. Like *Aquilegia* species, they do not come true from seed. Any dianthus flower that has been cross pollinated by other nearby species can produce anything other than the name written on the seed packet. This situation leads to the distribution of misleading and incorrect names.

Yet the "seen one, seen them all" reputation is undeserved, as the family provides a range of plants for every type of rock gardening, including the trough, raised beds, walls, and containers both large and small. There are tiny species for crevices in the choicest miniature schemes. There is plenty of challenge for the skilled grower. There are sun loving carpets of gray foliage and sheets of colors that delight in rocky ledges and slopes and demand little else. An occasional clipping with shears maintains neatness and often results in another crop of flowers.

Among their many good qualities is the fact that they flower after the mad rush of the early spring flowers. Obviously one cannot predict when a plant will start to flower in every garden, but in most regions it is safe to say they will start in May and June and may continue through much of the summer.

Alpine Species

D. alpinus. A true alpine plant from the higher elevations of Europe, *D. alpinus* has been in our rock gardens for many years. The leaves are green and make small mats of glossy foliage. Truly glorious flowers an inch or so across are carried singly on very short stems. They start to appear in mid-May and continue into summer. The species is variable in color. White flowers are not uncommon, and a few nurseries offer named color variations. All and any are worth a try. The wild plant is usually found in shades of rich pink to purple-pink. I am happy with whatever I get. This is a plant for that favorite little nook, requiring excellent drainage and a little extra leafmold. I have seen it flourishing in practically nothing but stone chips.

Dianthus alpinus 'Joan's Blood'

Now for the bad news. This species does not last for many years regardless of the little extras I give, including its own private topdressing of chippings. Therefore, try to maintain a supply of new seedlings for replacement. Seed is not hard to find and it germinates without a lot of fuss.

D. erinaceus is a singular species quite unlike other dianthus. In my garden, over a period of several years, it has grown into a large, dense, humped mound some two feet across with smaller mounds bulging from the surface. Planted on the edge of a sunny, west-facing outcrop it has expanded happily and now is beginning to flow over the vertical rocks of the outcrop. Close examination shows that the narrow, very short leaves are quite prickly. The numerous, stemless, crimson-

pink flowers make their appearance in early summer. The plant originates from limestone outcrops on Mt. Kaz Dag in the dry mountains of Turkey. In the garden it demands light, fast-draining soil, so plant in the higher parts of the rock garden to make sure there is no danger of wet soil in winter.

162

Dianthus erinaceus

I remember seeing this species in gardens of some of the Eastern States and, on checking with a friend in Pennsylvania, he tells me it has done well with him over the last ten years.

D. haematocalyx and its subspecies and varieties are all excellent subjects for small rock gardens and troughs. As a group they are all worth growing, for they enjoy sun and seem to be tolerant of winter's wetness. They are compact mounds or low flat spreading stems, not quite mats. Leaves are short and sharply pointed. Flower stems rise carrying branching heads of five-petalled flowers. Each petal is wedge shaped and raggedly toothed. Those of red-purple flowers each have a biscuit colored underside. In some forms the calyx behind each flower is particularly noticeable because of its strong red color.

D. h. ssp. pindicola is a `highly desirable high mountain form with a low, flat habit. The flowers are on extremely short stems with petals so large that they practically overlap one another. The very short stems of this form make it preferable for smaller plantings.

D. pavonius, D. glacialis and **D. freyneii** are different species that share the same broad features, and all are denizens of the close, stony, turf of the high mountains. There is some concern about their tolerance of limey soil, and where the soil is exceptionally limey it would be best to avoid them.

In meadows they form low tufts of green leaves that mingle with grass and other alpines. The stems are short enough for the small garden, growing up to four inches tall. They will be shorter if not crowded by taller plants. Flowers are in the light- to dark-pink range, with occasional darker forms.

D. simulans is a dense, cushion-forming plant with gray needlelike foliage that leads to a spiny tip. When grown under lean conditions the flower stems are very short. A plant growing in pure tufa has no flower stems whatsoever. *D. simulans* is a native of the mountains along the Bulgarian and Greek borders. Will Ingwersen describes the plants' habitat on Mount Ali Butusch, home of the popular *Sempervivum ciliosum* of that name; they share the same habitat, the scree slopes and adjacent sparse turf.

The plant survives in one of my troughs but is never rampant. The good, solid pink of the half-inch blooms makes it well worth the wait. There is some confusion among gardeners as to the true identity of this species as there seem to be several differing forms circulating.

Easy, Trouble-Free Dianthus

D. deltoides is available at springtime sales in local garden centers, and very tempting with bright and startlingly colored flowers so neat and tidy in their pot. I mention them here only to deliver this message. The gardener with a small rock garden must be strong and walk away from them, for they are too aggressive for limited spaces.

D. gratianopolitanus is from the limestone Mountains of West, South, and Central Europe. It has been described as *D.caesius* for ages and under this name countless rock garden books have noted the fact that it is a rare British Native species. Rare it is indeed, limited to small groups in the Cheddar Gorge, Somerset in England. The greater populations of the species range across the rocky clefts and stony meadows of Europe. The short, carnation-like leaves are gray-green and make large, low, flat mats that romp over contours. An excellent wall plant, it will cascade in sheets. A truly sun loving plant, it prefers light soil and lots of drainage. In May and June it starts to flower, covering the foliage with a mass of rose-pink, scented flowers. The large blooms are about an inch across on stems four or so inches tall. The plant is variable in cultivation for several reasons. Owing to the wide distribution in the wild, there are several different naturally occurring forms, even a double and a white.Over the years it has been propagated from garden seed and may well contain some hybrid blood. Nonetheless, where you have room it is a good choice.

D. myrtinervius is another easy, low carpeting species from high alpine meadows where it spreads its tiny, bright green leaves into closely set, thyme-like mats. The small flowers are bright pink. A lovely plant if kept in very lean soil to retain the natural alpine character, a constant watch must be kept over it to ensure that no seedlings escape to richer soil. If left to their own devices they will make significant clumps of taller and looser plants.

Rock Garden Hybrid Dianthus

Within the dianthus genus there are numerous intermediate hybrids well suited to the small garden. They are much smaller than either the border carnations or the old fashioned pinks, both of which, Will Ingwersen tactfully wrote "...are best confined to the more formal parts of the garden."

These hybrids fit into the rock garden scheme very well, since they are small, compact, and flower well with short stems. Some originate as accidental crosses in gardens and nurseries, others are deliberate selections aimed at introducing something new.

Check the nursery lists for varieties described as having tidy blue- gray tufts or mounds of foliage and short flower stems. Tall, floppy stems do not look right in an alpine garden. Look for double or semi- double flowers. These hybrids introduce a wider range of colors. *D.* 'Mars', is brilliant red, *D* 'Little Jock' is semi-double and rose-pink, and *D. gratianopolitanus* 'Tiny Rubies' has delightful, rosy-red double flowers.

D. 'La Bourboule' has an interesting background and is likely to have *D. gratianopolitanus* as a parent. It is very similar to *D. gratiano-politanus* but the flowers are a richer pink and the habit tends to be more tufted. There is a white variety also, *D.* 'La Bourboule Albus'; in my garden the white form is less vigorous. Spelling has always been an issue with this hybrid, which has also appeared as *D.* 'La Bour-boulle' and other variations.

I have a copy of Will Ingwersen's little monograph on rock garden *Dianthus*, dated 1949, and assumed he would know the correct spelling, since this is one of his favorite genera. I was surprised to see he listed it as 'La Bourbrille', with the comment that it was sometimes known as 'La Boulville', which I have never seen used. I then checked Alpine Garden Society's *Encyclopedia of Alpines* where it is listed as 'La Bourboule'. I spent some time looking back at the few very old catalogs and good old standard rock garden books I have, hoping for historical consistency, but even Ingwersen's Birch Farm Nursery changed the spelling over the years.

Draba

Many species of *Draba* make excellent subjects for miniature gardening chiefly because of their neat, tidy, bun shape. The foliage can be bright green or silvery gray, depending on the density of silky hairs on the leaves and stems. Most species produce yellow flowers dancing on threadlike stems no more than two or three inches high, while others have practically no stem at all. There are a couple of white flowered kinds.

There are quite a few species that are not worth including because of poor quality flowers or straggly growth habit. As you raise them from seed you will soon notice that many seedlings do not seem true to the species listed on the seed packet. This is not necessarily the supplier's fault but is a sign of the ease with which the plants hybridize with one another.

Draba mollissima

Drabas are among the first plants to flower in early spring, brightening the garden with their cheerful flowers for what seems too short a time. Unless seed is required, cut off the spent flowers and stems. Cut as close to the foliage as you can, for the drying stems spoil the appearance of the plant. Sometimes this encourages a second crop of flowers.

Culture. For the most part the drabas are easy, undemanding plants tolerant of varied climate and soil. Give them a spot in a trough, small rock garden, or raised bed. They are great pot plants, too. Giving them plenty of sun keeps them compact and the domes hard. When they have too much shade they become sloppy, with the cushions opening and sprawling in a weedy manner. For the gardener who likes to experiment with miniature containers and soil mixtures, they have few rivals. They produce seed that germinates readily, providing a supply of young plants with good root systems that can be transplanted into holes in lumps of tufa or similar nooks and crannies among rocks and stones.

It is surprising that these choice little alpine buns are members of the *Brassica* family, along with cabbages, rutabagas, turnips, and the unmentionable mustards. Fortunately this family is not restricted to vegetables, and many key rock garden plants are members: *Aubrieta, Hutchinsia, Erysimum* (the wallflowers), and *Iberis,* to name a few of the more popular ones.

166

Many are saxatile plants, which means they love to grow in association with and among rocks. If you ever get to see them at home on the mountains you will quickly realize how to exploit them in the crevices and ledges of the small rock garden. Basic rock garden soil with some extra gravel added will guarantee an attractive and floriferous plant.

Drabas come in several shapes and sizes, from ground-hugging carpets to domes and tiny pincushions easily mistaken for moss. As always, the choicest species are difficult, and this is true for those with dense, downy leaves. They cannot cope with winter wetness.

Grow plants in an alpine house, or place a piece of glass or clear plastic over them to shed rain but without restricting the vital movement of air around the cushions. A well established plant growing outside is worth the effort of keeping rain off the foliage. Often, trough-grown specimens develop into wonderful, iron-hard domes.

D. longisiliqua will not be found in older books, for it was introduced into horticulture in 1976 and is considered a recent discovery. It is found in the Russian Caucasus Mountains, where it inhabits sunny, hot, limestone cliffs that are brutally cold in winter. I have described it as the larger edition of *D. mollissima*, and equally as fussy when it comes to winter wetness.

D. mollissima, a woolly ball from the rocks and crevices of the dryer parts of the Caucasian mountains, is so covered with soft, fine, white hair it appears to be gray. It is a perennial plant that is dormant during the winter months, so dormant that the foliage is brown and easily taken for dead. Do not water the plant while it is dormant or it will *be* dead. As spring weather approaches it starts to turn green. Soon the thin flower stems appear and the heads of fresh lemon-yellow flowers blow in the breeze. It makes a refreshing sight and gives a great deal of satisfaction to the grower who succeeded in bringing it through the winter.

D. polytricha. If I were limited to one draba this would be my choice. It hails from the harsh mountains of Eastern Europe, growing under conditions similar to those for the preceding species.

It consists of masses of tiny rosettes of downy leaves packed tightly into a mound covered with rich yellow heads of flowers on stubby stems. A young specimen established in a tufa rock or planted in a crevice between two stones, in a rock garden or trough will develop into an iron-hard dome. Grown outside, development will be slow and during wet winters it will look extremely unhappy. As a pot-grown or alpine house plant it performs very well, growing into a large dome.

D. rigida and its subspecies and forms. *D. rigida* is a perfect alpine plant that loves to live in among rocks, crevices, troughs, and pots. From my observations, it seems to do well under many garden climates. The iron-hard bun is bright green. Mine dwells in a trough beside a well-traveled path, seen and admired by all. It even gets stroked. When it flowers it has those threadlike stems, which in this case will grow up to three inches tall. The flowers are in corymbs. I describe the color as lemon yellow, although many describe it as golden. Regardless of this small point, they are bright and cheerful.

D. rigida var. *bryoides* is another very choice species that looks like a smaller version of *D. rigida*. It has the same tiny leaves in a dense bun, but the flower stems grow only an inch high. There is an even smaller form called *D. r.* var. *imbricata* f. *compacta*. It is wise to treasure these smaller varieties, planting them in pots and alpine houses or a favorite trough.

The following three drabas have been around for a very long time and are often sold under the names I have used here. They can be found under these names in a number of classic rock garden books, but newer publications may list them as forms or subspecies of *Draba rigida*. That is something for the experts to sort out. My advice is to buy them all when the opportunity arises and then judge for yourself.

D. dedeana is one of the prime white-flowered species from Spain and the Pyrenees. It has dense tufts of broad but spike-tipped leaves with white flowers and is quite safe to plant in with other treasures.

D. x salomonii also has white flowers and is something of a mystery plant. It may be a hybrid of *D. brunifolia* and *D. dedeana*. It is another of the tight green-gray small mounds with very short flower stems and is an excellent candidate for a fine trough.

It is possible to list many more great drabas, but it would become just a list of green or gray mounds or cushions of varying size and density, as some are more semi-open carpets as opposed to having a mounding habit. While the flowers are essentially yellow they range from the palest lemon yellow to golden yellow, and the flower stems range from next to none to a few inches tall. Having said that, I cannot move on without at least drawing your attention to the *Draba* species of North America.

In a recent conversation with Roger Barlow of Beaver Creek Greenhouses he reminded me that there are many new species constantly being introduced from around the world that are hardier and of better quality than many of the forms we have grown. As a major alpine nurseryman he has to keep up with what the plant collectors are doing. He stressed that plant hunters who search the world for new plants for us have never been more active than at present. As an example he described a recent introduction of a superior form of *D. longisiliqua* with much brighter silvery foliage and good solid flowers.

He also notes that the plants are fertile, which is important to the propagation and distribution of a new introduction.

I do not enjoy just listing plant names without at least some descriptive or helpful comment. However, the following names are intended to guide the searcher in the direction of appealing North American *Draba* species. Check out *DD. oligosperma, paysonii, incerta, densifolium*, and *ventosa* from the Beartooth Mountains of Wyoming.

Erigeron

If you like daisies, then the genus *Erigeron*, the fleabanes, may offer good choices for your small rock garden or raised bed. There are many native species that are dwarf and non-invasive, providing a range of plant sizes and requirements. There are tiny, challenging species from the high Rocky Mountains and ground-hugging species from the deserts. There are so many that I have selected just a few of the more floriferous kinds.

E. aureus is a plant from the alpine zone of the mountains of Western Canada and the Coast Mountains of British Columbia, the Selkirk Range, following the Rocky Mountains in Alberta and Montana and southward. It seems to prefer the cool, higher elevations in its

natural habitat, so, in cultivation, provide well-drained garden soil with some extra humus added . It is best if it does not have a hot, full sun location. In my garden it starts to flower in June and continues over a long period. Golden-yellow flowers are carried on single stems four to five inches tall from a low tuft of spoon- shaped leaves. A well established plant can form a clump up to eight inches across. It is an interesting flower, about an inch across with a large center of disc florets and deep golden yellow radiating ray florets.

E. aureus 'Canary Bird' is a plant well worth growing if you enjoy bright, canary-yellow flowers. This variety has an interesting history since it was raised by Jack Drake of the famous nursery in Scotland, from wild-collected seed from Montana. He developed the cultivar from two seedlings that differed from the normal species by their stronger growth. They had slightly longer leaves and flower stems

E. chrysopsidis is a variable plant from dry open places in California, Washington, and Nevada and is often found near sagebrush. Usually it ranges in height from six to eight inches. Its solitary yellow daisies are an inch or two across.

E. c. 'Grand Ridge' is a selected form discovered in the Wallowa Mountains of eastern Oregon by Phil Pearson and Steve Doonan, of the Grand Ridge Nursery near Issaquah, Washington. Anything these two discover and introduce is worthy of note, and if there is space in the garden for one more yellow daisy, consider this one. It is a neat and compact plant and very floriferous; the flowers are bright-yellow and have so many petals that they appear to be double. I have heard that it can be short-lived or can collapse for no apparent reason, which suggests to me it might require a cool alpine environment rather than desert conditions.

E. karvinskianus is described in older books under E. mucronatus. I cannot leave the erigerons without at least introducing you to this particular favorite of mine. True, it might be considered a bit of a weed. If you have a place for it where it can flourish, it will provide you with a bountiful supply of little pink and white single daisies all summer long. The plant forms a billowing mass. It can carpet an area of up to two feet with thin twiggy stems and unobtrusive slender leaves. It is not for the choice trough or the exclusive raised bed, but it is wonderful when planted in a vertical wall or at the base of a raised bed. It may be admitted to smaller rock gardens where there is room. Plant it on the peripheries: let it cascade onto the walkway, so what! If it gets too rambunctious take the shears to it. It will soon bounce back. You will always have it since it will seed itself into the most incredible cracks and crevices. The species originated in Mexico and has now firmly established itself throughout Europe and beyond, despite the fact that it is not hardy in severe winters.

E. leiomerus has a special appeal to me since I first photographed it in Rick Lupp's sand-bed planter, where it formed a tight, solid mat of green spathulate foliage wedged into a crevice created by half submerging two flat rocks side by side. It has the most attractive large flowers of rich blue-violet. Its natural habitat is the higher elevations of the Southern Rockies.

E. scopulinus is a complete contrast from the tufted clumps of yellow daisies, since if grows into a tight mat of tiny glossy leaves, with almost stemless, ragged white flowers in summer. In my garden it grows happily in my scree in full sun and now covers about a square foot, making a completely flat mat of solid green. I cannot recommend the plant for the small trough, although a modest raised bed could accommodate it. The original collector, Sonia Lowzow, discovered it in Arizona, where she reported it quite close to a waterfall in partially shaded crevices. This is a valuable clue to those who may have trouble with it.

Erythronium

Not all gardeners want or can have the classic rock garden. Sometimes, a shady site is the only garden space available, and lots of gardeners live amid woodlands, where rock garden plants will not flourish, so a small shade garden planting is the only option.

Erythroniums are to found in the Eastern USA and in the Western mountains. In cultivation they are happier in a lightly wooded setting where they are protected from hot sun and will not become parched. Drainage is very important. No wet corners for them, so add some compost if the soil tends to be sandy or heavy. Avoid dense shade as they most likely will not flower as well there and it would be a waste to condemn these bright spring flowers to such a spot.

Hardiness is a hit or miss experience, and often a trial and error experience. The varieties listed on the next page have a good reputation for hardiness.

E. dens-canis is mainly from Europe and has been in cultivation for a long time. It bears the name of dog-toothed violet due to the shape of the bulb. I have mixed feelings about this species, as it sometimes is a shy bloomer and is not always a good pink shade. This plant might react better if given a little more sunshine. It must be a successful species because there are numerous color variations that are grown today as named varieties.

The names *E. d.* 'Charmer', 'White Splendour', and 'Snowflake' speak for themselves.

Here are a few more of the named color forms that give an idea of the range of shades found in this species.

E. d. 'Frans Hals'– deep violet purple

E. d. 'Lilac Wonder'

E. d. 'Pink Perfection' – clear, bright pink

E. d. 'Rose Queen'

E. revolutum is a West Coast species from the Coast Range Mountains spreading from British Columbia to California. It occurs in open forests, often close to streams and creeks. It has a reputation as a good garden plant. I have seen it rated to Zone 3. The bold flowers are an inch and three quarters in diameter, blooming in a deep shade of pink with a bright yellow center, sometimes with as many as four blooms per stem. Modest sized foliage is strikingly mottled with dark greeny-brown tones.

E. r. 'White Beauty' is a must and a good garden plant too. It is a beauty with glistening, creamy-white flowers that reflex very gracefully, exposing the yellow throat and the rusty-red ring at the center. Even when not in flower, the green and brown mottling of the leaves is striking.

E. tuolumnense comes from the dry semi-shaded woodlands of Tuolumne County in California, often referred to as a gateway to

172

Yosemite as much of the park is within the county. This is an important plant, and a surprisingly good garden plant. I call it a noble plant because the flower stems will elongate to 12 inches tall and the plant spreads by offsets, creating a large clump of bright green foliage. The leaves are up to six inches tall and several inches wide, even more in rich soil, so locate it in the garden with this thought in mind. I enjoy the good yellow flowers, several to a stem.

Where space is limited, plant one of the *E. tuolumnense* hybrids for a good show of yellow. *E.* 'Pagoda' is *E. tuolumnense* crossed with *E.* 'White Beauty' and has the best of both plants. Its good, rich yellow flowers are borne in quantity. The vigorous foliage is bright green but has some mottling. *E.* 'Kondo' is from the same stable and may even be taller than 'Pagoda'.

There are several intra-specific hybrids among the erythroniums and I recommend that you study the catalogs closely before making a selection. Garden hybrids, whether unintentional crosses or part of a deliberate breeding program, often have garden-worthy characteristics some of the wild species may not offer.

Gentiana

It is most likely that, after studying books and lists of rock garden plants, readers will know what a gentian flower is. Many others will remember the *Enzian* (gentian) from their homelands. One has only to look at a Swiss calendar to see the huge blue trumpets of the gentians featured amid the alpine rose and edelweiss. Not only are they among the finest wild plants of the Alps, they are delightful additions to the smallest rock garden.

Gentiana septemfida 'Latifolia'

173

You'll enjoy the bold trumpets of the trumpet gentian, *Gentiana acaulis*, which flowers in late spring. There are also the tiny starlike flowers of gorgeous blue of the spring gentian, *G. verna*, the first to flower very early in spring, sometimes so early they can hardly wait for the last traces of snow to melt. The early gentians fade as early summer moves into July and August, but there are still more gentians waiting to flower. The summer flowering species carry their trumpet flowers in clusters rather than one to a stem. Generally dark blue, some of them lean toward blue-purple shades; in clear weather the flower heads last into September.

As the flowers fade in September, the Himalayan gentians stage one final glorious display of brilliant blue to close the season before winter finally closes them down.

In their native hills, gentians favor open, sunny alpine turf and low grass pastures. They are not difficult in the rock garden if they are given a sufficient depth of soil to nourish and keep the roots cool and moist during the heat of summer.

Spring Flowering Gentians

G. acaulis is composed of basal rosettes of glossy deep green leaves an inch or so long and half an inch at the widest point. The plants increase by sending out small rosettes on slender underground roots from the edges of the parent plant. A thriving plant soon develops into a dense, healthy clump. In some gardens, as early as March, the huge gentian-blue trumpets start to open on their very short stems. There is an unseasonable flower on my plant right now, so I was able to accurately measure the flower. The trumpet from the calyx to the mouth of the trumpet is two inches long and an inch and a half across the corolla lobes. The flower gives the impression of being blue all over, but the outside of the corolla has broad vertical stripes of a greenish hue and similar light stripes with rows of darker spots inside the throat.

G. acaulis has a reputation as temperamental and reluctant to flower, so avoid disappointment by buying a plant in flower or get assurance from your nursery that they are selling you a flowering form. If after some time it has failed to flower, just dig up the plant and relocate it. For some unknown reason a non-flowering plant will sometimes flower happily if moved just a few feet. Bear in mind that in the Alps it prefers the open meadows, where it also can be found in association with rocks, but always in a good depth of soil.

The name *acaulis* is erroneously applied to many similar species and is still used as a synonym for others. Some books advocate that plants known by the name *G. acaulis* be considered as of garden origin with no connection to the wild species, while others regard *acaulis* as a group name covering a number of geographic forms of several very similar species. When checking through seed and plant lists, should you encounter plants and seeds of gentians with names like *GG. alpina, angustifolia, clusii, or kochiana*, take my advice and grab them.

G. verna, the spring gentian. This little treasure is widely distributed throughout the mountains of Europe and beyond, as far as Afghanistan. In my infrequent trips to the Alps I always look for the bright, sky-blue flowers among the trailside grasses or on banks peeping between large rocks. In nature it has a long flowering period because it follows the melting snow upward, enabling the summer tourists an opportunity to enjoy them.

In the garden it forms a loose mat of small green leaves with slender, ground-hugging stems that creep about just beneath the soil. It is reputed to be short-lived in cultivation and this rambling habit might be a reason. I noticed that it runs out of space in a trough. To encourage it to prosper I give it a good dressing of sharp sand mixed with screened leaf mold, but it only delays the inevitable. On the credit side I have often noticed self-sown seedlings that can be carefully harvested.

There is nothing prettier that a clump of *G. verna* in flower: its plentiful sky-blue starry blossoms totally obscure the foliage. An interesting flower, the long thin corolla tube flares out into the five-pointed lobes, centered by a tiny white star.

Plants of *G. verna* are available from mail order nurseries and so is the Caucasian variety *G. verna* var. *angulosa* which has slightly bolder flowers and a better garden temperament.

Summer Blooming Gentians

G. septemfida (see photo page 173). I am rash enough to call it everybody's gentian because it has such a good reputation as a successful plant under many conditions. It hails from the very harsh climates of the sub-alpine and alpine parts of Asia Minor and the Caucasus. Not only is it amenable to cultivation, it is beautiful too. I would like to clear up a common misunderstanding concerning the name. It is not a reference to the month of September but a botanical reference to seven parts of the flower.

Unlike the preceding species, it produces numerous erect but spreading leafy stems, variable in height from four to12 inches. It

175

grows into a bold clump of spreading stems that become erect to carry the flowers, so it has to have a depth of soil to sustain all the growth. Be sure to give it space to develop.

In July and August, sometimes a little earlier, it will start to flower. Its deep blue flowers are carried in heads of five to eight flowers each. The individual flowers are bell-shaped, but face upward and are about an inch and a half long and three-fourths of an inch across.

Fall Blooming Gentians

The fall blooming gentians differ widely from the neat, compact growth patterns of some of the European species, because they consist mainly of stems radiating from a central point. These thin, rambling stems are clothed with pairs of thin leaves, and root at the nodes wherever they touch the soil. Growth is luxuriant, soon creating a tangled mass of bright green. Prior to flowering, the ends of the stems turn upward and produce one long bud at each tip. The flowers open in September, depending on current weather conditions, lasting until well into November. The late fall rains usually ruin them in my garden.

There are several wonderful species that hail from the high mountains of Western China and Tibet; as a group they are informally referred to as the Asian, Chinese, or Himalayan gentians. All are very beautiful and highly desirable, but very hard to obtain and challenging to grow, to say the least. So I am not going to irritate you by describing plants we cannot acquire.

G. sino-ornata is listed in several mail order lists and is considered by many as one of the more successful species. It comes from the high and vast, rolling open mountain meadows of Western Yunnan and Tibet, where, I am told, the moisture in the turf may cover your shoes, a condition that does not last in that dry altitude.

The flowers of *G. sino-ornata* are the typical tubular shaped gentian flowers up to two and a half inches long and are a solid royal blue. A sizeable clump in full flower is an impressive sight. On closer examination the flowers show several bold vertical stripes of light and dark blues and greens on the exterior of each flower.

Can your garden offer a cool but sunny spot and be protected from direct sunshine at the same time? It must have bright light and still be partially shaded. Finally, the atmosphere must be cool and humid. I doubt there are many such gardens, at least in the places where we prefer to live—mine certainly is not like that. Failing such conditions, try growing them in a trough at least six inches deep inside. Fill it with rock garden soil that has a higher proportion of soil, since *G. sino ornata* needs a richer soil. Also keep it slightly moist.

My trough is on the east side of the house and is shaded by the shadow cast by the house in the afternoon. The southern aspect is tempered by a trellis.

The trough needs to be replanted every second year. Do it when the new shoots are just visible above the soil. Totally empty the trough of plants and soil and refill with new soil. The roots of the gentians are in clumps, like small white carrots, called thongs, so select the largest and replant them right away. If you pot up the extras, suddenly you will be very popular.

White Gentians and Hybrid Gentians

There are white-flowered forms of many gentians, which are more a collector's item than a must for the rock garden, as the blues are so perfect. On the other hand there is a little species from New Zealand that is white flowered and has an appeal of its own. It is not successful everywhere though it is listed regularly and has a good reputation. It is a confirmed lime hater.

It is deeply rooted and the branching, prostrate stems are clothed with small spoon-shaped dark, fleshy-looking leaves. It will form an attractive, compact mat. In July or August terminal clusters of white flowers bloom, usually two to five per cluster on two-inch stems.

At first glance it does not look like a gentian as the corolla is deeply divided at least halfway down and is cup-shaped when open.

The species grows in sand hills. While it enjoys a sunny rock garden it must have a depth of soil for the roots, as it is not a drought tolerant plant. It is compact enough to use in a deep trough.

The autumn flowering Asian gentians have been popular in England and Europe since their introduction into cultivation in the early 1900's. Expert s have hybridized them. Many great crosses were introduced and named, all of them wonderful shades of blue. Over the years they have become mixed. Much seed raising has diluted the purity. It is a gamble to buy them by name. In countries where they are still treasured and readily grown true to name, classic varieties are still available. 'Inverleith', 'Kingfisher', and 'Drake's Strain' are sometimes listed by our alpine nurseries. If you need to try some of these vigorous hybrids it never hurts to ask growers if they have unlisted plants. Sometimes they do not have enough stock to list it in the catalog.

Geranium

True geraniums (not to be confused with pelargoniums) are also known as cranesbills, a name which describes the developing seed heads perfectly: a small, rounded head with a large pointed bill. There are many lovely *Geranium* species which are too large for small rock gardens, being better suited to woodland gardens, the front edges of borders, or very large, informal rock gardens, since they grow very tall.

But as I stroll around my rock garden I notice that I have several smaller species growing well and behaving themselves. My plants of **G. dalmaticum** are now bold, solid mounds six inches tall and 18 inches across. I will be able to keep them for another year before I have to divide and relocate them. The solid mass of rich pink flowers in May and June earn them their space.

G. cinereum is a true alpine species from the Pyrenees and is a relatively easy going, sun-loving plant. A good form of it will have silvery leaves and pink flowers with darker veining, well worth a space. This species is a parent of several good hybrids, mentioned below. Along with superior forms and subspecies, these make a major contribution to the rock garden. All are sun loving and thrive in poorer soils. The three subspecies which follow are suitable for a good-sized trough.

178

G. c. subspecies Album, *G. c.* subspecies subcaulescens, and *G. c.* subspecies subcaulescens Splendens are similar in growth habit, each a crowded mound, 3 to 4 inches high and possibly spreading a few more inches, depending on soil conditions. The divided leaves are about an inch across and closely packed into a mound. The flowers are cup-shaped, half an inch across, and, except the white form, are found in shades of bright magenta with a black eye.

G. 'Ballerina' and G. 'Lawrence Flatman' are two similar hybrids derived from and similar to *G. cinereum* and its subspecies. They may grow a few inches taller, depending on cultural conditions. The chief difference is the color of the flowers. While principally pink, they are so heavily veined with red-purple that it is difficult to notice the base color. Both have the dark eye. 'Lawrence Flatman' is a slightly larger variety and the venation particularly heavy. Both excellent choices and hardy to Zone 5. It would be prudent to refrain from planting them in smaller plantings.

G. dalmaticum is a compact mat up to six inches high composed of a mass of creeping underground stolons and covered with deeply divided glossy-green leaves. Generous amounts of clear pink, flat-faced flowers an inch and a half across appear from June onward. It grows in Zones 4 to 8, in sun or part shade, but for winter color in the foliage, full sun is best. There is also a white form which often contains a delicate trace of pink.

G. farreri is, like many choice plants, difficult to keep for long. I regret that my plant has disappeared again and I suspect my dry summer air was the problem. Reginald Farrer introduced the plant from his S.W. China expedition in 1917, and it is still periodically available from a few sources. Why include it here if it is not easy to grow? Because it is such a lovely plant that it should be publicized. It has a quiet charm with flowers of delicate translucent pink. The green marks at the base of each petal provide a bright eye contrasting with the black anthers. Although one gardener has trouble growing it, others may not, and once the nurseries take an interest, it will become more available.

It is rated to Zone 4 and enjoys a gritty, humus-rich soil and a cool spot. Once established it is a semi-erect tuft of finely divided green leaves. It would probably not do well in trough because it is tap-rooted. In England it is often grown in cool alpine houses.

Gypsophila

Gypsophila (baby's breath) species are popular for perennial borders and florist bouquets. Better known species are too big for our small gardens.

G. aretioides is another of the minute gems from high in the mountains of Iran. It is probably the tightest, most compact of all the cushion plants, with iron-hard mounds of dark green foliage. Plant explorers talk of mature wild specimens capable of bearing their weight—with their mountaineering boots on. As far as I am concerned a large plant is two inches across, as it does not stay with me for many years even in the alpine house. I have only seen photographs of these large ancients.

It is a hardy species which will grow in well-drained alpine mix that is deep enough to allow the roots to penetrate deeply, and where there is likely to be moisture during hot, dry spells. A generous topdressing of chippings protects the plant from contact with warm wet soil and the ugliness of rain- splashed soil on the foliage. I have grown it both in a trough and a pot but my trouble was making certain it did not get too dry. Next time I get a plant I will put it in a trough. *G. aretioides 'Caucasica'* is an even more refined form for those who really enjoy the smallest plants.

Both these plants flower in the summer, but do not expect an instant riot of bloom on young plants. The blooms are typical baby's breath white flowers except that they are a borne singly with no visible stem, and never in large numbers.

G. briquetiana from the ridges and crevices of the limestone Turkish Mountains is a lovely rock garden plant. It is well worth reserving some valuable space for it. It likes rock garden soil with a little extra humus added. When established it will cover eight inches. It forms a neat and twiggy cushion of slightly fleshy looking green leaves, less than half an inch long. In late summer there is a generous display of wiry stems carrying one to eight notched, white to pink flowers with marvelous maroon centers.

Gypsophila briquetiana

180

G. cerastioides is another lovely gypsophila even if it derives its name from the weedy Cerastiums. The name only refers to the shape of the leaves. It forms a low mat of tufts of soft, distinctly spoon-shaped leaves. My plant has green leaves, the blades of which measure about half an inch. Many lists describe them as gray-green. The only hairs I can see are tiny ones along the leaf edges. Flowers are white with striking purple lines radiating from the center. Even though it lives on rocky Himalayan mountain slopes I find that it needs extra humus and at least partial shade from hot sun. It is rated as hardy to Zone 4, but without snow cover, protection is advisable.

G. repens is a handsome creeping and billowing type, often with a mist of pink flowers; there are white ones too. But they are for larger projects such as for use as a bold plant for the planter or raised bed, where there is space for the spreading, greedy roots. There are a few variations often listed such as 'Rosea'. 'Fratensis' is a rich pink form.

G. tenuifolia is another unusual looking gypsophila. It forms hard cushions of thin, grasslike leaves, slightly gray-green. It comes from the Caucasus and Turkey from rather tough habitats. For me, it grows very well on the rocks of an outcrop, in full sun with occasional water. Flower stems can be four to six inches tall with panicles of white flowers. There is a pink form described but I have never seen it.

Haberlea

Haberlea rhodopensis is a remarkable plant, a member of the *Gesneriaceae* and therefore a relative of the African violet. However, this plant comes from the mountains of Bulgaria and Greece and is

rated hardy to Zone 4. It dwells in cool, north-facing, shady crevices and is a valuable addition to the shady sides of a raised bed where it can be planted between the vertical joints. It can stand some sun providing that the plant is not allowed to suffer too long. It is able to wilt and wither and then recover once watered.

H. rhodopensis is composed of rosettes of soft but bold elliptical leaves, very strongly toothed and covered with short hairs. Leaves are dark green on the upper surface and lighter on the reverse. It is an

181

evergreen perennial. With or without flowers, a group of these plants growing vertically in a wall makes a pleasing sight.

The flowers start in spring to early summer, on short, stout stems bearing one to five flowers per stem (a cyme). Each flower is tubular with petals of uneven length creating lobed flowers. Each has pale lilac petals and golden spots in the throat.

H. r. 'Virginalis' is a lovely white form. *H. r. ferdinandi-coburgii* is sometimes described as a separate species (*H. ferdinandi-coburgii*), although some botanists who suggest it might be a superior form of *H. rhodopensis* do not recognize this. It is safe to buy the plant under either name.

Iris

Gardeners familiar with irises probably agree that they are too big for the small rock garden. Regrettably, for the most part this is true, and we must forego the lovely Pacific Coast Irises and several other intriguing species knowing that they are just too bountiful. Fortunately, there are several wonderful smaller species we can use. There are the iris bulbs — ideal subjects for pots in the alpine house or the open garden, and there are one or two plants for semi shade and another for sun.

I. cristata is an old favorite, all too often described in an offhand way as a native of North America, while some lists say Eastern US or

southern states. The late great plantsman, Roy Davidson of Seattle, says it is from the Appalachians and Ozarks. In its native habitat it lives on hillsides and stream sides. While it is not an alpine plant, it looks perfectly natural in sun and partial shade in a rock garden or raised bed. It is better treated as a fringe woodlander in warmer climates. For moisture retention, add leaf mold to the soil.

The plant can be a spreader, so watch it. It creeps across the soil and produces fans of four-inch, bright green iris leaves. Its typical iris flowers start to appear in May and can range in color from lilac-blue to violet and almost purple. The flowers are attractively marked with a white blotch and gold flecks.

I. c. 'Alba' is a lovely plant with pure white falls that display the golden flecks to perfection. Reverential references to this uncommon form are to be found in older books. It is offered today by several specialty nurseries.

I. lacustris, the dwarf lake iris, hails from the shores of the great lakes in Michigan. Wisconsin, and Ontario, Canada, and is on the endangered species list. This is the one to plant where space is at a premium. It is broadly similar to *I. cristata* but is much more refined in stature. It has deep blue, gold- flecked flowers up to an inch and a half wide, on short stems. The true plant is not easy to obtain, but perhaps a show of interest in it as it will prompt more nurseries to grow it. It is available in the horticultural trade, so there is no need for anyone to collect wild stock.

I. pumila is my last iris for this list and is in complete contrast to the previous two: first it is a sun lover and second it is no longer a true wild plant as it has been widely hybridized. It is offered in colors of white, yellow, blue, and purple. It seems like a small edition of the bearded iris. As such, it might be better planted where it will not clash with true alpines or semi-woodlanders. I enjoy the plant and grow it beside the main paths in my rock garden.

Lewisia

Lewisia species are North American plants that have found high regard in other places, particularly in Great Britain and Europe. Their story is similar to that of the phloxes. They, too, were introduced into Europe and were hybridized and returned to us with a huge range of bright colors. The lewisias are closely associated with many pioneer rock gardeners and plant hunters both here and in Europe. The

Lewisia 'Pinkie'

relatively recent discovery of a yellow flowered *L. cotyledon* helped to change the color spectrum of *L. cotyledon* hybrids we grow today.

The lewisias belong to the family *Portulacaceae* and so to some extent they are succulents. They have fleshy leaves, and some live in deserts and other dry places. However, do not think they are a pushover to grow, for they have definite cultural requirements.

Growing lewisias presents a challenge, so here are a few general comments which may be of some value. Protect all species from extreme heat and sun. Fast drainage is essential. It helps to understand the climate and habitat of the species, and its natural flowering time and resting period. This will help you decide when to water the plants and when to let them dry off. Where lewisias are difficult, container growing is a satisfying alternative, particularly when frames or alpine houses can be used to control conditions.

Lewisias tolerate a small amount of lime in the soil, but it is safer to avoid it where possible, particularly in potting soils. Their cultivation is not terribly difficult except for those gardens with high summer humidity or excessive winter wetness. There are few plants that rival lewisia as pot-grown specimens when conditions can be controlled. The picture on gallery page b shows what can be done.

We can introduce lewisias by dividing them into two groups. First, there are evergreen kinds, with large flat symmetrical rosettes of roughly spoon-shaped fleshy looking leaves. Lewisias *cotyledon, columbiana,* and *tweedyii* are popular examples. Then there are the summer deciduous species with neat, small foliage that dries off immediately after flowering. The plants remain dormant until fall rains begin. This is a large group composed of many species with a distinct beauty of their own. *Lewisias rediviva*, *brachycalyx* and *pygmaea* are examples of this group.

184

L. columbiana is a charming little evergreen species from the West. It has a narrow-leaved rosette, neat and symmetrical. Despite the fact that the foliage is green rather than silver, it is reminiscent of silver saxifrages. Quite a variable species, its rosettes range from just an inch up to four inches in diameter. Eight-inch airy stems carry sprays of small, pinkish flowers.

L. c. ssp. *rupicola* is described by Roy Davidson as a claret-flowered plant that is intermediate in size between the previous two plants. It is a good plant for a trough. Just add a few fist-sized rocks to provide some shelter for the roots and locate the trough where it can evade excessive heat and sun.

L. cotyledon (gallery page g) is a lovely species with dark green rosettes and bold flower stems bearing one- to two-inch blooms. In the wild the flowers are essentially white with broad stripes of pink, rose, or shades of magenta. The color and width of the stripes is so dominant that the white does not always register. The species is variable and produces a wide range of colors including pink, dark pink, yellow, apricot, magenta, and the occasional white. Since the species is so variable it was divided into varieties based upon the variations in foliage. Not everyone agrees with the way these distinctions have been made and probably there will never be a complete resolution. Nevertheless, the introduction of these variations into horticulture is the reason we have such an incredible range of colors available to us in lewisias today.

The cultivation of *L. cotyledon* and its hybrids is not difficult once it is understood that the species is accustomed to receive plenty of moisture in the spring and drier conditions as summer advances. They prefer gentler summer treatment than the desert species. If you can maintain a balance between very wet soil and desert-dry conditions, and provide shelter from very hot sun, *L. cotyledon* will flourish. It is evident that if it is exposed to prolonged heat and drought it will go into a dormant state and remain so until cooler weather arrives.

Any well-meaning attempts to break this dormancy by watering either pot grown or garden plants will encourage rot in the caudex, a common cause of death in lewisias.

L. cotyledon hybrids. A quick look at a few catalogs will soon show the wide range of hybrids available to us today. Jack Drake of the famous Inshriach Nursery introduced the 'Sunset Group'. It created quite a stir when first introduced, with flower colors of lemon yellow, apricot, peach, and bronze along with pink, rose, and red shades.

Lewisia hybrids can be bench-grown or pot-grown in an alpine house.

The term 'strain' means the plants are the results of planned and repeated crossing of selected plants to produce certain traits or colors. Consequently, saving ones own seed from such a strain does not mean that the resulting seedlings will be exact duplicates of the strain. To obtain exact duplicates, cuttings must be taken.

The Ashwood Strain from the West Midlands in England also caused much attention when it burst upon the scene some 20 years ago. It too has a full range of wonderful colors, including crimson, scarlet, orange, and magenta. There are double-flowered forms that would be fun to try.

The Carousel hybrids from Ashwood Nurseries Ltd. are a recent introduction providing a series of equally colorful but smaller and more compact plants which bloom from late spring to early summer. The nursery states that this group is tolerant of winter wetness and is hardy to 10 to 15 degrees F.

From Germany comes a gold medal series called 'Regenbogen', meaning rainbow, an apt word for its wide range of bright colors; there are excellent doubles too.

L. rediviva is probably the most well known lewisia, but not the easiest to grow. It is widely spread in the West from mountains to flat dry areas. It is heat and cold resistant provided it has a drying period in the summer. The life cycle begins in late summer when the narrow leaves begin to appear. They continue to develop through the winter, with or without snow cover. When the weather warms up in spring, the leaves start to dry up and the huge flowers begin to show. They are typically found in shades of pink, but pale, almost white ones are not uncommon.

L. tweedii is recognized by gardeners as the queen of the lewisias. Residents of Washington State refer to it as the mountain rose, although I fail to see any resemblance to a rose. It is found principally in the Wenatchee Mountains of Central Washington and can also be found in a small region just across the border in southern British Columbia. It chooses rocky places where drainage is rapid, but it can be found in open places at higher elevations. At lower elevations, where it is much hotter, the plants seek the shade of pines and grow in the forest duff beneath them. It is a bold looking plant; the first sighting of a good clump is never forgotten. Large fleshy leaves form loose tufts that can be four to ten inches high, depending on the richness of the habitat. Glorious apricot colored flowers up to an inch and a half wide are freely produced. Several color variations are

187

known, even white ones, but do not worry about color—be satisfied to grow any of them.

This great native family merits far more than my few introductory comments, but the details are beyond the scope of this book. It is a satisfying group of plants to grow. Seeds and plants are not difficult to obtain and are fun to grow and collect. Understanding the life cycle of each species is important to successful cultivation. Study the plant's natural habitat, for its natural life cycle will help you understand when to water or let them dry off. All the species require a light, open soil, and fast drainage is a must. Protect all species from extreme heat and sun even though some of them come from our hottest places.

Pot and container growing is a satisfying alternative, particularly when frames or alpine houses are available to guarantee complete control of cultivation. Once confidence has been gained from growing them for a while, it is time to branch out and experiment. The bright and colorful *L. cotyledon* hybrids make wonderful pot plants if the soil is enriched with organic matter. It is even possible to feed them with fertilizers and produce huge plants with hundreds of blooms. Some garden centers are now selling them as summer bedding plants. Don't let this shock the purist within you, since they are manmade hybrids anyway. There are still the pure species to return to.

Lewisia tweedii growing in the Wenatchee Mountains, in Washington State.

188

Papaver

Tiny alpine poppies have all the characteristics rock gardeners enjoy. They have low, tufted, gray-green foliage, sometimes covered with an abundance of dark hairs. The airy flower stems can be up to six or so inches tall and dance in the ever-present mountain winds. They bear impossibly large flowers as much as two inches across. They have a crinkled texture reminiscent of artificial flowers made from tissue paper.

Papaver alpinum is the collective name often applied to this group. Other species are sometimes covered under this name also, but do not let names deter you as long as the suppler indicates that the poppies are truly dwarf.

In cultivation and in the wild, wild poppies are known to hybridize among themselves, resulting in the normal white and yellow plus a wider range including orange and the odd red.

Seed of is sometimes available from rock garden seed lists, and alpine nurseries periodically offer seed or plants. The naming is extremely complicated and confusing and mainly of interest to the serious botanist.

Avoid *P. nudicaule,* however tempting it may sound. It is truly a lovely poppy but too big for the small garden.

These little alpine poppies are excellent for special pockets in the rock garden or raised bed. They enjoy well drained soil and it is a good plan to add extra gravel.

Most are perennial, at least in the wild, but are considered short-lived, and this certainly is true in many gardens. Where the appeal of these mountain flowers is too great to resist, why not save a few seeds for next year and lightly rake them into the soil. From then on regularly remove spent flowers so the plants will continue to bloom and not spend all its energy making seeds.

Penstemon

I grow a few *Penstemon* species in the rock garden, plus a few of the taller varieties in the areas surrounding it. I cut back the penstemons after the first flush of flowers so they become bushy and flower continuously. This is a good thing to do with many of the wild species,

189

since they have a tendency to flower themselves to death if left to set seed without any control.

Recently, as I renovated part of the rock garden, it occurred to me that my sunny, south facing slope might provide the right microclimate for some of the wild penstemon species I had encountered in my travels, despite my Mediterranean climate with wet winters and rainless summers.

Penstemon is a huge genus (250 species or more) native to North America, occurring as far south as Guatemala, and extending northward into several Canadian Provinces. Penstemons can be difficult to grow and have a reputation for being short-lived. They can be found in all manner of habitats which include high mountains, low plains, deserts, sagebrush country, and woodlands. With such an extensive distribution they are exceedingly variable in size and appearance, ranging from tiny crevice plants to tall statuesque spires along the roadsides. Since they occur in widely differing habitats and climates, the various species have diverse cultural requirements.

I did some reading to see which varieties would be suitable for my project and soon found myself captivated by the genus. There are not that many species suitable for the small rock garden. Consider not only the ultimate height but the spread also. Many are woody and shrublike, even evergreen, and can be used in that role on a miniature mountainside. The low, compact kinds can be planted in close association with rocks. Where convenient, allow them to spread out onto the path. Start with species that are comparatively easy to grow. For me, many of the best choices originate in the mountains of British Columbia, Washington State, and Oregon, where cooler, moister conditions exist.

Nurserymen offer several of these species plus interesting introduced forms. These may be smaller or have flowers that are superior in size or color (see cover photo). Should you be tempted by the descriptions of native plants from Arizona, New Mexico, Colorado, or Utah, choices become more experimental. Some species require diligent searches to locate or involve raising them from seed yourself.

The drought tolerance of some species makes them prime candidates for inclusion in waterless gardening or xeriscaping. Although they have good drought tolerance, they do not necessarily prefer being overly dry. Their tolerance is not to be interpreted as their preference.

Drought tolerant penstemons from the Great Basin (Western USA) must be given a fighting chance in order to become established in a new environment. They require a sufficient depth of soil for the roots to find sustenance and protection from heat and drought. Light they must have, although they will appreciate some high shade during the hottest weeks of summer and sufficient water to help them re-establish. Coax them along with meager but consistent watering.

We know one of the reasons they are considered to be short-lived is the effort they make to produce masses of flowers followed by the additional demands of a heavy seed crop. This is more than the plant can do. As gardeners we can help the plants in our care by removing spent flowering branches and cutting back the plant to at least half.

Where seed is required, a few branches left to go to seed will not risk the plant's demise. Once this is accomplished, check around the plant, do a little gardening, remove any competing weeds or competing plants to ensure air circulation. Then lightly cultivate the surrounding soil and resist the urge to add fertilizer. If the soil is dry, apply a penetrating application of water and walk away! Allow the plant to make the rosettes, buds, or laterals that are vital for the following season's growth. The plant will be able to face the winter with ripened tissues which assures the next season's growth.

Rock and Crevice Dwellers

For reliable summer-flowering plants for a small rock garden, look no further than the mountains of Vancouver Island, coastal British Columbia, and the Cascade Mountains of Washington and Oregon.

Penstemon davidsonii and its varieties are widespread. It can be found virtually at sea level on Vancouver Island. It then runs south through the Cascade and Coast Mountains of Washington and into Oregon and flows into California. It is commonly found on cliffs, steep rocky banks, and slopes of broken rock. A mat forming plant, the twigs and stems are buried beneath the host of short leafy shoots, heavily clothed with small glossy, evergreen leaves. In the wild the flowers begin to appear in June and can continue into August.

The tubular flowers vary in length from three-fourths of an inch to over an inch long. They are carried in a raceme on three- to four-inch flower stems. Flowers are shades of lavender and are not the most inspiring display, but can bloom from June to August. If you take a drive through the canyon of the Fraser River on a sunny morning when the variety **P. davidsonii var. menziesii** is in full flower, you'll see that the walls of the canyon glow.

P. davidsonii can spread, so where space is critical, consider some of the other dwarf kinds. **P. davidsonii var. davidsonii** is closely related but has a wider range of preferred altitude and a more southerly distribution. It is a smaller plant with toothed leaves.

191

These two varieties have given gardeners several notable variations which the nursery trade often makes available. They are offered in white, pink, and pretty blue shades. For the small garden there are a couple of small scale varieties. *P. davidsonii* 'Mt. Adams Dwarf' is a fine example. It makes a low, flat, compact mat no more than one inch tall. Its elfin flower stems are well under one inch.

The variety ***P. davidsonii* var. *menziesii*** gives several choices, including a good pink form, a white, and a very compact form named 'Microphyllus' which is a fine choice for a deep trough.

Finally, *P. davidsonii* gives us a noble variety from the Steens Mountains of Oregon, with the ungainly name ***P. d.* var. *praeteritus*.** It has very large flowers of rich lavender. Highly rated as a garden plant, it is available from several nurseries in Washington and Oregon. The color is hard to describe but it ranges through shades of bluish-lavender to violet, and is very appealing. It has tiny leaves and a low compact habit, and is a mountain dweller happy among the rocks. The State of Oregon lists this plant among rare and endangered species. It is extremely attractive and worth seeking at specialist nurseries, for use in the not-so-small rock garden.

P. rupicola. Before leaving the mat-forming, cliff dwelling penstemons of the *davidsonii* style, *P. rupicola* is a gem that I cannot be without. A cliff dweller by name and by nature, it is native to the Washington, Oregon, and Northern Californian mountains. Those lucky enough to have seen this plant in the wild will agree on the magnificence of a healthy clump hanging from a cliff in full startling color, contrasting with the grays of the rock.

It is a mat forming plant, although in my garden it tends to be a loose mat. It is very pleasing with grayish, slightly toothed leaves and a light, open habit. It flowers on short stems, with several individual tubular blooms per stem. And the color! Every description I read has a different name for it. It can be rich rose pink, reddish pink, or rich red—it is a stunning color range.

It prefers a site in close association with rocks where its roots can delve, and a degree of shade in the hottest months is always appreciated. It does not thrive in troughs.

Several years ago I went with Boyd C. Kline up the steep road to Fiddler Mountain in the Siskiyou Mountains to see a favorite group of *P. rupicola*. They were compact and the leaves were strikingly gray, with masses of dark red flowers. On another long day in the mountains, Boyd took me to Diamond Lake to see the original plants that were introduced by Siskiyou Rare Plant Nursery as *P. rupicola*

'Diamond Lake'. In this group the flowers were consistently rich pink. Regrettably I do not have a photograph of this group. While there, I ran around frantically taking pictures, only to find out there was no film in the camera. I still have not told Boyd. There is a white-flowered form and also a dark pink variation with compact gray-green foliage, called *P. rupicola* 'Myrtle Hebert'.

The alpine nurseries on the West Coast offer fine hybrid penstemons. Among the smaller varieties are a few worth trying. Check the catalogs and select varieties that tempt you, watching out for ultimate height and spread. Among the crosses discovered in the wild is *P.* 'Breitenbush Blue'. While it is not a pure blue, it is as near to blue as lavender can get. This plant was introduced by the late, longtime NARGS member Roy Davidson of Seattle. When he spots a good plant you can bank on it! I have only seen it in flower once, growing in an old trough, quite starved but full of flowers. It is listed as six inches tall, but this plant was closer to a 12-inch mound of blue.

I cannot resist mentioning *P.* 'Pink Holly', whose leaves have the prickly look of tiny holly leaves. The tubular flowers are a delightful shade of pink. It can attain six inches in height and spread twice as much; where space is available it is a joy to behold.

Other Garden Penstemons

There are some totally different penstemons with different site preferences. ***P. procerus*** has several attractive dwarf forms. These are more suitable for the small rock garden since the species can grow to 12 inches or more. The available dwarf varieties are much more tolerant of garden conditions and are more tractable than the dryland or desert species. Plant them in a sunny spot in good rock garden soil. You need a location where the water drains rapidly because they will not tolerate standing water. They are winter hardy in many zones.

The dwarfs are loose mats of ovate leaves from which slender flower stems with heads of tiny flowers arise. They compensate for their diminutive individual size by sheer numbers. Their color is mainly in the lavender to blue range.

Look for ***P. procerus* var. *brachyanthus*, *formosus*, *aberrans***, or especially ***tolmei***. Any of these will be dwarf, around four to five inches. Variety *P. procerus formosus* is highly rated with bright blue flowers on short stems over gray-green compact mats. Var. *tolmei* has flowers from blue-purple to an astounding bright blue. Occasionally it is found in pale yellow, white, or pink. Local plant explorers Mark McDonough and Rick Lupp have introduced many specimens. There is one with pink and white flowers, a clear pink, and a creamy yellow.

P. pinifolius provides foliage contrast. As the name suggests, the leaves are thin and needle-like and are borne on sprawling stems that rise to six inches or so. Small, narrow, tubular flowers are generously produced in early summer and are a bright orange-red. There has been a satisfactory yellow form available for several years. It was discovered as a sport in a garden in West Mersea in England. When introduced to the nursery trade it was listed as *P. pinifolius* 'Mursea Yellow'. Recently a NARGS member discovered another yellow clone while plant hunting in New Mexico. Fortunately he was able to propagate it vegatively and it too is now available and has the romantic name *P. pinifolius* 'Magdalena Sunshine' after the mountains in New Mexico where it was found.

P. pinifolius has a very good garden record and seems to thrive in a wide variety of climates given light rock garden soil. My specimen is in the lee of a small *Cryptomeria* and is protected from the hottest sun. A bit of shade is advisable.

The western plants have received all the attention since there are not many eastern penstemons suitable for the small rock garden. One first-rate dwarf which has proved successful for a great many years in a range of garden conditions is *P. hirsutus* 'Pygmaeus'. *P. hirsutus* itself germinates readily from seed and regularly produces dwarf forms making it possible to create a fine colony of dwarfs simply by selecting the smaller forms and rejecting taller plants. Planted in light shade it forms a pleasing clump of green foliage almost covered with heads of tubular flowers. Height ranges between four and six inches. The flowers are an attractive shade of violet with white tips and a white throat, blooming over a period from May to June with intermittent heads appearing for most of the season.

Phlox

Low growing phlox species are in complete contrast to the tall, hardy perennial border phlox, with their tall stems and huge heads of bright colors. These low-growing, carpeting kinds are usually sold as moss phlox or rock phlox. Doretta Klaber, the renowned pioneer rock plant grower and garden writer who lived at Cloud Hill, in Quakertown, Pennsylvania, used to call it the mountain pink. The botanical name of this wildflower is *Phlox subulata* and the species contains many splendid and colorful hybrids. Unfortunately, too few of the good ones are seen in garden centers.

In nature it grows on open, rocky, gravelly, and sandy slopes. In the wild it ranges throughout Pennsylvania to eastern Ohio, lower Michigan, and western New York. It occurs spottily in New Jersey.

Phlox douglasii 'Rosea'

Considering that this phlox is so well known and easily recognized, there is relatively little written about it, or the rest of this great American genus of plants.

You will always find phlox for sale, but customarily the plants offered are ordinary varieties comprising a mass of green foliage and magenta or pinkish flowers. They are easy, fast growing, undemanding plants, giving full value for the money. As a rule, the subulata phloxes grow too fast and take too much room for small rock gardens, so we will not dwell on them. Nevertheless, we can appreciate their role in the development of the choicer rock garden phloxes.

Many years ago, several phloxes found their way to Europe. In all probability they were selected forms with good colors. They settled down happily and were well cared for and actively cultivated. As more color variations were discovered and selected, no doubt some hybridizing was done, producing more new varieties. Some of these were exported back to their homeland bearing European names.

It is frustrating to read the descriptions of some of the many varieties offered in overseas catalogs, realizing that they are not available here, particularly as newer varieties of other rock plants are regularly being introduced into this country. Acknowledging the time and money that has to be spent on plant introduction, I am certain that if new, brightly colored *Phlox subulata* varieties were offered, they would be popular and sell well.

Among these returning exiles are a series of more compact phloxes that are not as aggressive as some of the basic types seen in garden centers. The parentage and origin of these useful dwarf plants is still something of a mystery, but they are often listed as hybrids between *Phlox subulata* and the Western native, *P. douglasii*. The plot thickens because it is now recognized that the name *P. douglasii,* which was used to include several different but similar species, is no longer valid as a distinct species name. Now that these plants have specific names of their own, it is unlikely we will ever know which of the several plants classed under the old name *douglasii* was the parent.

Some nursery catalogs list them as *Phlox x douglasii*, others omit the *douglasii* and use only the cultivar name. The few plants described here will be found by searching domestic rock plant nurseries.

P. d. 'Boothman's Variety' was most likely introduced by Stuart Boothman of the celebrated Nightingale Nursery in England, long since closed. It forms a neat cushion with rounded lavender flowers with a darker circular eye.

P. d. 'Crackerjack' with crimson-red flowers is not easily missed and is regularly offered.

P. d. 'Eva' is a good pink with a crimson eye.

P. d. 'Rose Queen' or 'Rosea' is one of my favorites, I like the pure clear pink of the flowers. It has to be clipped periodically to keep it compact.

P. d. 'Sileneflora'. One phlox I would suggest for walls or terraces is *P. d.*'Sileneflora', another choice introduction by H. Lincoln Foster. It is a *subulata* selection but is very low growing and forms a neat cushion with small pink flowers. He named it 'Sileneflora' because the plant reminded him of the mossy carpets of a true alpine plant, the moss campion, *Silene acaulis*. This variety is grown successfully in many Eastern gardens but unfortunately is not as widely distributed as it should be.

P. d. 'Waterloo' is listed with violet-purple flowers.

Occasionally varieties are listed with names other than the familiar ones. If they are described as dwarf, neat, or compact, and *douglasii* is attached to the name, I would buy them. If you are fortunate enough to visit a nursery when they are in bloom, you cannot go wrong.

There are many more lovely phloxes growing in the mountains and dry lands of North America. They can be found from the sandy flats of the Great Plains to the sagebrush country, and from the deserts of Arizona to the heights of the western mountains. All are compact low mats composed of tiny leaves, some so narrow as to be needle-like. Pastel flowers practically smother the foliage. Some are fragrant.

I would be amiss if I did not cite them; readers may then pursue them further if they are intrigued. They are not easy to grow and not many nurseries stock them. An enthusiast with the inclination to take up the challenge will have to search specialist seed lists.

I would particularly enjoy the challenge of growing *P. alaskensis* from the stony slopes of Alaska or the flat mats of *P. albomarginata* that live on the harsh screes of Montana's Big Belt Mountains. Also of value are some of the tiny gems from the Great Plains such as *P. andicola* and *P. hoodii* ssp. *muscoides*. There is a wonderful purple-flowered form of *P. kelseyi* from Idaho named 'Lemhi Purple'. The list goes on. *Phlox* is only one of many genera of native alpines that challenge the experts.

Primula

As we consider the gigantic genus, *Primula*, I remind myself not to attempt to describe every species. My role is to suggest a few that will grow and flower in a small space along with other alpine plants. *Primula* species include hundreds of kinds of plants coming from cool and moist regions of the northern hemisphere, in particular the Himalayan Mountains, China, Europe, and North America.

It would be easy to plant a whole garden with nothing but primulas; in fact, many have done so. There is a particular primula for practically every garden condition. There are types for shady woodlands, boggy conditions, and sunny beds and rock gardens. Many are ideally suited to a small garden. Some of the alpine species are classic crevice plants, just right for pots and containers.

Even the tiniest garden should provide room for a plant of *P. juliae*, one of the parents of the Juliana Hybrids, such as the famous 'Wanda'. The true species is small enough to tuck into small shady crevices where it will produce occasional flowers throughout the year, starting as soon as early spring weather permits the main display. It makes flat mats of the small, red-stemmed, crinkly leaves. Purplish-pink flowers with notched petals with bright yellow, star-shaped eyes are borne on the shortest of stems.

There is a group composed of European species that have been referred to as the rock primulas because they prefer to inhabit cliffs and similar rocky places. They are not overly demanding about soil as long as it contains some decent loam plus gravel for fast draining. The plants can be planted in the rock garden in any crevices available. A simple crevice can be created by placing two rocks side by side. As long as the roots are able to find rock nearby, providing them a cool haven, they are able to withstand a fair amount of sun. This group contains good trough plants which are excellent subjects for pot culture. Grown under glass, the delicate coloring of the flowers can be enjoyed, and the farina, the white, floury dust that coats parts of some of the plants, is not washed off.

P. hirsuta is a rocky ledge dweller with leathery leaves, and is somewhat sticky. The pink or mauve blooms are produced in heads of several individual flowers, upon stems two to three inches tall. There are finer colored forms available in clear pinks and bright reds.

P. marginata is a popular plant providing several color forms and numerous hybrids. It comes to us from rocky places in the Maritime Alps. It has a strange habit of making long, woody-looking stems (probably correctly called rhizomes) the ends of which carry remarkable light green, tufted and scalloped leaves. The flowers are borne in heads, in colors ranging from pale lavender to shades of blue and purple. This is a very variable plant and named forms have been in cultivation for years. Look for 'Prichard's Variety' or 'Linda Pope'. Parts of this plant are covered with white farina, particularly the edges of the leaves and parts of the flower.

P. minima is another tiny plant from the Alps that may be tricky but is too good not to give it a try (see photo on page 81). In the wild it is often described as forming tight mats covering several square feet. There is little danger of that happening in our gardens. The plant consists of small, flat rosettes of wedge-shaped leaves with sharply pointed margins. The rosettes sit tightly on the surface as if they were pinned to the soil. The average size of rosettes is up to three quarters of an inch across. Bright rose-pink flowers with a small white eye appear in March. Flowers will vary from half an inch across to just over an inch, each with five narrow petals deeply notched, sometimes so deeply that they appear to be ten petals.

Find a cool and safe place for this little gem of a plant. Give it additional peat or leaf mold. It is happy in a cool trough where there is an adequate volume of soil.

P. x pubescens is a title given by botanists to a large group of hybrids and I will leave it at that. Some of these hybrids have rock primulas as parents along with other wild species. Listed under *P.* x *pubescens* are hybrids of the most brilliantly colored and free-flowering varieties. The flowers retain their color and the blooms last longer if they get some shelter from midday sun. Look for 'Mrs. J. H. Wilson', 'Faldonside', and 'The General'.

Pulsatilla

The Pasque Flowers (*Pulsatilla* species) have delightful spring flowers in many colors, and are enjoyed by many gardeners. **P. vulgaris,** the common Pasque flower, normally has flowers in a deep rich purple, but the color variations include shades of purple, pink, and crimson, plus the ubiquitous white form. Those acquainted with this plant will agree that, as lovely as it is, it is not an alpine plant suited to small spaces. These pulsatillas require a generous depth of soil for their woody crowns and deeply penetrating fibrous root mass. *P. vulgaris* may be successfully grown in pots if they are large enough to provide a sufficient volume of soil, enough to prevent starvation and drying.

P. vernalis, on the other hand, is most certainly an alpine plant. It is a compact little mound of tightly packed, divided leaves. The buds, when you are lucky enough to see them, are nestled deep within the tuft of leaves, each bud clothed with golden-bronze fur. It is a spring flowering plant and the two inch flowers are carried on very short stems. The whole plant in flower rarely exceeds four inches tall. The flowers are white with a tint of violet-blue on the underside and have bold golden stamens. Of course it is far more beautiful than I can describe. Other writers speak of chalices, goblets, opalescence, and iridescence.

In cultivation it is a hater of winter wetness. It demands a richer soil than the usual alpine starvation diet and it must be well drained. This species will flower if the foliage can be protected from spring and winter rains and you do not deprive it of light. The alpine house, cold frame, or trough make for easier management of this lovely hardy plant.

Pulsatilla vernalis

Saponaria

Saponaria species, known as the soapworts chiefly for the age-old plant know as *S. officinalis,* and eventually for the double flowered forms *S. o.*'Alba Plena', *S. o.*'Rubra Plena', and S. o.'Rosea Plena'. Popularly known as bouncing bet, it is a perennial known for the soapy quality of the juices from the leaves. There are several species compact enough for rock gardening. The varieties below are safe for smaller projects.

S. 'Bressingham' bears the name of the famous nursery that produced it, operated by the Bloom family of the U.K. This plant is the one for us since it is a cross between *S. ocymoides*, a true alpine plant but a bit too big, and a cushion forming hybrid, *S. x olivana.* It gives us the trailing, leafy habit of one parent, *S. ocymoides*, and the compact-ness of the other. It forms a carpet of soft, hairy leaves and stems. When it blooms the plants are covered by heads containing several deep pink, white-eyed flowers on short stems. It enjoys a gritty soil but not an arid site, and lasts longer with a degree of shade. It flowers from June to September.

S. ocymoides 'Rubra Compacta' was popular several years ago but seems to have slipped in popularity since it gained a reputation of being short-lived. This little plant has such an impact and is small enough for a trough garden. I would give it a try and take a few cuttings as well. It covers its two-inch height in the brightest rich red flowers possible. It is still offered by a few nurseries and may take a bit of searching for, so be sure you are getting the true dwarf form.

S. x olivana (pictured on page 127) is an old hybrid that dates back to the 1930's. Named for the Olivana Botanic Garden in Danzig where it was raised, it offers a pleasant contrast, with a large, low mound of narrow, green, fleshy looking leaves and the habit of a typical alpine plant. It is capable of growing into an undulating mat some 12 inches across which is covered from May to July with clear, rose-pink flowers measuring nearly one inch across. Plant it where the taproot is free to penetrate deeply into a freely draining but not rich soil. *S. pumilio* and *S. caespitosa* are its parents and are sometimes available when the hybrid is not. Both are similar in habit and stature but the color is not as delicate. The species will have more crimson to purple tones. Either species may be used in small projects, but remember to allow room for the taproots.

200

In the author's garden, *Sempervivum octopodes*, above, has colorful rosettes about an inch in diameter. Below, *Tanacetum densum* subsp. *amanum* contrasts well with clipped golden box (*Buxus suffruticosa*).

a

Lewisia hybrids thriving in Roxie Gevjan's Pennsylvania alpine house.

b

Above, *Saxifraga* Rainsley Seedling. Below, *Saxifraga* 'Southside Seedling Boerdum', a gift to the author from Beryl Bland, the holder of the British National Collection of Silver Saxifrages.

Draba siberica forms a spreading mound of tiny dark leaves, practically covered with yellow flowers on threadlike stems. Below, *Narcissus bulbocodium*, the hoop petticoat daffodil, dots alpine meadows and is excellent for open slopes.

d

Part of the author's gently sloping rock garden in the middle of May.

e

The beauty of androsace is its late season of flowering. The plants have lavender-pink flowers and soft, silvery hairs on the foliage. Above, *Androsace sarmentosa.* Below, *Androsace lanuginosa.*

f

Campanula haylodgensis (above) has flowers that are so double that they resemble old fashioned roses. It's a bit on the fussy side and sometimes does not overwinter, so the author keeps it going by rooting cuttings in the alpine house. It looks best growing with cool roots where the flowers won't be splashed with soil.

Above, Lewisia 'Pinkie' is truly a jewel of the rock garden.

Above, fall-blooming colchicum in the New York Botanical Garden rock garden.
Below, a stacked collection of new and vintage troughs at Wave Hill in New York.

h

Saxifraga

Saxifraga is one of the backbone genera of the rock garden, but in North America it has a poor reputation. It is not that saxifrages are not admired, for they certainly are—one has only to watch the speed with which they sell at plant sales. There is no doubt that gardeners find them very difficult to grow, particularly in hot, humid climates.

They cannot stand the heat. The rise in soil temperature effectively shuts down the plants' root systems. Eventually the foliage begins to die from what amounts to drought. Even in ideal climates, rock gardeners guard against this problem with heavy topdressings of stone chippings to keep the soil cool.

The saxes are hardy enough as far as cold temperatures are concerned, but do not like to be stressesd in the middle of winter with freezing and thawing. Under snow cover they are content.

The rock gardener can succeed if the garden is situated in a protected place and the right growing methods are used. Alpine houses or frames are a help. I know I am hopelessly biased, but *Saxifraga* is an ideal genus for the collector with little space.

For convenience I have divided the saxifrages into three distinct groups: the Dwarf Cushion Saxifrages (the Kabschias); the Silver Saxifrages or Encrusted Saxifrages; and the Mossy Saxifrages.

Dwarf Cushion Saxifrages

The dwarf cushion saxes are properly named the Porphyrion group. For many years they were named the Kabschia saxifrages

Saxifraga iranica

after a German botanist, Wilhelm Kabsch (1835-1864). This group comprises many wild species and hundreds of hybrids raised in England, Germany, and the Czech Republic. It would not do to overlook the significant contributions made to these hybrids by H. Lincoln Foster of Falls Village, Connecticut. These wild species are true alpine plants, forming hard cushions of needle-like gray-green leaves with large flowers on very short stems. The species originated in the mountains of Europe, Iran, Yunnan, and the Himalaya.

Since mass hybridizing began, the original flower colors, white, yellow, and purple-red have blossomed into a full range of shades including deep purple, striking red, many shades of pink, and pale reds. Orange and beige are popular and the breeders are still producing new colors.

As a group they are early spring flowering, commencing in January and running into April, sometimes into May. The Saxifrage Society estimates there are well over 600 hybrids listed today.

There are many suggestions published for their culture, but so much depends on where you live. There is little doubt that they are most successful when grown in pots and troughs or planted directly into tufa. The normal potting mix for potted alpines is adequate providing that there is an additional part of a good sharp grit.

Saxifrages for Small Gardens

The flowers of older saxifrage hybrids do not compare in size or color with the newer varieties. Nonetheless, their bright flowers will be appreciated in early spring, especially since the newer, larger-flowered varieties are not very likely to succeed in the open rock garden. Use the following dependable saxes for small gardens, raised beds, walls. and terraces.

S. x apiculata **'Gregor Mendel'** is a very old and durable hybrid formerly known as *S. apiculata*. It forms a flat mat of bright green foliage and two-inch stems bearing ten to 12 flowers of primrose yellow per stem. There is a white variety of this plant that goes by the old name of *S. apiculata alba*.

S. x eudoxiana **'Haagii'** is another tough old hybrid dating back to 1908. It grows as a green cushion with rich golden flowers on three-inch stems. The quantity of flowers compensates for the smallness of individual blossoms.

S. sancta is another tough old bird, a species from Northwest Anatolia. It is one of the parents of the hybrids described above. It forms loose rosettes of dark green with sharply pointed leaves and two-inch stems with heads of yellow flowers.

Saxifrages for Pots, Troughs and Tufa Rock

With so many varieties available for containers, how should we choose? The first thing is to check all the current mail order catalogs and see just what is readily available. Then divide the list of saxes into two groups: one featuring a few older varieties that have stood the test of time, and the other a list of the newer varieties.

There are other points we can consider, such as all year round appeal. Saxifrages flower for less than a month, so the appearance of the plant is important. Foliage may form green or silver-gray mounds. Individual leaves may be either needlelike or broad at the base, while the plants may be large and leafy or small, tightly compacted dwarfs.

OLD VARIETIES THAT HAVE STOOD THE TEST OF TIME

S. x elizabethae 'Boston Spa', primrose-yellow flowers, and green
  spiky foliage, robust.

S. burderiana 'Brookside' and S. 'Gloria', two of the greatest whites.

S. x boydii 'Cherrytrees', yellow flowers and dense gray foliage.

S. x anglica 'Cranbourne', pink flowers on short stems, blue-gray foliage.

S. jenkinsiae, reliable, soft pink flowers on two-inch stems, gray mound.

S. x irvingii, introduced in1909, now named 'Walter Irving'. Has lilac-pink flowers and forms a very low and compact mound of silvery-gray.

S. marginata var. rocheliana is a species with shining white flowers. The plant is composed of small rosettes, and loves a trough and tufa.

Recent Cultivars

Here are a few of the newer sax cultivars which I have selected from some of the current breeders. The Czech Republic has for many years pioneered the introduction of new and striking cultivars. The Allendale and Lismore Series originate from two English breeders.

S. 'Bohemia' is a strong grower and flowers in an interesting orange shade.

S. x *megaseaeflora* 'Jan Neruda' is a favorite of mine with large flowers in a bright shade of yellowish pink.

S. 'Louis Armstrong' belongs to a new group from the Czech Republic. Jan Burgel, the breeder, named them the Blues Group and they bloom in a striking range of deep red-purples.

S. x *goringiana* 'Nancye' is slightly different in form. These plants grow with flat, open, dark green rosettes; the flowers open deep cerise pink and fade to lilac-pink.

S. 'Peach Blossom' is described as having creamy-pink flowers and gray-green foliage.

The Silver Saxifrages

If I were limited to one group of plants for my small garden, this would be my choice. The silver saxes embody the true feeling of the mountains and love to live with and among rocks. They are ideal crevice plants and live contentedly in pots. The variety of shapes and sizes they provide is enormous, from tiny clumps to huge rosettes capable of producing flower plumes over two feet long. Unfortunately they are not the easiest plants for many of us to grow, for they cannot survive high temperatures, hot sun, or high summer humidity. It is for this reason that they are not popularly grown in North America or stocked in much variety at nurseries.

However, I see no reason why they would not prosper if you give them a spot with some protection from the midday sun where they can live among rocks and a free draining soil mixture with some organic matter and lots of stone chippings mixed in, plus a generous layer of chippings spread around the plants. They certainly lend themselves to trough and pot culture, and the alpine house is an ideal home for them. At least, under these conditions the gardener has a fighting chance to manage the unwelcome heat and humidity.

The appearance of the plants themselves has on more than one occasion worked against them. The leaves have a thick leathery appearance and are arranged in rosettes suggestive of many of the succulents. Of course, they are not succulents, nor do they want

204

Silver saxes in the wall garden of Harry Jans.

anything to do with sun and drought. In their natural habitat, principally the mountains of Europe, they seek some shade. Even in the hot, sunny Maritime Alps where they thrive, it may be dry but they always arrange to grow where they will get some shade.

Having dwelled on the need for some shade I hope I have not gone too far, for the silver saxes are not shade plants. If given too much shade, they become loose in form and lose their attractive alpine compactness.

They make the most beautiful contribution to the trough garden landscape. With their silvery foliage contrasting with a couple of the green leaved species, the designer can play with the differences between large rosetted kinds and the tiniest. Leave space for a couple of plants that produce gracefully arching plumes of pure white flowers, for they look so natural, gracefully drooping over the sides of the trough.

They flower prolifically and the display lasts several weeks; the cooler the weather, the longer they last. White is the dominant color but there are many degrees of white, from the stark chalk-white previously mentioned, through whites that really are off whites with creamy tones. Some of the species with white flowers have red spots on the petals, sometimes so many that the flowers appear rusty colored. The red spots can join together, forming large blotches. *Saxifraga* 'Southside Seedling' has large, dull crimson blotches at the center of each flower, and it glows. There are a few other rosy-colored varieties plus two pale yellows. Aim to include these colors in your collection.

To gain a quick grasp of the silver saxifrages we need to know that there are four principal species and multitudinous hybrids created among them. This is an oversimplification, but, in the interest

205

of helping readers choose a few saxifrages to start their rock gardens, it will suffice.

S. callosa is a variable species occurring in the Maritime Alps and is considered by many as the finest of the encrusted saxes. The rosettes are symmetrical and beautifully silvered. The leaves are long and narrow, gray with pronounced silvery margins. The flowers are a good clear white and sometimes carried on dark red stems.

S. cochlearis in its dwarf forms is probably the most widely grown of the silvers. The smallest ones form domes of tightly packed, heavily encrusted, spoon-shaped leaves. They provide pure white flowers on arching mahogany colored stems, about six inches long.

S. cotyledon grows in fleshy looking rosettes with wide leaves and rounded tips, with finely toothed margins. They are mostly on the green side of glaucous. This variable species is capable of growing huge rosettes with massive pyramidal panicles of white flowers, or white flowers with numerous red spots. My Zone 8 garden has too much sun for this plant to be easily grown. Interestingly enough, this is one of the few saxifrages that prefers to grow on granite or slate in the wild, so don't feed it lime.

S. oppositifolia, the purple saxifrage, occurs all through Europe, North America, and Asia. It thrives in cool environments where it can be found on rocky ledges, scree slopes, cliffs, and gravel bars in mountain streams, both on limestone and igneous rock.

It forms low flat carpets of creeping stems set with tiny leaves that can be obscured when it flowers. The flowers arrive in May and June and are virtually stemless. Colors range through purple, purplish-pink and deep red. It is a bit tricky in the garden. Since it is a true alpine from the cool regions , it must be shielded from midday suns. I once saw a wonderful specimen growing on a piece of tufa set deep in a trough. There are several cultivars described and raved about, both here and in Europe. *S. o.* 'Theoden', rose-purple, and *S. o.* 'Ruth Draper', rich crimson, head the list. There is a pure white form available, but it usually gets disparaging comments on the quality of the flowers.

S. paniculata has the widest distribution in nature of all the silver saxes and includes several zones in Canada and the USA. As a result, the species is infinitely variable and includes a great many geographic forms and natural hybrids. It is notorious for hybridizing with almost every saxifrage that grows near it. The result is that too many similar plants have been named and published in catalogs. Here are a few that I consider distinct enough to be recognized, listed here more for convenience than for botanical accuracy. They should add interest to a collection.

S. p. 'Balcana' seems to be widely grown—at least the name appears often. It is one of the smaller kinds, with rosettes only an inch across with noticeable strong reddish six-inch flowers stems. The individual flowers may be heavily spotted.

S. p. 'Hirtella' (also listed as *S.* 'Hirtifolia', so take either or both if the chance arises) is one of the few silvers with fuzzy leaves, or perhaps I should say velvety gray leaves, makes a great trough plant with white flowers.

S. p. 'Lutea' dates back to Farrer's time,1919. It may be a hybrid. Rosettes are on the larger side, two inches or so, and pale green and strap-like with serrated margins. Its pale yellow flowers bloom on stems nine to 12 inches tall.

S. p. 'Minutifolia' is a popular little species that is often confused with *S. p. baldensis*, which Reginald Farrer found on Monte Baldo near Lake Garda, Italy. The plant we grow today is very compact. It forms a low-growing mat of small, silvery rosettes. Rosettes range in size from only a fourth to half an inch wide. Two-inch high stems carry a generous display of the creamy-white flowers.

S. p. 'Rex' is another of Farrer's introductions and is still considered one of the better paniculatas. It is well silvered and bears creamy white flowers on ten-inch mahogany stems.

S. p. 'Rosea' is another of Farrer's early finds from Bulgaria. It grows into flat mats of numerous lightly silvered rosettes with rose-pink flowers freely borne on six- to nine-inch stems.

S. p. 'Venetia' is also one of the smaller forms. The small rosettes are silver-edged and green with a distinct mahogany-red on the underside of the leaves, blooming on short stems with white flowers.

Here are a couple of very choice hybrids:

S. x burnatii **'Emile Burnat'**, a cross between *S. paniculata* and *S. cochlearis*, is truly a jewel among the silvers. Its heavily silvered leaves, narrow recurved, give the rosette a light airy look, which is completed with arching plumes of white flowers.

S. **'Whitehill'** probably needs no introduction from me. The distinct silvery-blue leaves with reddened bases are a regular sight in many gardens. I was told that Whitehill is the name of a garden in England that may have had something to do with the introduction of this plant.

S. **'Winifred Bevington'** is another of these well dispersed little hybrids that seems to grow everywhere. It must be given a fair amount of shade, but not total shade or it will not flower profusely. It is a hybrid between a silver saxifrage and one of the London Pride Group of saxifrages. It is an exceptionally neat, high quality plant. The foliage forms rosettes, mid-green and slightly notched along the margins. It has the look of London Pride despite the *paniculata* blood in the rosette. The flowers are white but covered with spots and flushed with pink, so they often appear to be pink.

The Mossy Saxifrages

There are very few mossies small enough for our purpose, but two names regularly appear in catalogs, so they must be popular.

S. **'Hi Ace'** is a tight little bun of variegated green and yellow leaves, the yellow so pale it can easily be taken for white. Flowers are bright red.

S. exarata ssp. *moshata* **'Cloth of Gold'** is a little clump of mossy golden leaves with a bronze cast. Its short stems carry white flowers with a golden center. Unfortunately, even with light shade and the coolest trough, it may collapse without warning. To prevent losing it, make sure to take a constant supply of young cuttings.

This account has gone on longer than I intended and I hope it has helped with this key genus for the small alpine garden.

Sedum

The sedums share a reputation for invasive behavior and weediness. In my garden they are often overlooked in favor of more colorful plants. It is only in the summer when there is little else in flower that they become noticed and credited with the attention they deserve. The fact that there are autumn-flowering sedums choice enough for the smallest garden is rarely understood or exploited.

True sedum enthusiasts complain that too many gardeners do not give the genus enough consideration when choosing which sedums to plant. As a result, varieties are planted in the wrong growing conditions so they either swamp their neighbors or they fail to prosper. This bring unjustified scorn down on all the sedums.

Sedums come from many diverse climates in many places ranging from the tundra of the Arctic Circle to the shores of the Mediterranean. They are found in the Himalayas, Japanese Islands, European mountains and North America, from high to low elevations. It is a wise move to check out the natural habitat of any sedum species you are considering, to be sure it will accept your local conditions. They can be touchy about dry summers, rainy humid summers, wet winters, or icy winters.

The hardy sedums will survive in almost any soil providing it is well drained: they will not tolerate overly damp or waterlogged soils. It is a good policy to add generous amounts of very coarse sand and or gravel. Lime does not seem to be an issue one way or the other. Their greatest asset is their love of sunshine. They are not averse to a shortage of water. However, do not let this stop you from watering other plants nearby. Those with a great deal of shade will be pleased to know that there are sedums that need it.

Sedums where space is not critical

These spreading sedums are generally similar to one another in that they are evergreen, low, compact mats with creeping stems of small, fat, fleshy leaves.

I like them and recommend them, for they are easy, bright, and colorful, but they come with a warning. Given a decent soil, some watering, and normal garden conditions, they will respond by growing fat and green and will take over the whole site. On the other hand, if they are kept to a lean soil, a mere few inches of soil in full sun, with minimal irrigation, they are capable of producing a wonderful tapestry of foliage colors. During the summer the picture changes as the yellow, gold, white, and pink flowers appear. Just be sure to exclude weeds and remove the dead flowers and untidy growth.

Using the garden shears works well; do not be concerned that every piece that falls to the ground will root.

S. acre is very ordinary and might be best left for larger plantings. *S. a.* 'Aureum' is a bit more refined and very pretty, as the new growth is tipped with gold.

S. album has white flowers and the same advice prevails as with *S. acre*.

S. a. 'Coral Carpet' is quite well behaved. It makes a low mat only an inch or so high. The foliage will assume very attractive red shades. Flowers are pink.

S. a. 'Murale' is very similar and should be included as the foliage is found in very dark shades of brown, bronze, and purple. Its small flowers are also pink.

S. hispanicum var. minus is a small, tufted plant that is capable of developing into a dense carpet. The leaves are small and bright blue-green. The star-shaped white flowers are heavily flushed with pink and are borne on one-inch stems.

S. sexangulare has yellow flowers and should be included for variety, for the fleshy leaves are tightly concentrated at the tops of the stems, giving the plant a different form. During drought, the green leaves turn a pleasing bronze shade.

S. spurium is another of the easy-going sedums, and will get out of hand if not controlled. However, it can make a contribution to the sedum garden as it has attractive, colorful foliage and excellent flower colors. Keep it restricted to places with shallow soil or a rocky site. It will tolerate partial shade, but not too much or it will grow lax and make a poor flower display.

The plant makes a spreading tangle of matted light brown stems. The broad, fleshy leaves are concentrated at the upper part of the stems, in attractive whorls. Several forms are listed in catalogs with green or dark red leaves, and there is one with tricolored leaves.

There are other forms to be found in the lists. Buy by sight or on the description, as the names tend to be a bit creative. The three varieties listed are among the least vigorous.

S. s. var. *album* has green leaves and white flowers, shyly produced.

S. s. 'Schorbuser Blut' (commonly known as 'Dragon's Blood') has green foliage that soon becomes very heavily darkened with red. The flowers are the darkest of all, hence the name. This is one of the least aggressive cultivars.

S. s. 'Variegatum', *also found as S. s.* 'Tricolor' is named for the colors of the foliage, mainly green but edged with yellow variegation that itself becomes tinged with red.

Sedums for the small garden or trough garden

Most sedums are very successful planted in a trough or other small space. They are often too successful and end up hogging all the space. But the two plants described here are safe. Yes, they will get bigger, but they will remain good tenants for the long haul.

S. cauticolum is a Japanese species that, if I were limited to one sedum, would be my choice. It is not invasive and is very handsome in habit, foliage, and flower. It is safe for the smallest scheme and it flowers into September and October. Nothing is prettier than a large plant in full flower flowing over the sides of a trough. It is a deciduous perennial with numerous drooping stems set with round blue-gray leaves with large heads of small rosy-purple flowers. I have found that this species needs slightly better living conditions than harsh sunbaked sites.

S. pachyclados is a recent introduction from the mountains of Afghanistan and Pakistan, and it seems to be hardy. It is offered by several mail order nurseries and most rate it hardy north to Zone 5. It does well in England and my wet winters in Victoria do not harm it. I have read that in England it makes a plant 18 inches across. If it does that with us on this continent then we have a great plant. It would make a nice trough plant providing it does not grow too big. The plant is very noticeable because of it light colored, glaucous blue rosettes—a quick glance and you think it is a saxifrage. The flowers are white but so far they have been sparse on my plants, not that it matters. The foliage of this carpeting plant is sufficient. I have grown this species in a light soil in a raised bed so it has the advantage of a depth of soil and occasional irrigation.

Sempervivum

Gardeners will recognize these plants under their popular name, hen and chicks, or refer to them as succulents rather than their scientific name, *Sempervivum* species. The familiar name of hen and chicks arises from the way they produce their offsets, or young plants: these are baby rosettes grown on very short and brittle runners, permitting the little round offsets to roll from the parent plant to the ground where they quickly root, clustered around the plant in a way that suggests chicks around the mother hen. In earlier times in Europe some of the larger species were planted on the roofs of farmhouses and chalets as protection from fire and lightening. They were named *hauswurz* and in England the name became houseleek.

Should anyone be moved to try this, a garden shed is a good place to start, particularly if the pitch is not too steep. Acquire some sempervivums with large rosettes and then mix up a batch of clay and fresh farmyard manure until it has the constituency of mortar. It should be wet enough to handle and not run when slapped on the roof. Plant the rosettes right away before the mixture dries. That is normally all that is required for the houseleeks to live and prosper for a long time.

The Latin name is informative. The first part, *semper*, means ever or always, and *vivum* means living, forming a name that describes these plants which survive with minimal care.

Although they belong to the family Crassulaceae, which contains popular succulents of the greenhouse and window sill, they are alpine plants used to the cool climate of the mountains. They occur in the mountains of Europe and eastward across to the Middle East and Central Asia. There are no sempervivums native to North America.

As with other species that cover a wide geographic area, they are extremely variable, originating from differing altitudes and habitats ranging from rocky crevices to alpine meadows. Their uniform

rosettes are one of their most appealing characteristics. Consisting of a flowerlike cluster of fleshy leaves arranged in circles, the rosette may be open and flat or may be tightly incurved, forming a solid globular shape. Occasionally, they can resemble little wooly balls perched upon the soil. One attractive species has weblike white threads running from leaf to leaf tip in a precise pattern.

A planting that takes advantage of the many shapes, sizes, and colors available within this huge family requires no further embellishment. Choose them in growth at a garden or nursery. You will get exactly the size, shape, and color you want. There are excellent nurseries that grow them under ideal conditions, so that each species retains its own natural personality. This is important to the garden designer, as plants grown in rich soil may be somewhat out of character. Seldom is permanent damage done and they will eventually return to their proper appearance when grown in the rock garden.

When planting a trough, look for varieties with small rosettes with lots of bright colors. Where space is not critical it is safe to collect larger rosettes. When it comes to flowers, some gardeners are of the opinion that it would be better if they did not flower at all! With a few exceptions it is hard to call them pretty. Words like bold, noble, or stately could be used instead.

The flowers are produced on powerful, thick, leafy stems which erupt from the center of mature rosettes. Some stems will grow as much as eight inches tall. Luckily there are lots of varieties that provide a choice of much smaller and less extreme flower stems. The flowers themselves tend to be of dowdy colors, somber reds and purples and few bright yellows. Without a doubt, my all-time favorite is *S. arachnoideum*. This is the one with the fine threads on the leaf tips and bright pink flowers on short stems.

Sempervivum	_Jovibarba_
S. arachnoideum	J. allionii
S. a. var. Album	J. arenaria
S. a. 'Minor'	J. heuffelii*
S. ciliosum	J. hirta
S. c. 'Borisii'	
S. c. 'Mali Hat'	
S. dolomiticum	
S. giuseppii	
S. ingwersenii	
S. marmoreum *	
S. montanum	
S. octopodes*	
S. pumilum	* forms worth searching for.
S. tectorum*	

After the flowers have finished, both the old flower stem and the rosette that produced it will die. While this not harmful to the plants it does make extra work for the gardener who will have to pull out the dead stems.

The sempervivums grow and spread by producing stolons, very similar to the strawberry plant. These stolons radiate from the bases of mature rosettes and terminate with a young plant at their tip. Some varieties produce a large number of these stolons and the young plants soon establish and grow, providing a supply of young plants.

These stolons also come in a full range of sizes, from long, stout ones up to several inches long to thin, threadlike ones. There some that are almost invisible. They offer excellent design opportunities, for long masses of stolons are ideal for cascading over ledges, while neat plants with few or no runners are suited to crevices. The larger species make accent plants and the smaller species are for troughs and small containers.

Sempervivums are wild alpine plants and so are true species, but there are a exceptions where natural hybrids occur in the wild. For rock gardeners who are purists and grow only species, there are many to choose from.

On the other hand there are hundreds of man-made hybrids of diverse shapes and sizes. The foliage colors of these are particularly attractive. Look for nursery lists illustrated with colored photographs.

Cultivation

Due to their water-holding capacity, sempervivums will survive for a long time without water and are fairly tolerant of sunshine, but they are not true desert plants. While they will live in near tropical zones, they seldom retain the compact habit of the true alpine in these conditions. They become fat and loose, their bright colors usually end up green, and their rosettes open and spread rather than remain formed into tight globes.

Semps are not fussy about soil requirements and will survive under poor conditions, but with a little attention we can grow them to perfection. They will look a lot better if given three or four inches of well-drained rock garden soil. They do not like shady damp soils. Sunny, outcropping rocks are their preferred habitat. However, in hot, sunny climates a little shade from tfull sun is advisable. Once they establish they will spread into semi-barren spots of their choosing.

Sempervivum and Jovibarba. As you are make selections from nursery lists, pay attention to the name *Jovibarba*. These plants were classed as Sempervivums until they were put into the genus *Jovibarba*, based on the different arrangement of the flower parts.

As I study several listings of *Sempervivum* and *Jovibarba* offered for sale I notice name changes. Varieties I have known for years have disappeared and newer varieties are listed which I am not familiar with. With this in mind I have listed a few varieties that are attractive and distinct enough to order sight unseen, which are also choice enough for smaller projects.

S. marmoreum has forms and varieties of the deepest reds imaginable.

S. octopodes may not be durable in the colder zones.

S. tectorum contains some of the most ordinary varieties imaginable and some very attractive forms. Look for Mrs Giuseppi, Sunset, and var. *Alpinum.*

J. heuffelii has a wide range green, bronzes to purplish browns. There is even a dwarf form.

Silene

Silene acaulis, with its hard, bright green moss-like mounds composed of small, tightly knit foliage, is easily spotted in the mountains whether in flower or not. It has a wide range both in Europe and North America. It is unfortunate that it is not as generous with the bright pink flowers in the garden as it is in the wild. It is amenable to a range of sites in the rock garden, thriving in crevices or open slopes, and in walls, terraces, troughs, and pots.

This silene is usually available with lovely pink stemless flowers, although there are variations such as *S. a. pedunculata*, a name which means that the flowers are borne on short stems. This one is well worth growing and it flowers well. *S. a.* 'Alba' is one of several white forms in the trade, although I have yet to see one that rivals the pink flowering ones.

S. alpestris always pleases me in May or June as the clumps of stems tumble down a rock or wall. It is a simple flower of pure white with attractively fringed petals set against small dark green leaves. Stems about three inches tall make a solid cushion covered with heads of flowers. The plant is usually offered under the name *S. alpestris* although others may be used. *S. a.* 'Flore Pleno' is a double flowered form that even the alpine gardening purist would agree to use.

S. schafta may not be the greatest color in the world, but in late summer and early fall it is noticed. The plant is ideally suited to wall plantings, raised beds, and rock gardens in sun or part shade. It forms a central woody rootstock from which thin stems radiate to cover up to 12 inches in width and ascend to around six inches tall. It is capable of responding to favorable soil conditions, so keep it clear of smaller treasures. Stems carry one or two flowers, each about an inch across, composed of five narrow petals, deeply notched at the tips. Opinions differ on the color. Rose-magenta might be the closest although I have also seen it described as a strident pink.

Soldanella

It is not possible to list every alpine plant, but I can hardly overlook the appealing little *Soldanella* species even if they are difficult to manage. I think everyone should at least try some, for the rewards are worth any effort. What makes them so special? Their delicate, pendant, bell-like flowers carried on light stems, often with two or three flowers to a stem. The heavily fringed edges make them tempting enough, but the color blends of lavender-blue to violet are so lovely they

Soldanella montana

are hard to describe. For the most part, they have small, rounded, dark green, leathery leaves and develop into tufts of leaves from underground runners.

They are tricky to manage in the open rock garden, but will grow well if given a northern aspect and a gritty but well draining soil with plenty of humus added. Do not let them become dry during their spring growing period. The fact that they begin to make their flowers in the fall for an early start in spring is their weakness, for the tiny buds are easy prey for pests. They are plants of the melting alpine snows, often so impatient to burst into flower that they pop up through several inches of snow. A pot or pan of them in the alpine house offers a better chance to flower these gems. Protect the buds from tiny slugs and sow bugs (also known as wood lice and pillbugs).

S. alpina is the alpine snowbell and is one of the choicer species with deeply frilled bells of rich blue-violet; it's not one of the easiest.

S. carpatica has larger leaves with dark red undersides. Flower stems run to six inches tall. The fringed bells are deep blue-purple.

S. montana (pictured on page 216) is a popular species that does extremely well here on the West Coast, where it makes large mats covered in purple pendant bells.   This plant is sometimes confused with or sold as *S. hungarica* or *S. montana* subsp. *hungarica.* Regardless of the name, plant it.

S. villosa is much larger than the other soldanellas. Some gardeners may even describe it as coarse. The large, kidney-shaped leaves can grow to two inches or more and the flower stems grow to six inches or more. It owes the name *villosa* to the silky hairs covering stems, leaves, and flower buds. It certainly lacks the elfin quality of the others. Nonetheless, given a cool, moist spot, it responds well and will not become invasive.

Thymus

Thyme (*Thymus* species) is very important in the rock garden. Yes, it is useful as a neat green mat sprawling across the paths, perhaps clothing a wall or tumbling down from a raised bed. Its true value comes in summer when the pink, red, or purple flowers cover the plants. The sun-warmed plants smell of summer and hum with bees. Enough of this romanticism—even the lowest, tiniest plants will

217

Thymus hybrid, variegated

spread, but you know this in advance, so plant them where they may spread without creating problems. If they are happy they will grow onto rock, paving, and even sidewalks. If there is sufficient space, the shrubby thymes make colorful small shrubs and they respond to shearing. There are so may thymes to choose from it is hard to know which to select. Not only that, they are hard to identify just from descriptions in lists because of nomenclature issues.

Thymus neiceffii is a choice plant allegedly from Anatolia that I admired in the rock gardens of Denver, Colorado. A superb, slow growing, ground hugging little thyme, it forms a low, gray-green mat that follows the contours of the rocks. This species is noticeably different from other creeping thymes due to the arrangement of the foliage, which is closely grouped together, especially at the tips of the shoots. Some gardeners describe this characteristic as similar to larch needles. Long, silky hairs on the leaves heighten the silvery appearance. It loves sun and must have very rapidly draining soil. I was told that the flowers are pink but it also has been described as magenta; regardless of color, grow it for its foliage and form.

T. serpyllum (T. polytrichus). When I describe *T. serphyllum*, I have a picture in my mind of the native species from Europe and Britain, not one of the semi-hardy Mediterranean species. I remember gardens where it grew as a very low, prostate plant composed of many sprawling, threadlike branches clothed with tiny aromatic green leaves; of course, all thymes are aromatic. Most of all I see colorful carpets made from the various color forms of this plant, from pure white through shades of pink, lavender, rose-pink, and rich crimson.

218

For a long time these colorful horticultural forms were sold as *T. serphyllum* and many nurseries still list them under *T. serphyllum*. Some current authorities list them under the name *T. polytrichus*.

I am unhappy when I see lists of names of plants that I am unable to purchase and am reluctant to produce one, but in this case my list may be of use. The nursery will know exactly what thymes you are seeking regardless of the current name. Also, if there is more demand for colored thymes, the nurseries will soon meet it.

These are some of the varieties of *T. serpyllum* (*T. polytrichus*) that may be found for sale:

'Albus', white flowers.

'Annie Hall', light flesh-pink flowers.

'Carol Ann', golden variegated foliage.

'Elfin', which is safe for the smallest garden. It contrasts with the others in the group by forming a tight, compact bun of dark-green rather than a carpet. Flowers are few and scattered, and are of a light lavender shade.

'Coccineus', crimson pink flowers.

'Minor', sometimes 'Minus'. The true plant forms a tidy, slow-growing mat with pink flowers.

'Pink Chintz', gray-green leaves and pink flowers.

'Ruby Glow', dark leaves and ruby red flowers.

'Russetings', bronzy leaves and deep mauve flowers.

I know I have painted a romantic picture, for such plantings were possible when these named forms could be purchased readily. The fly in the ointment with these gorgeous thyme carpets was self seeding; the bees knew no difference between the named forms. Consequently, year by year, the distinct colors began to fade into lavenders and poor purples as the open-pollinated seedlings began to take over. The only way to maintain the purity of the planting was with painstakingly weeding out of the poorer colors or buying new plants and starting again.

Other Thymes

T. pseudolanuginosus is a gray, woolly leaved variety with pallid pink flowers, but the flowers are not important since it is the gray mat we are after. In some catalogs this plant is included with the *serpyllums* while others list it as a separate species. Just be sure you get a low, flat plant.

219

T. **'Doone Valley'** adds color with its gold-tipped green leaves and crimson flower buds. This plant will grow into a cushion five inches high with lavender flowers. Use it if there is room, for it has the valuable role of providing foliage contrast in a thyme planting.

T. **'Doretta Klaber'** is a popular small thyme and listed and recommended by several leading alpine nurseries. It only grows half an inch high and spreads into a flat mass about 12 inches across. The small leaves are slightly hairy, adding texture to the plant.

Trillium

Talking about trilliums in the same breath as small garden spaces may seem a little contradictory, since we know how large many trilliums can grow. Besides, few of them could be classed as alpine plants because they are woodland plants. However, there are a couple of delightful species that are truly rock plants and are ideal for semi-shaded gardens. They have such similar botanical names that it is worth taking a moment to explain. *Nivale* refers to snow, or growing near the snowline, hence the name snow trillium. *Rivale*, on the other hand, refers to brooks or growing near a brook, so it is called the brook trillium. Mind you, it has other local names.

T. nivale, the little snow trillium of the Eastern USA with distribution among several states, is never a common plant. Not an alpine plant, it can be found among the crooks and crannies of limestone outcrops. It has an affinity for alkaline talus slopes that form at the base of limestone ledges. In the rock garden it prefers an open, gritty soil to which some limestone chippings may be added. No extra leafmold is required where the soil has been prepared according to directions in chapter 5.

The small flowers start to show in mid-March until April. Of course, since it has such a wide distribution, timing will vary. The little white flowers with their bright yellow stamens start out on short stems varying from one to two inches, and continue to grow to three or four inches. The ultimate height depends on your particular plant and your garden conditions such as shade, soil fertility, and moisture. The leaves are blue-green and attractively veined, completing the picture of a choice rock garden plant.

T. rivale, the brook trillium, is a delightful little species from the Siskiyou Mountains of Oregon and California, an area of great beauty

This coveted dwarf pink trillium in the author's collection is a cross made by Boyd Kline, and is one of his selections of forms of *Trillium rivale.*

and wonderful plants. The species is found on the slopes and travels west toward the Pacific Coast, where it dwells in the cool forests.

There is no doubt that winters are cold in these mountains, but whether the plant will survive under tough winters elsewhere is doubtful. Even with protection, it might never really settle down. It is suggested that Zones 5 to 9 would be safer, although I expect that it would be worth the gamble in a favored spot in Zone 4. It is a white-flowered species, but pink forms occur regularly. Some types have petals spotted with purple, with the spots becoming more numerous as they approach the center of the flower. There are pink forms in varying degrees of intensity. Particularly sought after are the rich pinks with lots of intense purple spotting.

T. r. 'Purple Heart' is a popular variation since the spots are so concentrated at the center of the flower. The name says it all.

Boyd Kline, one of the original partners of the Siskiyou Rare Plant Nursery who has long been a connoisseur, has deliberately crossed a good form of 'Purple Heart' with a rich pink form he discovered to produce a glorious deep pink flower with the mass of purple at the heart. There are several of these selections getting into the nurseries, but so far none of the names have been formally recognized. Of course, as long as they continue to be raised from seed, it is unlikely any particular form will ever be stabilized.

Veronica

Veronica species. Very little beats good blue flowers, and the veronicas (speedwells) certainly can supply them. Most of the rock garden varieties grow into pretty sizable clumps and have a solid mass of roots. Knowing this, plant them where there is room. You may have to decide that they are just too large for the space available.

V. armena is a delightful sun lover, happy to creep over rocks. Its prostrate stems radiate from a central rootstock, making a mat of finely divided, gray-green leaves, each half an inch long. In summer the plant is covered with loose spikes of bright blue flowers. The plant remains low and will easily cover a square foot.

V. bombycina is not for every rock garden, but for those with a dry, sunny garden it might do well. The rest of us have to grow it under protection from too much rain. It hails from the screes and rocks of Lebanon and Turkey, which gives some indication of its requirements: plenty of moisture during the growing season and minimal wetting in the winter. A well grown specimen will be a mound about two inches high covered with white-felted leaves. In summer you will see the lavender-blue flowers, perhaps closer to mauve. It is not a true blue but is ideally suited to the plant.

V. pectinata **'Rosea'** is obviously not blue. It is another attractive trailing species for a sunny spot with densely hairy gray leaves and deep pink flowers in the summer. It is a good, trouble-free plant, but it is too vigorous for the trough or other select neighborhoods.

V. prostrata to me is the perfect veronica. The flowers are intensely blue. It is easy and showy, usually flowering from May and June into summer. The name implies that it is a creeping plant, but it is more of a mat forming plant composed of decumbent to ascending stems. It makes a good solid plant of green foliage and is covered with spikes of rich deep blue. It is listed as anywhere from six to nine inches tall. My own plant is certainly nine inches tall and 18 inches across. There are other color forms available, ranging from white through the pink shades to the lighter blues to dark blue.

Veronica spicata

V. p. 'Trehane' is a six-inch high, floppy mound of golden-yellow foliage with spikes of good blue flowers. I am tempted to comment, for those who need a golden veronica. I have one and like the bright contribution of the yellow leaves. It is on an open western slope in full sun and it would appreciate a bit more shade, as a few leaves show sun damage.

V. spicata will surely be too much for many smaller projects, but, centered in a sunny raised bed where the surface is large enough, it makes a fine accent plant for a summer's day. The larger varieties are considered to be herbaceous border plants. They make dense mats of oval leaves; expect them to grow to two feet in height. They produce long thin spikes of tiny flowers, available from white to the pinks to shades of rose, blue, and purple. *V. s.* ssp. *incana* 'Nana', on the other hand, is only four inches tall in flower from a low mat of green foliage.

Crocus tomasinianus

10. Small Bulbs

Bulbs and bulblike plants require a different approach than that for other rock plants. Non-botanists use the word bulb as a general term to cover other plants that look something like bulbs, for example, corms, tubers, and, sometimes, rhizomes, and I am including them all in this chapter.

Some bulbs are native to countries with absolutely dry summers; the bulbous part of the plant allows it to store food and moisture during the long dry months while it is dormant. The plants grow during cool, moist months, flowering in spring. After flowering they continue growing leaves long enough to produce enough stored food for the next season.

They should be purchased and planted in the early fall, something I sometimes have trouble getting around to at the proper time, and they are not difficult to handle. They can be the answer for some gardeners who cannot do customary plants and gardening because they do not have adequate facilities. A few potted bulbs are the answer also to those who have to be away from home a great deal. Once the bulbs are planted they can be enjoyed as they grow and flower, and then given to a friend who has a garden.

Many of the small bulbs we will be growing are alpine plants, so the rock garden with its fast-draining soil mixture will suit them admirably. Certain species require a degree of shade, and perhaps there will be just such a spot in the rock garden.

Listed here is a sampling of important bulbs to use in the rock garden or grow in raised beds, troughs, or pots. Do not overlook these wonderful plants or the pleasure they offer.

Using Bulbs

There are several basic ways to use bulbs in alpine gardens, ranging from planting a few bulbs or bulblike plants in the soil to growing them in pots or in specially designed structures (see Chapter 7) such as cool greenhouses and bulb frames (pages 117 to 119). Bulb frames (similar to cold frames) can be designed to grow challenging bulbs that require a totally dry summer, or they can be made and used differently for growing bulbs that need controlled winter rainfall.

From initial success with easy-to-grow, spring-flowering bulbs, it is natural to progress to growing a greater variety because there are

Galanthus nivalis 'Flore Pleno', the double form of the common snowdrop.

so many wonderful bulbs to enjoy. Once you become involved, it is easy to overdo it. Just because they are small with short flower stems, alpine garden bulbs do not appear to take up much space. But just wait until spring, when their foliage may overwhelm the other tiny alpines you have planted.

I have stressed that gardening in small spaces forces us to evaluate every plant we might like to use to be sure it justifies the valuable space it will occupy. This certainly applies to the use of bulbs, particularly in the small rock garden. They are extremely valuable for early color, but what will we do with their space when they are resting and the foliage has dried off?

The traditional garden approach is to plant summer annuals in the space, either on top of the dormant bulb or by removing the bulbs for the summer and replanting them in the fall. This plan has its drawbacks, particularly if the bulbs demand a dry summer resting cycle. They will not tolerate the moisture necessary to satisfy summer flowers. Digging up and storing bulbs after flowering is a chore. If they are to be used again the following fall, they have to be given the chance to fatten themselves up for subsequent flowering. That means a space will have to found for them where they can be cared for and nurtured. In a small garden, where can we find the space?

Many writers advocate growing bulbs under carpeting rock garden plants. This works in some cases where there is adequate room for carpeting plants robust enough to cope with a suffocating mass of bulb foliage. The tiny narcissus are safe to use under smaller rock garden plants, but the lovely dwarf crocuses produce a huge amount of foliage that even stress my tough woody plants of *Globularia cordifolia*.

Gardeners tend to plant dwarf bulbs in tight little groups. Concentrated in this manner, they make a better show. There is nothing wrong with this where room exists for group plantings. But, I wonder, is this nature's way? I have seen bulbs in the mountains scattered singly or in twos and threes across mountain sides. Are they less effective this way? I think not. When we follow this practice in the rock garden, summer foliage is not concentrated in one spot and is less overpowering.

Naturalizing bulbs in rough grass, lawns, light woodlands, and shrub borders is a wonderful way of gardening but can hardly be called gardening in small spaces. Yet the smallest lawn would be a great complement to the rock garden if it were planted with lots of the small anemone, crocus, erianthis, small snowdrops and narcissus. They will have finished flowering and matured enough by the time the lawn needs its first mowing.

Planting Dwarf Bulbs

Planting small bulbs is similar to planting larger bulbs such as hybrid tulips and daffodils. However, the planting depth is shallower, and fertilizer is not required with rock garden dwarf bulbs.

227

Galanthus nivalis foliage remains after bloom has ended.

The soil in the rock garden or raised bed, if prepared according to the directions given in chapter 5, is correct for bulbs. It should be light, open, and free draining, and contain enough nutrients to sustain the bulbs for at least one season.

How deep should the small bulbs be planted? An old rule of thumb advises, 'set a bulb in the soil to a depth twice that of the bulb's height.' Using this guide, a bulb one-inch high would be planted with two inches of soil above it. In colder climates I have seen bulbs planted with three to four inches of soil over them. Since the difference between the two is only a matter of an inch or so, not much harm will been done using either method. More bulbs are killed by planting them too shallowly than too deeply.

There are many ways to plant bulbs and almost as many special tools for the job. There is no real need to go out and buy a bulb planting tool to plant a few dozen rock garden bulbs. How do you rate yourself as a planter? I use my regular garden trowel for all my alpines and bulbs. With one swift movement, I make the hole and know from experience how deep it is.

Planting Method. Here is a safe and accurate method of getting the correct depth. Once the planting spot has been found for, say, a dozen small bulbs, mark the shape of the proposed grouping and remove enough soil to provide the necessary depth. The finished excavation should look like a tiny, flat-bottomed, empty pond. If the soil in the bottom is hard or compacted, now is the time to loosen it with a garden fork and add some organic matter and gravel and firm it slightly.

Now lay out the bulbs on the newly prepared base. This is where crea- tive skills are employed. The space between each bulb is usually twice the width of each bulb. This is a fair guide, but for a natural looking group, vary the distances. Once in a while be drastic and let bulbs touch. In the wild, you would be unlikely to see evenly spaced bulbs. Once satisfied with the arrangement, carefully replace the soil without disturbing the bulbs and firm the soil. Water well if the soil is dry and rain is not expected.

Squirrels and chipmunks favor certain bulbs and cats have an overpowering desire to visit neat patches of soft soil. To forestall their activities, spread pieces of chicken wire over freshly planted groups. The wire can be disguised with a layer of appropriate mulch.

Bulbs in Flowerpots

The gardener with limited space, having read this far, must be getting depressed about having no spare room for bulbs. Cheer up! There is always the trusty flower pot.

Where to start. First we must acquire the bulbs, and this cannot be done very easily until the garden centers have them available, which is early fall, around September. You have had plenty of time to study bulb lists and make your selections and purchase the packets of bulbs. There are many excellent mail order suppliers you might consider in addition. The illustrated lists they supply can be very helpful. Some of these suppliers are specialist growers, concentrating on specific genera, including small bulbs for the rock garden. These nurseries will become very important to you as you develop your interest in bulbs.

Terracotta bulb pans (see Chapter 6) are designed for growing bulbs and come in standard diameters of five, six, and seven inches, measured at the inside rim of the pot. These are efficient sizes, not too small and not susceptible to rapid drying. On the other hand, they do not contain a large volume of soil that could stay wet. These sizes hold enough bulbs to make a worthwhile display.

How many bulbs to a pan? It is tough to generalize, for clearly the size of the bulbs is a factor. Standard tulip bulbs take up more space than tiny narcissus or rock garden tulips. Little anemones can be planted almost touching each other, as they will carpet the surface with leaves and the flowers will float above the foliage. Tulips will send up stems generating quite large flowers that do not want to be crowded or the individual beauty of each flower is lost. Therefore, five tulip bulbs to a six-inch pan makes sense. If you are an advocate of odd numbers, stick with five. If not, the pan can safely accommodate six tulips.

As a general rule of thumb, I suggest spacing each bulb just over its own width away from the next. A one-inch bulb would be placed just over an inch from its neighbor. The soil for potted bulbs can be the same as that recommended for alpines in pots (Chapter 5) It must be light, airy, and fast draining. Nutrients and fertilizer are not required at planting time. The bulb is virtually self- sufficient at this time; the flower buds are already formed within the bulb and rich soil will only encourage foliar growth at the cost of flowers.

Pot up the bulbs as soon as possible after receiving them. We need to get as much root growth going as possible before heavy frost sets in and stops all growth.

Adding lots of drainage material to the bottom of the pot is not necessary if the planted pots are set in a dry location. It is wise to put a small square of fine screening over the drainage hole to exclude worms and other creatures that would make a winter home in the pot. Place the screen over the hole and hold it as you add a little soil to keep the screen in place. Then fill the pot halfway with soil, firming it by pressing it down with your fingertips. There is no need to pack it heavily.

Space the bulbs over the surface and make any adjustments you feel need to be made. Halfway down the pot is a safe measurement of planting depth because there is little danger of fatally burying a small bulb, and larger bulbs have to manage with the depth the pot permits. A free lesson in planting depths will be gained when it is time to repot the plants later in the year. Note the depth that various species have managed to find or adjust for themselves.

Now fill the pots with potting mixture and carefully label them with the names of the inhabitants and the planting date. What is next? The ideal area for their development is a cold frame or a cool pit. Where these are not available, a cool cellar free from rodents will suffice. Careful management of water is vital, for the bulbs must be kept moist but not wet, and must not be allowed to dry out.

If space can be found in the garden, dig a trench 12 inches deep, long and wide enough to hold all the pots. Pick an area where water will not collect. Place a layer of gravel in the trench a few inches thick and level it. This makes a base for the pots to stand on and ensures free drainage for the pots. The next step is to set the pots in the trench and backfill. I have found it easier to work peat between the pots as they are set into the trench rather than trying to work the peat between the pots once they are all in place. Next fill in the trench to the top with either peat or the excavated soil. It is necessary at this time that the soil in the pots be moist but not soaking wet. I recommend a watering if the weather is dry. Fall weather will take care of the watering from then on.

After the trench is backfilled, nature can take its course until frost puts a meaningful crust on the soil surface. Now is the time to add a layer of mulch over the trench. This can be leaves, straw, compost, or any convenient material. This is not intended to protect the bulbs from freezing, for they are hardy. It is to keep the soil in the trench from freezing so that you can access the bulbs at any time. Providing that nothing untoward happens, the bulbs are safe until the spring. They will have made lots of roots but the tops will not have sprouted because they are in darkness. They are at the same stage as bulbs planted in the garden.

Checking the bulbs. At some time in the new year, curiosity will build and you will want to check the bulbs. The reason for the mulching now becomes apparent. It would be very difficult to check the bulbs with the whole trench frozen solid. Perhaps you would like to bring a few pots into the house. By all means do so, but you must follow the following procedure.

1. Select those that show plenty of roots, which are often visible growing through the drainage hole. There may also be some indication of a shoot poking through the top.

2. Put the pots in a light, cool, frost-free room such as a sunporch, with a temperature no higher than 50 degrees. Water as required. Don't allow strong sunshine to come through the glass. Shading with newspaper will do the job. This will allow stems and leaves to develop naturally and prevent premature flowering. I cannot put a time limit on this phase as there are too many imponderables. As long as the bulbs continue to receive plenty of light and air they will develop naturally.

3. Once they have achieved their natural stems and leaves, take them to a warm sunny room where you want them to flower. Flowers will last longer if the pots are returned to the cooler room at night.

4. If the bulbs are to be retained after flowering they must be returned to the cool room and be cultivated as a growing plant would be, until it is safe for them to go outside. Then they can be put somewhere to be fed and watered until they go into their summer resting period.

Cultivation

When you see bulbs at the garden center packed in neat colorful packages, it is easy to overlook the fact that they all originated as wild plants from many lands with widely differing growing conditions.

It is helpful to know that some bulbs are native to countries with very harsh, dry summers; the bulbous part of the plant allows it to remain dormant all summer long. Growth commences during the fall, winter, and spring with the advent of cool, wet weather. After flowering in spring, the bulbs continue to grow leaves until they produce enough stored food to sustain them for the next season.

There are also bulbs living under the opposite conditions, where winter is cool and dry and summer is hot and wet. Growth then occurs in summer. These are the extremes, and in many areas of the world the conditions are in between these extremes. This knowledge goes a long way in our understanding a species' requirements, and why a particular type of bulb thrives or dies. In his helpful book, *Growing*

231

Bulbs*, Martyn Rix describes native areas in some detail, and this is well worth studying.

Where no rock garden exists, the raised bed makes an excellent place to grow small bulbs because the raised soil level guarantees good drainage at the same time it makes closer inspection of the flowers much easier.

The smallest garden can find a home for a few potted bulbs. If a cold frame is available, so much the better, as it will keep excessive rain and snow from soaking the pots during the resting period and protect the growing bulbs. The ultimate luxury for growing bulbs is of course the alpine house with its high degree of climate control. Here, potted bulbs may sit on benches or be kept on the floor beneath the benches until more daylight is required.

Best Bulbs for Alpine Gardens

My greatest difficulty when it comes to small bulbs is that I forget to order them soon enough in the fall. Then I think of it when I enjoy them in flower in other people's gardens the next spring. Planting time is dictated to some extent by when the suppliers receive their stocks. Ideally, planting can start in the late summer and early fall. Here are my descriptions of the best bulb choices for rock gardeners.

Anemone

Anemone blanda (right) is a pretty blue daisy-shaped flower arising above a loose mat of dissected foliage. It prefers a little extra leaf mold in the soil and a little dappled shade in the lee of a shrub. Spring flowering usually is about six inches high.

There are other colors available and it is wise to buy them by named variety. *A. b. atrocaerulea* is dark blue; *A. b.* 'Charmer' is deep rose-red; *A. b.* 'Radar' is red with a white center; and *A. b.* 'White Splendour' is pure white.

* Rix, Martin, and Croom Helm. *Growing Bulbs. Portland;* Timber Press, 1983.

Bulbocodium

Bulbocodium vernum is generally overlooked when considering small bulbs. It is an alpine species and looks something like a narrow-petalled, reflexed crocus flower. The purplish blooms arrive before the foliage. I would be inclined to try it in a pan in a cool frame or greenhouse.

Chionodoxa

Species and varieties of *Chionodoxa* (glory of the snow, below) have been grown in gardens for over 200 years, so they must have something going for them. Their star-shaped flowers in shades of blue are cheerful on cold spring days. There are choices in shades of blue and lavender. All have a white eye and are in the range of six inches in height. They are hardy in Zones 5 to 8. The names you will see on the packets will differ from store to store, since confusion still reigns as to which is the correct name. The very same plant may be found under every name I have listed here: *C. forbesii, C. gigantea, C. luciliae* and *C. sardensis.* Why worry, just go through the lists and pick out the ones that appeal to you.

Chionodoxa species are by nature carpeters, growing in drifts. They will settle down if given some shade from deciduous shrubs. Unlike many bulbs, they do not respond to a summer of baking soil. They seed around and can be thinned and transplanted while the leaves are still green.

Crocus

Crocus hardly needs an introduction, since everyone appreciates these bright spring flowers after a long winter. Most of the crocus we see around are the Dutch crocus. They are man-made hybrids developed from wild species in order to produce plants with large, showy flowers.

The smaller wild species and their countless forms and selections are still with us, and just as beautiful. Generally they are not that difficult to grow and some will make themselves at home and naturalize. This is a good thing to some extent, but where space is limited, it is something to guard against.

The small species of crocus provide a huge range of different varieties in an array of colors based upon shades and combinations of white, yellow, blue, lilac-blue and purple. Their value is increased because in addition to the spring flowering types there are several varieties that naturally flower in the fall. The expression "one for every occasion" can be applied to the dwarf crocus, or amended to "a color for every occasion."

There are so many choices I cannot begin to describe them all, so my advice is to go shopping yourself and pick those that appeal to you. For the most part, they are not difficult to grow. The prepared rock garden soil is ideal most of the year. It is only in summer that they appreciate being a bit on the dry side.

Fall-Flowering *Crocus* Varieties

It would be better to plant fall blooming crocus earlier than they are customarily sold in the early fall. Therefore, get the bulbs as soon as possible and get them planted right away. This is the accepted practice and it works. Here are several small species:

C. laevigatus **'Fontenayi'** has blooms with pale violet and dark purple stripes, and yellow centers.

C. pulchellus. Flowers are blue with a deep yellow throat.

C. speciosus. Blossoms are violet-blue with intricate dark veins. There are several named varieties available.

Spring-Flowering *Crocus* Varieties

C. ancyrensis has one of the nicer golden colors. This species is referred to as 'Golden Bunch' and 'Cloth of Gold'. The smallest flowers are one and a quarter inch in diameter and a bright golden yellow. In some locations it will begin flowering in winter and very early spring.

C. chrysanthus is a deep rich golden yellow species from Greece, but is seldom offered because the many selected forms and crosses are preferred. Again my advice is to check them out yourself. Look for names like 'Advance', soft blue; 'Blue Pearl', lobelia-blue; 'Cream Beauty', lilac-brown; and 'Lady Killer', purple-blue. There are interesting yellows, bronzes, and creamy whites — good hunting!

C. sieberii favors the lilac-blue shades set off by the striking golden throat. Several varieties are available. *C. s.* 'Hubert Edelsten' is a popular deep violet-purple, and 'Violet Queen' is rich blue.

C. tommasinianus (see page 224) has small slender flowers of pale lilac-blue with a prominent white tube. It is a simple, very early little plant that I would not be without. It makes few demands and will naturalize. For those who require a little more color, try *C. t.* 'Ruby Giant' for it has deep ruby-purple flowers. *C. t.* 'Whitewell Purple' is purple with a striking inside of silvery purple.

There are so many great *Crocus* varieties that it would take pages to describe them, and new ones appear often. Read about them and examine as many bulb catalogs as you can.

Eranthis

Eranthis hyemalis, the winter aconite, is hardy to Zone 5. It appears and blooms as soon as winter lets up a little, sometimes as early as January and February. The golden yellow, cup-shaped flowers are surrounded by a ruff of foliage. They grow from two to four inches, subject to growing conditions. A native of southern Europe where it prefers the light woodlands, it will do well in the rock garden if it is not completely baked in summer. It will colonize when it finds acceptable conditions, so use it with care. It is an excellent little plant for practically any use. It is sold along with other dry bulbs, but does not always respond when planted.

It helps if the little corms are soaked in water for a couple of days before planting. Buy them as early as you can. As the soil begins to seriously cool down there is a real danger of their rotting before they start to grow. Alternatively, they can be grown in a pot and planted out in the spring. The best way is to plant them is 'in the green,' which simply means that you can move them anytime right after flowering, while they are in active growth.

There are several other kinds available. Some of these are slightly larger, but it is safe to plant any of the winter aconites. Yet I am not sure that winter aconites have a place in the small rock garden, chiefly because by nature they grow in broad sweeps in semi-shade and slightly moist soil. They will not thrive in a raised bed unless it is in partial shade and the soil will not dry and bake in summer.

Galanthus

I am sure there is no one who does not like *Galanthus* species (snowdrops). I certainly look for their cheerful pendant white flowers in spring. If you want some in the small garden by all means include them. Just be prepared for some hefty leaves and for the bulbs to multiply rapidly. There is always the option of growing a few in a pot in the alpine house or cold frame.

There are two further points to consider. First, snowdrops continue to be a passion to many collectors. As a result there is a lot of action among suppliers, and rare and tricky bulbs are available that require some expertise and special conditions. If they come your way, try them.

Secondly, if at all possible, obtain your snowdrops "in the green" when they are in active growth just after flowering, since dried bulbs can sometimes be difficult to establish.

G. nivalis (see photo on page 226) is called the common snowdrop. To my mind it is one of the most dainty plants with its narrow, gray-green leaves and elegantly shaped flowers at six inches in height. *G. n.* 'Flore Pleno' is a very double form. In my opinion it lacks the elfin quality of the *nivalis*, but makes a nice, short, compact plant. *G. n.* 'Viridapicis' is different by having green tips to the otherwise pure white outer segments as well as to the inner ones.

Iris

Of the many *Iris* species, either plants or bulbs, the small spring flowering bulbous irises from the open mountain slopes and alpine meadows of Russian Armenia, Turkey, Iran, and Iraq are the best for the smaller garden. They must be very tough to survive in this harsh climate. It never ceases to amaze me when I see these seemingly tender flowers braving the often foul early spring days. Even so, I would prefer to grow them in pots or pans in the protection of a frame or alpine house, where they can be enjoyed in safety and comfort, perhaps closer to eye level.

I. reticulata is regularly recommended for rock garden use. The plants are small enough, flowering at four to six inches tall. The flowers are large for the size of the plant, about two and a half inches across. However, the slender foliage will elongate to 14 to16 inches after the flowers fade. *I. reticulata* has dark velvety-purple blooms

236

with bright orange markings on the falls (certain petals) so often found on irises.

Here are a few varieties that offer a change in color.

I. r. 'Cantab' is pale blue.

I. r. 'Harmony' is royal blue.

I. r. 'Ida' is lobelia-blue.

I. r. 'J. S. Dijt' is a reddish purple.

I. r. 'Natascha' is almost white with a tinge of blue.

Narcissus

The daffodils (*Narcissus* species) are a large group with many choice and sometimes rare species that may be a little difficult to keep in cultivation. When in flower they are so captivating it is worth a certain amount of effort to acquire a few bulbs and try them, perhaps under controlled conditions for one season. The few varieties described below give an idea of their diversity and only their general cultural requirements.

N. asturiensis now and then will be found under the name *N. minimus.* It is a perfect miniature daffodil only four inches tall with narrow gray foliage and deep yellow flowers only an inch long. Coming from Spain, it enjoys spring moisture and well-drained soil for the summer.

N. bulbocodium (see photo on gallery page d) has the descriptive name of hoop petticoat daffodil owing to the wide funnel shape of the flower. It has a frilled edge. In the wild, it has a wide distribution in western France, Spain, Portugal, and North Africa, so it will vary in stature. Flowers range from deep to pale yellow. There is a remarkable white one too. Flowers are one to a stem and held almost horizontally. It naturally haunts the slopes and thin turf of the mountainsides where there is ample moisture in spring. The sites gradually dry as the season progresses. Try to discover the size and color of any bulbs you intend to purchase.

N. cyclamineus. I only mention this marvelous wild species should you see it described elsewhere and wish to grow it. I hope to forestall the frustration you may encounter when trying to buy this species. It is a wonderful little narcissus, owing its name to a

237

resemblance to the cyclamen flower. Like its namesake it has reflexed petals or perianth segments giving the flower a long, tubular look. The nodding flowers are carried singly on stems from six to 12 inches tall and are a lovely rich yellow.

If you find some bulbs, plant them in moist soil with partial shade and do not let them become totally dried out in the summer. Chances are you will see this plant described in books and possibly in the occasional bulb list. This species may well be endangered, but is not on the CITES List of Endangered Species (see below), so it is not forbidden to the horticultural trade. As the bulbs are difficult to buy, gardeners resort to growing them from seed, a long term project at the best of times. This can be extremely frustrating if at the end of the long road, they flower and are not what they are supposed to be. It is a fact of life that not all seeds turn out to be precisely what is written on the packet.

Current bulb catalogs list many attractive hybrid bulbs under the headings of *N. cyclamineus* and *N. triandrus*. Do not get too excited since delightful as these varieties might be, they are a bit tall for our small rock garden projects. There is no need to let this stop you from growing a few in pots if you wish.

What is CITES

CITES stands for the Convention on International Trade in Endangered Species of Wild Fauna and Flora. Once its full name is seen, the function is very clear. We all hear terrible stories of what goes on in the trade concerning endangered species of animals and there are similar stories of whole populations of plants and bulbs being almost wiped out.

CITES is a voluntary agreement, and those countries that join agree to adhere to the Convention, which does not take the place of national laws.

Today more than 30,000 species of animals and plants are accorded degrees of protection through a licensing system that controls the movement of selected species.

N. triandrus bears several creamy white flowers per stem and the height will vary from six to eight inches. Somehow these few extra inches don't seem to matter because the foliage is narrow and dark green. The individual flowers are pendant with a cup-shaped corona and the perianth segments are folded back, reflexed like a cyclamen.

There are many more *Narcissus* species, too numerous to be included. Some are too tall for our small garden project but are ideal for pot growing or the bulb frame. Furthermore, there are delightful dwarf hybrids listed in the bulb lists, so take a look at them and see if any fit your criteria. Be sure to check the ultimate size before you buy.

Puschkinia

Formerly known as *Puschkinia libanotica*, **Puschkinia scilloides** is similar to and closely related to *Scilla*. Growing to around four to six inches high with minimal foliage in early spring, it produces massive heads of blooms, each bloom half an inch in diameter. The flowers are china-blue, and each segment has a dark blue stripe along the center. It would be safe to plant this species under the same conditions as *Scilla siberica*.

Scilla

Scilla siberica has always been a great favorite of mine because it has the most beautiful shade of blue. It flowers very early here in Victoria. I always look for the deep glowing blue flowers on a neighbor's grassy bank. They remind me of the gentian, *Gentiana acaulis*, for they have the same wonderful blue. They carry up to five pendant, bell-shaped flowers per two- to four-inch stem; each flower measures up to three quarters of an inch long. By nature a naturalizing species ideal on gentle banks or in light woodland situations, it fits in well in the rock garden. Preferring a cool spot, it does not require the hot, dry summer treatment.

S. s. 'Spring Beauty' is often listed and is indeed a handsome plant, slightly larger than the species and said to be an even richer blue. *S. s.* 'Alba' is the pure white form and it is a choice and noble plant, but really! Why choose white when there is this gorgeous blue?

Tulipa

Tulipa species (tulip). Tulips come in a variety of sizes, but most are too large for small spaces. However, there is no reason why some of the dwarf species could not be planted in suitable surroundings in the fall. The flowers can be enjoyed during the spring. The bulbs must be allowed to continue the foliage growth until it dies down in its own

Tulipa tarda

time; they can then be stored in warm dry conditions. If it is not convenient to leave them in the rock garden for this process, dig them up in full leaf and replant elsewhere or pot them, continuing to water them until they go dormant. Then store them dry and plant in fall.

The tulips listed below are all safe to use where space is limited, if the foliage is allowed to ripen. Plant them in pots, in the rock garden, or in raised beds. Many of these tulips have attractive foliage, which can be green or gray and may appear in flat rosettes on the soil. It may be plain or wavy edged. Read descriptions carefully and select those that most appeal to you.

T. batalinii, pale yellow flowers on four-inch stems.

T. clusiana, a slender species up to 12 inches high whose white flowers are flushed with crimson on the outside.

T. humilis, a tiny species three to four inches high, magenta-pink with a yellow center.

T. kaufmanniana, called the waterlily tulip, with bright red and yellow, wide open flowers. There are many hybrids with a range of attractive colors.

T. linifolia, four- to six-inch stems, bright red flowers.

T. sprengeri, late flowering, 12 inches tall, scarlet-red.

T. tarda, four inches tall with several white flowers per stem, each with a large yellow center.

T. turkestanica, eight inches tall with small white flowers, several to a stem.

T. urumiensis, four to six inches tall with large yellow flowers.

Conclusion

I have excluded *Cyclamen*, *Corydalis*, and some *Erythronium* from this section (they are in the herbaceous section), mainly because they thrive better if bought when in growth and treated as herbaceous plants rather than as dry bulbs. Many popular genera were excluded for being too big for the scope of garden I am considering. There are other lovely genera you might wish to check. The smaller alliums and brodiaeas are sun lovers. *Fritillaria* is a huge genus full of lots of small and challenging species.

Add new plants with caution, for some are invasive. The English bluebell is a gorgeous sight in the English woods, and there it should have remained, for in my garden it is an absolute terror, even if it does flower in pretty shades of blue, pink, and white. They are attractive in the shrub border, but when they start popping up in the middle of one of the Kabschia saxifrages it is not appreciated. Just watch out for this pest, as it has even changed its name to slip under our guard. Originally it was called *Scilla nutans* and then *S. non-scripta*. Now it is found under the name *Hyacinthoides non-scripta*.

Another terror is *Muscari*, the grape hyacinth, with its pretty spikes of dense blue flowers. It seeds into every plant I have and is difficult to remove from choice alpine mounds. I would keep a wary eye on some of the *Chionodoxa*, too.

The author's rock garden.

11. Dwarf Trees and Shrubs

When it comes to trees for the alpine garden, the operative word is small. Whatever tree is planted can only be effective when it is in scale with the rest of the plants, and the rocks also. Clearly the tree cannot be several feet high and take up a lot of space because there is so little to spare.

Here in this section of *Plant Talk* you will find small woody species that fill the role of trees and shrubs. They are chosen because they are slow growing and have small stature and tiny foliage. Several of the genera described in the following list contain many more varieties and forms than I can fit into the space available. Very often the differences are so slight that they are difficult to describe in a few meaningful sentences. Therefore, let my examples lead you to study further varieties that you might consider as garden candidates.

During planting, one way to get an idea of how a tree might look in the future would be to place a stake marked with measured increments of height where a tree might be planted. This will show the height that the tree may achieve in a few years.

Another issue is the authenticity of the mountain landscape. If you are recreating part of an alpine scene, be sure to plant only those species that would be able to survive in alpine conditions, or, at least, alternative varieties that would pass for them. Use small-leaved plants because large-leaved deciduous trees or broad-leaved evergreens would be totally out of place at such altitudes.

In mountain forests, as the elevation climbs, some tree species are replaced by species better adapted to life in the harsher climate. As the elevation continues to rise, more changes occur. The trees become narrower and the branches become shorter and more flexible, enabling them to shed snow loads.

At even higher elevations, life becomes harder. The soil is thin and poor, resulting in very little annual growth. Freezing winter gales regularly kill growth buds, twigs, and leaves. Trees become stunted, contorted, shrubby, and dense. The accepted term for these trees is *krummholtz*, a very descriptive German word meaning 'crooked wood' or 'elfin timber.' Eventually those few trees that survive become prostrate carpets. Any growth exposed to the drying, freezing wind is instantly killed. At the highest elevations, trees cease to grow, as the environment is just too hostile for them to survive.

Ecological patterns are interesting, but how do they relate to the rock garden? I hope that the observations offered in this chapter will help you to consider and select suitable trees. The tree species found in alpine conditions are normally the same evergreen species found in the lower subalpine forests. Very few deciduous trees are found at this altitude since they cannot withstand the harsh climate.

Evergreen Trees

It is tempting to plant an attractive pyramidal dwarf evergreen tree, and I have succumbed on more than one occasion and used such plants. They have such an appealing shape. Unfortunately they suggest a tall, stately forest specimen rather than a timberline dwarf. Such a specimen would never survive at the higher elevations.

Where the rock garden is not designed to represent any particular ecological zone, wonderful effects can be created using conical evergreens. A dwarf spruce planted beside an outcropping rock, not on top but at the base, makes the small rock appear to be a towering cliff.

It is usually more effective if the outcrop is at the lower reaches of the garden, where upright trees suggest the forest. As we move upward the trees should take on more rounded, shrublike shapes. Alternatively, there are informal and irregular shape varieties suggestive of the krummholz.

Finally, nearing the summit, resist the temptation to stick a nice upright tree on top. Instead, choose from among lovely low, flat, creeping specimens.

If there is an impression that the small rock garden project should be filled with lots of trees, it is not intended. I know that many small rock gardeners will be hard pressed to find space for even one tree or shrub. There is no law that says that trees are required. In my garden I keep one or two trees in pots and sink them, pot and all, into the ground. They stay in place winter and summer until they need to be repotted into larger pots.

Dwarf Conifers for Small Projects

Abies

***Abies* species.** *Abies balsamea* 'Nana' is a fine choice. (It may be listed as *A. b. Hudsonia* and there is still discussion among the experts suggesting that there may be some difference in the needle structure, hence the two names.) Either plant is fine; just be sure that the plant you buy is truly slow growing.

It was discovered in the White Mountains of New Hampshire and has been in cultivation for many years. It is hardy and makes an attractive flattened globe shaped bush with dark green needles. I had a very satisfactory specimen in a trough measuring 18 by 24 by 6 inches, which happily survived for over ten years before it got untidy from starvation. In my West Coast rock garden a 12-year old specimen is now 12 inches high and 24 inches across. It looks natural where it is but it would not pass for krummholz.

There are species of *Abies* (balsam or true firs) that produce a few dwarf variants, so if you are an *Abies* fan, keep in regular contact with specialist nurseries who periodically have rare forms for sale.

Chamaecyparis

Chamaecyparis, or false cypress, is mainly a genus of tall forest trees from North America and Japan. All have produced some excellent dwarfs. For our purpose the Japanese *C. obtusa*, the Hinoki cypress of gardens, is the best. These are shrubs with handsome, dark green foliage. Branches spread out in flat, fan-shaped tiers. The selections listed below will help when searching lists. There are many forms of this plant listed because it is a popular collector's plant: be on your guard, for collecting it is contagious!

Chamaecyparis obtusa 'Juniperoides' in the Wave Hill rock garden collection.

C. o. 'Caespitosa', the smallest and slowest growing, is a dense, bun-shaped bush with crowded foliage.

C. o. 'Intermedia' has dark-green foliage and is slightly conical.

C. o. 'Juniperoides' is a great little dwarf with a rounded shape and flattened, slightly opened branches.

245

These are examples of the smallest and most compact varieties for pot, trough or other situations where slow growth is important. Mature plants are hard to find and can be expensive. Regrettably, they are not plants for every climate for they suffer from wind burn and definitely need protection from severe cold.

Juniperus communis 'Compressa'

Juniperus

***Juniperus communis* 'Compressa'** is an old favorite as it can be relied on to remain small for years. It is not reliably hardy in all climates but makes an excellent subject for alpine houses, pot growing, troughs, and special projects. Its attractions are the tiny, prickly leaves, the narrowly fastigiate habit, and the sharp pointed tips.

Picea

Picea, or spruce, is common in the mountains here and in Europe.

Picea abies. *The Norway spruce, P. abies,* has provided us with a full range of dwarfs and semi dwarfs ranging from upright to broadly spreading, mounding, or globose cushion forms. As a group they all have the typical spruce needle-like leaves, a crowded branch system, and the typical conical red-brown buds.

Picea abies 'Little Gem'

P. a. 'Clanbrassiliana' is a small, dense, flat-topped bush, eventually wider than high.

P. a. 'Gregoryana' is a good old variety similar to *echiniformis*

P. a. 'Little Gem' is a dense globe, slightly flattened, with tiny

needles. It will live in a trough for several years and remain small, but in the the garden it will, in time, grow to two feet tall and two to three feet across.

P. glauca, the white spruce, offers the delightful 'Pixie', a perfect pointed dwarf tree that is ideal for the trough. *P. g.* 'Echiniformis' is a slow growing hedgehog shaped cushion.

P. mariana **'Nana',** a dwarf form of the northern black spruce, is highly rated as a dwarf shrub for the rock garden. It has gray-green leaves and is low and compact. It is a good plant for krummholtz.

Picea glauca 'Pixie'

Pinus

It is unfortunate that *Pinus*, a great genus with a definite presence in the high alpine regions, has so few dwarf forms. I know there are dwarf forms out there, but dwarf is a relative term. If and when you decide to go after really dwarf pines you will need time to do some reading. The subject is more involved than can be covered in this small overview, for some of these pines are exceedingly rare and hard to find or to grow.

A forty-year old specimen of Mugo pine, like this one in Roxie Gevjan's garden, makes a low but broad carpet.

247

P. mugo, the mountain pine, is a variable species with a wide distribution throughout Europe, so there are different names associated with it. They will be listed as *mughus* or var. *mugo, pumilio,* or 'Compacta'. Then there will be horticultural names such as 'Gnom', 'Humpy', and 'Mops', as well as others. All will eventually take up too much space and have to be moved. Meanwhile, why not resort to growing them in pots and plunging the pot in the rock garden or the raised bed. Then, at least you will have the enjoyment of them until that day dawns when they no longer fit into their allotted space.

Tsuga

Tsuga canadensis, the Eastern hemlock, offers a wide range of sizes and habits, as well as diverse foliage colors. There are true miniature trees, mounding specimens, and completely prostrate plants. Several are ideally suited to trough work, rock gardens, and the raised bed. The choice depends upon the role the gardener wishes them to fulfill. A small treelike shape sets a perfect focus in a trough, while one of the mounding types will fit nicely into the conventional rock garden. Nothing is as attractive as the long, flat-to- the-ground branches of the creeping kinds flowing down from a raised bed.

Protect them from excessively hot sun and drying winds in summer. They are quite tough under winter conditions .

T. c. 'Cole's Prostrate' lies flat on the ground. Its typical hemlock twigs follow the contours. As the plant grows and spreads, the center of the plant becomes almost bare, displaying intricate branch patterns. It is an excellent plant, but too large for troughs or small rock gardens.

T. c. 'Jeddeloh' contrasts in form to 'Jervis' by growing into a graceful flat-topped little tree with horizontally tiered branches with drooping tips. Maybe it is not the ideal candidate to portray the austere alpine atmosphere, but it makes a wonderful picture when it is featured in a sizeable trough, and it makes a good pot specimen too.

T. c. 'Jervis' was found by Mr. Guy Nearing, the famous rhododendron breeder from New Jersey. It is an excellent rock garden subject with a slow, growing upright form. The irregular branch patterns give the plant an informal shape.

T. c. 'Minuta'; 'Pygmaea'; and 'Hussii' are among the dwarfest and slowest growing hemlocks and sometimes are hard to obtain, but where a really dwarf tree with congested branches and tiny needles is required, any of these will fill the bill. They are effective because they look like species that might occur naturally at the very limits of the treeline. Be on your guard and make sure the varieties are truly dwarf and slow growing. Even though they are hardy, local climate can have disastrous effects on some dwarf conifers.

Deciduous Dwarf Trees and Shrubs

Is a dwarf tree really a shrub? What is the difference? A tree is defined as a woody plant with a single trunk, while a shrub can have many stems branching from the base and no obvious main trunk. As long as the plants we use in alpine gardens to represent trees are convincing in appearance, it matters little whether they are properly called trees or shrubs.

Most of the upright dwarf trees available to us, such as birch, willow, elm, maple, and mountain ash, may have the shape of a miniature tree and will, in time, grow three to four feet high and wide.

Rather than ban all trees from the small landscape, you can use a young plant and dig it up when it gets too big. Alternatively, grow it in a series of larger pots until it shows signs of distress caused by a solid mass of roots.

Evergreen shrubs add another dimension to the winter scene with their shapes and colors. A few deciduous trees and shrubs provide a bit of fall color to the rock garden, while others provide spring and summer flowers. Last but not least are the broad-leaved evergreens that contribute both flowers and evergreen leaves.

Betula

Betula nana. The birches are picturesque in any landscape and the rock garden is no exception. *B. nana* is a dwarf which will eventually grow into a twiggy mass. There is nothing more appealing than its reddish stems clothed with perfectly miniature birch leaves. However, once it starts to grow in earnest it can lose much of its charm, and pruning just adds to the problem. With repeated pruning it can develop a hedgehog shape with no more character than a green mound. When this happens, it is time to remove the plant and replace it with something smaller.

Salix

There are always willows (*Salix* species) growing on the mountains, from the lowest elevation to the very highest limit of plant life. We are not concerned with the trees of the lower elevations, but as the willows ascend the mountainside they become shorter and more shrublike until finally they resemble those incredibly colored species we see in tantalizing photographs taken on the tundra.

Salix hasta 'Werhahnnii' is close in habit to *S. lanata* 'Stuartii' but with green leaves. The catkins first show as little wooly balls but mature and lengthen as they develop. Stamens gradually turn yellow, while younger twigs are mahogany.

Salix lanata, S. l. 'Stuartii', and *S. lapponum* could all be called woolly willows because they all have similar silvery, downy leaves. The strong, woody stems are upright. All have attractive catkins in the spring: there are creamy white catkins on *S. lanata* and silky gray ones on *S. laponicum*. Both species are great favorites of mine; just bear in mind that they will eventually attain three feet in height.

S. 'Boydii'. Since I have already stepped over the line by introducing taller plants, I might as well tell you of the "ultimate willow" though I risk frustrating readers. This willow is almost impossible to buy in North America. It is not a rare plant in cultivation elsewhere, so if we create a demand for it, our nurseries will soon provide it. If ever you come across a supply of this fabled plant, buy it and call me!

It is a natural wild hybrid between two local species in Scotland and was discovered by botanist W. B. Boyd back in the 1880's. Luckily, he introduced a few cuttings into cultivation and from those the plant has survived and found its way to many parts of the world. It is amazing that this particular hybrid has never been found again.

The plant has stiff, upright, gnarled branches that slowly develop into a dwarf tree. The leaves are appealing in shape and color. The dark gray-green upper surface is deeply veined (reticulated) and silvery white beneath. It is the perfect trough plant where there is enough depth of soil to retain some moisture, a good pot plant, and a sure prize winner at the show bench.

250

S. herbacea, S. retusa and *S. reticulata* are attractive, small, low, flat species from the mountains. They creep about among the rocks and late melting snow patches. In the garden they are effective if given flat rocks to drape over where they show their open branch structure between the tiny leaves. The leaves are rounded. *S. herbacea* and *S. retusa* have shiny oval, yellow leaves while the leaves of *S. reticulata* have a dark upper surface heavily netted with veins.

Sorbus

Sorbus reducta is the right name for this little reduced mountain ash relative. It is a thicket of suckering branches up to two feet tall with the red-stemmed, pinnate leaves that are typical of the family. Sprays of small white flowers are followed by clusters of red berries. Do not overlook the lovely bronze and reddish fall color.

Ulmus

Ulmus parvifolia, the Chinese elm, has produced several truly dwarf forms much favored by bonsai specialists, as several Japanese named cultivars will confirm. They are truly treelike with a tiny trunk and perfect miniature leaves. *U. p.* 'Hokkiado' and *U. p.* 'Seiju' are two popular varieties. Check out the nursery lists and select what appeals to you, but bear in mind they may eventually put on growth. In Zones 7 and 8, I have seen some pretty big specimens that were supposed to be dwarfs.

Ulmus parvifolia

Dwarf Evergreen Flowering Shrubs

Evergreen flowering shrubs, as their name suggests, provide form and shape during winter months. They provide contrast to the needles of dwarf conifers and the brown foliage of sleeping perennials.

There is great variety within this loose category of plants. Foliage size, shape, and color are only part. There are drought-loving species with silvery and gray leaves. These plants contrast with the dark greens of small woodland and high mountain, acid-loving species.

251

For color there is little that can compete with the masses of flowers produced by dwarf rhododendrons.

Andromeda

Andromeda polifolia. Called bog rosemary because the leaves resemble true rosemary, this is the plant to use to suggest a boggy area. It certainly can inhabit bogs, but also does well under rock garden conditions. Put it in a little shade where you have added extra peat to the soil. Given moist, peaty soil, it will tolerate quite a lot of sun and may well grow into a bush two feet tall.

A. p. 'Compacta' is from Japan. As the name suggests, it is much smaller, normally growing only to six to eight inches, and spreading very slowly. The striking foliage has a leathery appearance. About an inch long, the narrow leaves are gray-green on the upper surface and silvery on the underside. Clusters of pink, urn-shaped flowers are borne at the end of the stems.

A. p. 'Compacta Alba' has similar habit with pure white flowers and green foliage.

In recent catalogs, several striking cultivars from Japan are described, all about eight inches high, and are worth considering.

Arcterica

Arcterica nana is a tiny evergreen shrublet ideal for use in a miniature landscape designed to represent a cool, northern, shady woodland. The plant is very hardy under cool peaty conditions, but not in dry, sunny troughs. It is happy to creep among rocks or raised beds and usually attains a height of two to three inches. Under favorable conditions it may go a bit taller. It spreads modestly by way of underground stems. It forms a mat of short woody stems clothed with small glossy-green leaves, followed in spring by a crop of urn-shaped, creamy white flowers. This little plant has had several previous generic names including *Andromeda* and *Pieris,* but the name now seems secure.

Convolvulus

Convolulus cneorum. Before you read further, let me say that this is not a weed although it is related to bindweeds which are terrible pests. *C. cneorum* is a shrubby, sun loving, shimmering, silvery-leaved plant from the Mediterranean. Depending on cultural conditions, it can grow up to two feet or so. The leaves are two inches long. The white, pink-flushed flowers are in umbels at the tips of the growth. Each bloom is an inch and a half across. The flowering time ranges from June to September. It is so beautiful that I wanted to bring it to your attention. It is only reliably hardy to Zone 7. Even there it occasionally gets frozen. For a potted specimen in an alpine house or other protected housing it is a great plant.

Daphne

Daphne species. The daphnes are among the most desirable of the true alpine plants, for the rock garden types are among the most beautiful of the crevice dwelling, tight little mats. Some attain venerable age.

There is a wild daphne to fill every situation the rock gardener may have. Certainly the trough grower can use several types. There are daphnes for the alpine house, where they can be placed in the rock garden under glass or grown in pots. There is a daphne or two for raised beds and, of course, for the rock garden itself.

The daphnes have a deserved reputation for being tricky subjects to cultivate and, until recently, hard to find. Some are still rare, but their recent resurgence has promoted the formation of a society devoted to them and the noticeable increase of varieties available in the nurseries.

Some of them are high alpine plants and as such are exacting about their climate. We cannot do much about the weather despite our efforts. By including daphne in this chapter I may well frustrate some gardeners (again). On the other hand, by not including them, I could deprive others of a great treat. They are handsome plants with a neat habit and lots of colorful sweet smelling flowers. They are great fun to collect and try to grow.

D. arbuscula is a delightful little semi-prostrate evergreen shrublet that may reach six inches high depending on the form or variety, for some are taller. It looks perfect in a raised trough garden where the small, dark green, shiny leaves can be easily enjoyed. Sweet smelling, deep rose-pink flowers begin to appear in summer. They grow in terminal clusters of three to eight individual, half-inch long, tubular flowers.

D. cneorum, the popular garland flower, has trailing stems and huge heads of fragrant pink flowers. It is just too much of a good thing in limited space. Luckily, there are dwarf varieties we can use. *D. c.* var. *pygmaea*, only three inches tall, is compact and a slow spreader. It has deep red-pink fragrant flowers. It is another plant for the trough garden or small, choice rock garden. For those who want it, there is a white flowered form usually listed as *D. c.* var. *pygmaea* 'Alba'.

D. jasminea is a low mat of radiating woody branches clothed with short, blue-gray leaves. Flowers are white and tubular shaped, opening at the mouth to a four-pointed star. The touch of color in the white flowers comes from the red to purple tinting of the tube. It too is nicely fragrant. This species is considered hardy and may do well if planted with lots of drainage through the winter. Plant it in a sunny spot in the rock garden or raised bed and add some extra humus to the soil. It is an excellent plant for the careful alpine house operator.

Daphne petraea

D. petraea and its superior variety *D. p.* 'Grandiflora' are considered by expert alpine gardeners to be the finest of the daphnes. A good sized specimen in full flower in a pot is a sight to remember; imagine what it must be like to see a whole limestone cliff face studded with ancient mats smothered by masses of deep pink flowers. In the wild it is limited to a restricted area of the Italian Alps where it inhabits cracks and crannies in full sun. The plant is a bushlet composed of short, stout branches clothed with tiny, oval, dark green leaves. In my garden it flowers during June and July, and, as with other daphnes, the flower heads hold clusters of tubular, heavily fragrant flowers.

It is a demanding plant and perhaps it belongs in pot in a well managed alpine house. Plant it in a lean, Spartan soil mixture and carefully manage the watering. In a trough it will grow best when wedged between two pieces of tufa. Use a trough big enough to contain a good volume of soil to be sure the roots are not continually drying out. Although it is a cliff dweller used to the scorching sun, the roots are deep within rock crevices where they never experience fluctuations of temperature and moisture.

254

D. retusa is an Asian species, from regions including China and Tibet, where it occurs in the mountains in rocky areas and pinewoods. It will eventually grow into a densely mounded shrub up to two feet tall, with a similar spread. The leaves are a lustrous deep green with a noticeable notch at the apex. Each leaf has a slightly rolled margin. The dense heads of purple-pink buds open into white flowers that are enhanced by the deeper colors of unopened blossoms nearby.

It is not considered that hardy, and Zone 6 is listed as the northern limit. I grew it as a pot plant for several years, but it is not a happy pot plant. As a rule as it needs more root space. I planted it in my rock garden in full sun in my ordinary rock garden soil and it has, over ten years, attained the prescribed two feet. However, hot as the sun may be in my Zone 8 garden, I am sure it does not compare with the heat in many other gardens, therefore I recommend planting it where it can enjoy some protection from full sun.

Pieris

For a small planting in shade or partial shade, consider smaller forms of **Pieris japonica**. This species enjoys organic soil, somewhat moist and slightly acid. It is normally hardy from Zone 5 to Zone 8, and under ideal conditions is successful in Zone 4.

The plants form green bushes of tightly packed dark green leaves and form solid small bushes. Some varieties produce typical white lily of the valley flowers. There are several dwarf cultivars:

P. j. 'Bisbee Dwarf' is an older variety with an attractive twist to each leaf and its beauty is not always spoiled by flowers. The variety is upright in growth habit.

P. j. 'Bonsai' is one of the smallest reputed to make a mound some 12 inches tall. Under favorable conditions it will exceed 12 inches.

P. j. 'Cavatine' will attain 18 inches to two feet and the red new growth makes it a valued addition where space permits.

P. j. 'Debutante' grows to around 12 inches.

P. j. 'Nana', despite the implication in the name, will form a dense globe of dark green and grow to two or three feet.

New cultivars regularly appear in lists so check for the variety that best fits your requirements.

Rhododendron

The idea of making a garden planted entirely with dwarf rhododendrons frequently returns to me. I envision a slightly sloping site, maybe with a little undulation here and there, with flowing mounds of dwarf rhododendrons gently growing together to form a carpet. The idea is reluctantly put aside for lack of garden space.

The word dwarf, when applied to rhododendrons, is relative, since they are large shrubs, some of which are capable of assuming treelike proportions. Therefore, a plant that is, let us say, under three or four feet can be considered a dwarf to rhododendron growers but is not dwarf enough for the alpine gardener with limited space.

Deciduous *Rhododendron* 'Pink Diamond' has bright pink blossoms in early spring.

Famous plant hunters past and present have written appealing descriptions of hills and moorlands of the Himalayas where dwarf rhododendrons clothe the ground as does the heather on the hills and dales of Great Britain. This sounds encouraging and just strengthens my desire for such a garden, until further reading reveals that this shrubby carpet of plants can be two or three feet high. Furthermore, individual plants spread by several feet, forming an almost impenetrable mass.

Mr. Peter A. Cox, in his book, *The Smaller Rhododendrons*, describes a plan for incorporating a few rhododendron specimens into a relatively small garden. He suggests informally dotting them about in a proposed rock garden site to provide interesting contours where none exist. Then he suggests using the spaces between them as protected spots for companion plants comparable to those found in the natural habitat of these rhododendrons. Lots of great plants spring to mind: small primulas, gentians, small, non-invasive vacciniums, and cassiopes.

If undertaking a garden based upon this strategy, take care that no herbaceous plants are allowed to overshadow, crowd, or invade the foliage of the rhododendrons. The rhodies will resent it and show it by defoliating, or become leggy and hardly producing any flowers.

Truly dwarf rhododendrons have strong appeal to the rock gardener because they are neat and compact. The foliage and branch

structure are all in scale. Above all, rhododendrons flower prolifically. Despite the disadvantages of ultimate size, many species make excellent subjects for pot grown specimens and they are delightful in a substantial trough. Over the years I have seen several collections of dwarf rhododendrons grown in pots and they are very appealing. Even when not in flower, the contrasts of the various foliage colors and shapes plus the growth habits of each individual species all add to the appeal. Such a collection will require regular care and maintenance plus periodic repotting. Containers should be displayed to their best advantage, much as bonsai trees are featured nicely and also housed with a modicum of protection from sun and wind.

Site and Soil Requirements. The basic rock garden soil recommended in the chapter on soils will be adequate for rhododendrons providing it does not contain heavy concentrations of lime. Where the native soil contains large amounts of lime, raised beds of specially imported lime-free prepared soil is the only option. The Alpen Rose of Europe, *R. hirsutum*, occurs in limestone areas and is lime tolerant, but it is not the easiest plant to grow in any soil.

While a well-drained site is necessary, it should not be allowed to reach drought conditions, as the rhododendrons will not tolerate prolonged drought. If dry soil is expected, prepare the site with deep cultivation to allow good root penetration, away from the drying surface. An addition of extra peat or other organic material will further aid moisture retention. Mulching is a wise practice but only do it when the soil is thoroughly moistened. Do not overdo the depth because rhododendrons can be suffocated by heavy mulching.

Dwarf rhododendrons enjoy full sun under all but the most extreme conditions and are surprisingly cold hardy. They make excellent subjects for open northern slopes, if there are no overhanging trees, since heavy shade or root competition will ruin the compact character of the plants and seriously limit the number and quality of the blooms.

R. calostrotum ssp. keleticum for a long time was referred to as *R. radicans*, and, without a doubt, it is one of the best for a partially shaded trough, although it will take sun if not neglected. It is neatness

257

itself with tiny, shiny, dark green leaves with brown indumentum on the underside.

Quite variable in habit, it ranges from very low and creeping to low mounds. The smallest varieties, having tiny leaves no longer than a quarter of an inch, are favored by many rock gardeners. Nurseries usually indicate any special forms they offer. The flowers are solitary with short stems are an open-funnel shape, about an inch across. The color can be depths of purple to a rosy-purple.

R. campylogynum is a variable species. Many forms are available, but try to obtain one of the low creeping or low mounding types. I particularly like *R. c.* Myrtilloides Group, which is widely recognized as one of the smaller varieties. Eventually it may grow too large for a small project, but in the confines of pots and troughs it will remain dwarf long enough to justify itself. Moreover, once it has served in one capacity, it can always be planted somewhere else.

Regardless of the eventual stature, I will always have one of these around because the small, plum-colored, thimble-shaped (campanulate) flowers on their short stems really appeal to me. It is easy to become attached to this species and to start collecting plants that reflect the range of colors from deep purple through the reds to pink or white.

I find that this species does well if given protection from drying winds and scorching sun, since in Upper Burma and Southwest Yunnan it is accustomed to moist moorlands.

R. camtschaticum, despite the name, has a much wider distribution than Kamtchatka and Siberia. It is also found from Northern Japan to Alaska. It is not a readily available plant nor a species seen all that often in gardens. I have never grown it myself, but a friend living nearby is growing a plant in a round trough that I have admired for several years, and his success prompts me to recommend it. It seems very content where my friend grows it, in partial shade cast by the house. The plant requires a balance of sun and a cool moist compost, and, since the trough is easy to move, he can adjust conditions as required.

It makes a fine trough plant with a prostrate habit and gains very little height. The branches root as they creep along the surface. The flat, open flowers are carried on short, erect stems, usually three to four inches high. It is found in shades of rosy purple with prominent stamens and darker blotches on the petals.

258

R. impeditum is too good to leave out, even though under good conditions it will grow to two feet or so. Under trough or pot conditions it will grow slowly, which prolongs the desired stature. Best described as a pleasingly shaped compact mound of small leaves, it is enhanced by the gray effect of the combined green of the upper surface of the leaf and the tiny scales on the underside.

The flowers are often described as purple, but I see it as a very bright blue-purple. Carried in terminal clusters, they often appear in such abundance that the foliage is almost obscured. This species usually flowers in April to May or longer, and it has the reputation of disliking heat.

R. keiskei from Japan is a yellow-flowered species far too tall and spindly for the alpine gardener. Fortunately there are dwarf forms available. *R. k.* var. *ozawae* 'Yaku Fairy' is extremely popular and is one of the low-growing, ground-hugging varieties. In time and under favorable conditions, it can make a mound up to six inches high. The small green leaves form a solid carpet over the flat branches, making it the perfect choice for the trough garden. The lemon-yellow flowers appear in April and May and almost completely hide the leaves. Individual blooms are an inch and three quarters across and held in trusses of two to five.

This plant is used to make many hybrids and several are just within our size requirement, although eventuallythey grow to 18 inches. Check out these USA hybrids: 'Ginny Gee' with pink, white tinged flowers; 'Too Bee' sometimes called 'Wee Bee' with its pendant rose-pink blooms; and the popular 'Patty Bee' in clear yellow.

The renowned Scottish nursery, Glendoick Gardens Ltd., owned and operated by the Cox family, have long been known for producing really dwarf hybrids, and they still do. It is an enjoyable experience to study one of their lists of dwarf rhododendrons. There is a series of dwarf and semi dwarf hybrids named after birds: 'Razorbill', 'Snipe', 'Ptarmigan', and 'Pipit' are a few that readily come to mind.

There are many beguiling small rhododendrons to consider, and it is great fun to check them out. Take tours and see as many as you can, and check the books and lists. Alas, we must exercise a bit of restraint as we make our choices, for space is always too limited in alpine gardens.

The alpine region of Mt. Ranier.

Resources

I hope this book has whetted your appetite for more information about alpine plants and rock gardening. You may want to learn more about unusual plants that will do well in your garden, or find local sources for them. Perhaps you would like to visit established public and private rock gardens, read specialized publications, or even do some plant exploration with a group of fellow enthusiasts.

NARGS. These things and more are available to members of the North American Rock Garden Society (NARGS). Membership is open to anyone who is captivated by alpine and rock gardening.

The American Rock Garden Society was formed in 1944 by a small group of rock gardeners in New York. The society grew rapidly over the years, so in 1994 the name was changed to The North American Rock Garden Society to reflect a growing membership across North America, including Canada.

Today there are 35 chapters of the society, five of which are in Canada. These semi-independent groups have their own executive boards and run their own programs. The NARGS has a slate of officers, directors of the board, and managers who contribute to the smooth running of the society, providing valuable services to the members. As I write this synopsis, the society has a total of 4,500 members in the USA, Canada, and thirty other nations.

The purpose of the society is to encourage and promote:

- The cultivation, conservation, and knowledge of rock garden plants, and their value, habits, and geographical distribution;
- Interest in good design and construction of rock gardens;
- Meetings and exhibitions;
- Plant exploration and introduction of new species and forms;
- Study of history and literature on the subject;
- Acquaintance between members resulting in mutual exchange of experience and knowledge.

Membership in NARGS affords privileges such as:

- NARGS Book Service, which offers discounts on new books and good buys on society publications.

⇛ A lending library, arranged with the Pennsylvania Horticultural Society, which permits you to borrow any book on the library's circulating list.

⇛ A well-stocked slide and video library, maintained by NARGS.

⇛ The society's journal, *Rock Garden Quarterly*, which is published every three months. A subscription comes with your annual membership. The articles and color pictures are contributed by members around the world on a wide range of subjects involving alpines and other wildflowers. The advertisements are carefully monitored and provide excellent sources for rock gardeners; many of them will not be found elsewhere.

Local chapters in Canada and the United States meet throughout the year for lectures, exchanges of plants and seeds, plant shows, and garden visits. NARGS sponsors a lecture tour whereby recognized international authorities speak to local chapters. There are educational annual meetings held in fascinating locations, often in mountainous states. NARGS' Winter Study Weekends are held annually, usually about the end of February, one in the East and one in the West. These weekend meetings are designed to chase the winter blues away and provide horticultural education at the same time.

NARGS maintains an up-to-date website (**www.nargs.org**) full of helpful information and links to many other organizations of interest. Obtain membership information on the website or by writing to:

Executive Secretary
NARGS
P.O. Box 67
Millwood, NY 10546

Rock Garden Books

A great deal can be learned from books on rock gardening. There are hundreds of them to choose from, some dating back to the early days of rock gardening. These are often written in the Victorian style of the early 1900's. If you find them heavy going, there are later books written in the more speedy modern style. There are books translated from European languages and also books by American authors.

It was not all that many years ago that nearly all rock gardening books were written in Great Britain and Europe. Consequently, all our knowledge was then based on European practices. That was not necessarily a bad thing except that, in parts of North America, many of these European principles do not work. More often than not, the problem is the failure of the European alpine plants to prosper in the more rigorous climates on this side of the Atlantic.

Magnificent rock gardens on the grand scale appeared across the land, built by expert landscapers. Hundreds of plants were imported from Europe for authentic planting schemes.

Long ago at a famous alpine nursery in England, I worked on one alpine plant order from a New Jersey customer. The order was so big that it took all the staff a week to collect and pack it. Once the plants were shipped off to New Jersey, the owner of the nursery went there too, to supervise their planting. Despite all the attention by several experts, many of the European alpines failed to prosper.

In North American gardens, the rocks, or the lack of them, can be a problem. A great deal of effort and expense is sometimes expended seeking the right rock, sometimes with disappointing results. Another problem is shade, for many gardeners live and garden in deciduous woodland. Every gardener knows the value of shade during the summer, but many have also learned that alpine and rock plants are not among those that thrive in it.

There were North American gardeners who, after experiencing these woes, began to modify the design for their rock gardens and to grow plants that were better equipped for the local climate.

Fortunately, several of these pioneers wrote articles and books about their experiences, so today we have valuable guidance in creating the North American rock garden. Of course, there can be no single rock garden design in a region that comprises so many widely differing climates and kinds of topography.

My Favorite Garden Books

These eclectic books are always close at hand. Often I will skim through one or two, just looking at the pictures, and I always stumble across something interesting. The encyclopedia, of course, is a must and I use it as the authority for the majority of plant names.

A few of these favorites are quite old now and may be hard to find or replace, but the content is timeless.

Natural Rock Gardening, by B.H.B. Symon Jeune, was published in 1932 by *Country Life*. London. This book is for those who want to thoroughly understand the anatomy of outcropping rocks before building an outcrop, however small. I am not suggesting that you try to replicate the stratification of rocks below the ground level, but the instructions for surface layout are excellent. There are diagrams on the natural positioning of rocks and some helpful rock garden plans. All the black and white photographs are excellent and inspirational.

Alpine & Rock Gardening is Volume 2 in a series called *The Ullswater Library*, founded by Viscount Ullswater, and was published in 1961. The authors are a group of prominent British rock gardeners. The subjects range widely, and the large and detailed portion covering rock garden construction was written by Will Ingwersen, my principal mentor. Once again, the black and white photographs are extremely helpful.

My copies of these two books are showing their age and falling apart, but I regularly look through them.

The Rock Garden and its Plants, by Graham Stuart Thomas OBE VMH DHM VMM, was published by Sagapress, Inc. and Timber Press Inc. in 1989. The author was for many years Gardens Consultant to the National Trust of Britain. He was a recognized authority on many topics, particularly old roses. I still read his rose books as if they were novels. I enjoy the history within the pages.

Long ago, as the new head gardener to Mrs. Constance Spry, I was responsible for her collection of old roses, a famous collection that had been put together by Graham Thomas. I was incredibly fortunate that he was retained as a consultant, and so I got to work with him. He knew those roses so well he could identify them from the leaves alone.

His rock garden book is one I constantly return to as it is so full of wonderful information. The subtitle is *From Grotto to Alpine House* and it covers the history of rock gardening. I think it is a must for the rock gardener, but to get the best from this book it might be better to delay reading it until you are really hooked on rock gardens.

Rock Gardening, a manual on rock gardens and alpine plants by H. Lincoln Foster, was first published in 1968 by Houghton Mifflin Company, Boston. *Cuttings from a Rock Garden*, by H. Lincoln and Laura Louise Foster, a book of essays and plant portraits, was published in 1990 by Atlantic Monthly Press, New York, and reprinted in 1997. These two books are a distillation of all the first-hand experience gained by two great gardeners who were high among the pioneers of rock gardening in the United States. They are ideal for anyone considering growing alpines in North America.

The Encyclopaedia of Alpines, first published by the Alpine Garden Society in 1994, is a huge masterpiece in two large volumes. It was well edited and the contributing writers are all well known experts in their own fields. Unfortunately it still maintains a high price, so perhaps purchase of this reference work can come later.

My list of favorite books would not be complete without two by Will Ingwersen. His *Manual of Alpine Plants* was published by Will Ingwersen & Dunnsprint Ltd., Great Britain, in 1978. While it has been in print for well over 30 years and is getting out of date with current plant nomenclature and new plant introductions, there is hardly a day that goes by that I do not consult this book.

Alpines, by Will Ingwersen, was published by John Murray Publishers Ltd., London, in 1991. Will never saw the bound book, for he died shortly after finishing the manuscript. In this book, unlike his manual, the plants are not listed in alphabetical order. Rather, the book is written as a pleasurable browse, not as a complete reference book. There is an index for those seeking rapid information on specific plants.

Journals

Despite all the wonderful alpine gardening books, I could not survive for long without my collection of journals. There are three sets I try to maintain, as each provides special knowledge and advice.

The *Rock Garden Quarterly*, the Bulletin of the North American Rock Garden Society, is a must for gardeners in North America. It is a balanced mixture of topics with accounts of plants in the wild, rock plants in cultivation, rock garden design, and personal experiences with growing plants from many states (see http://www.nargs.com).

The Alpine Gardener is the quarterly bulletin of the Alpine Garden Society (AGS) of Great Britain. Membership in the group is welcomed from anywhere in the world. This journal maintains a high standard of excellence. It contains information for beginners as well as experts. The plant names are up to date and new introductions are featured along with top quality photographs. For more information, go to http://www.alpinegardensociety.org/ online.

The Rock Gardener is the journal of the Scottish Rock Garden Club and is equal in quality and content to *The Alpine Gardener*. The climate of Scotland is unique and the Scots are able to grow many plants others have great difficulty with. Scotland has its own widely recognized rock garden experts who regularly contribute articles. For more information, go to http://www.srgc.org.uk/ online.

Annotated Bibliography and Book List

There are hundreds more books written about rock and alpine gardens, covering a wide spectrum, so I have selected a few that focus on the subjects discussed in this book.

Balzer, Donna. *The Prairie Rock Garden*. Calgary, Canada. Red Deer Press, 2000. A great book for cold climate gardeners, it is full of excellent ideas and very well illustrated.

Beckett, Kenneth A. *Growing Under Glass.* London. Mitchell Beazley Publishers, 1981, in cooperation with the Royal Horticultural Society.

Carl, Joachim. *Miniature Gardens*. Germany,1978 and later published in English by Timber Press Inc., Portland. This book deals mainly with troughs and planters and small rock gardens.

Davidson, B. LeRoy. *Lewisias.* Portland, OR. Timber Press, 2000.

Fingerut, Joyce, and Rex Murfitt. *Creating and Planting Garden Troughs.* Wayne, PA. B. B. Mackey Books, 1999.

Grey-Wilson, C. *A Manual of Alpine and Rock Garden Plants.* Portland, OR. Timber Press, 1989.

Heath, Royton E. *Rock Plants for Small Gardens*. England. Collingridge Books, 1957. Heath is a prolific English rock garden writer always worth reading. Although his books seem somewhat dated now, many of his ideas can still motivate the reader.

Hinckley, Daniel J. *The Explorer's Garden.* Portland, OR. Timber Press, 1999.

Lowe, Duncan B. *Cushion Plants for the Rock Garden*. London. B. T. Batsford Ltd, 1995. The two books by Duncan Lowe are favorites of mine which I heartily recommend. I admire the late Duncan Lowe and his skills, for to me he personifies the spirit of alpine gardening. The ideas and high quality photographs are tied together with his incredible drawings.

Lowe, Duncan B. *Growing Alpines In Raised Beds, Troughs And Tufa*. London. B. T. Batsford Ltd., 1991.

Malby, Reginald A. *The Story of My Rock Garden.* London. Headley Brothers, 1912.

Mathew, Brian. *The Genus Lewisia*. Portland, OR. Timber Press, 1989.

Mathew, Brian. *The Smaller Bulbs*. London. B. T. Batsford Ltd., 1987. This comprehensive book dealing with dwarf bulbs was written by a man who really knows his subject.

McGary, Jane (editor). *Bulbs of North America*. Portland, OR. Timber Press & North American Rock Garden Society, 2001. A comprehensive work on North American native bulbs, this book will be excellent for growers of dwarf bulbs. The contributors are skilled and enthusiastic gardeners who know the bulbs both in their natural habitats and in the garden.

McGary, Jane (editor). *Rock Garden Plants of North America.* Portland, OR. Timber Press and the North American Rock Garden Society, 1996. This large book preceded Bulbs of North America and was also edited by Jane McGary. It offers contributions by many experts and the information covers diverse climatic regions.

Mineo, Baldassare. *Rock Garden Plants.* Portland, OR. Timber Press, 1999.

Nicholls, Graham, and Rick Lupp. *Alpine Plants of North America*: *An Encyclopedia of Mountain Flowers from the Rockies to Alaska.* Portland, OR. Timber Press, 2002. This is an excellent book co-written by a British nurseryman who specialized in growing American alpines, receiving many prestigious awards for his skillfully grown plants. He has made several visits to the US studying native alpines. Anyone growing these plants, regardless of where they live, will find this book invaluable.

North American Rock Garden Society. Jane McGary, editor. *Rock Garden Design and Construction*. Portland, OR. Timber Press, 2003. I am safe in saying that anyone on this continent contemplating building or creating any form of alpine garden should first read this informative book. NARGS members conceived the idea of the book and an editorial committee commissioned the various authors to write their contributions. It covers design and materials, types of rock gardens, regional considerations, and gardens to visit.

Rix, Martin, and Croom Helm. *Growing Bulbs*. Portland, OR. Timber Press, 1983.

Rolf, Robert. *The Alpine House*. Portland, OR. Timber Press, 1990. Written in England, it deals principally with local issues but nonetheless is good reading for anyone who is considering getting an alpine house.

Wilder, Louise Beebe. *The Rock Garden.* New York. Doubleday, 1933. Reprinted in several editions. Wilder was a pioneer US writer who is still well worth reading.

About the Author

Born in England, Rex Murfitt trained as a nurseryman, later specializing in alpine plants at the famous W. E. Th. Ingwersen, Birch Farm Hardy Plant Nursery at Gravetye, Sussex. There, he trained under Walter Ingwersen VMH and his son Will Ingwersen VMH, who taught him the art of propagation and cultivation of alpine plants. He traveled widely with Will Ingwersen, building rock gardens for clients. From these great gardeners he learned the romance and lore of alpine plants.

Rex Murfitt

Later he worked in large English gardens including J. Spedan Lewis's gardens at Longstock Park in Hampshire, caring for the greenhouses and orchid collection, as well as a collection of alpine plants. Eventually he became Head Gardener to Mrs. Constance Spry at Winkfield Place, near Windsor, where plants were grown for her famous flower arrangements. He helped develop her white garden, based on the one at Sissinghurst Castle. Under the guidance of Graham Stuart Thomas, he undertook the care of a large collection of old fashioned roses.

He later moved to New York, and with Frank and Anne Cabot, started Stonecrop Nurseries, Inc., at Cold Spring On Hudson, an alpine nursery based on English traditional methods. Stonecrop displayed rock gardens at flower shows in New York City and Philadelphia.

Rex Murfitt now grows alpines for pleasure at home in Victoria, B.C., Canada, and is an author and lecturer. His particular interests include collecting saxifrages, and he has a growing love for North American alpines. When not in the garden, he devotes time to photographing alpine plants and recording the efforts of the distinguished alpine gardeners he was fortunate enough to have known.

He was coauthor with Joyce Fingerut of the book, *Creating and Planting Garden Troughs* (B. B. Mackey Books, Wayne, PA). It received a "Book of the Year 2000" award from the American Horticultural Society.

In 2002, he received the Carleton R. Worth Award for distinguished writing about rock gardening and rock plants from the North American Rock Garden Society.

Index

Abies species, 244
Acantholimon 135-136
    -acerosum, 136
    -bracteatum, 136
    -ulicinum, 136
access, to garden site, 12
acclimatization, of plants, 124-125
Achillea
    -ageratifolia, 137
    - x jaborneggii, 137
    - x lewisii 'King Edward', 137
Aethionema
    -armenum, 138
    -caespitosum, 138
    -grandiflora, 81
    -'Warley Rose', 138
Ageratum varieties, 134
Alpine Garden Society of Great
    Britain, 265
alpine houses, 98-114, gallery p. b
Alyssum, 134
    -montanum, 139
    -propinquum, 139
    -ptilotrichum, 139
    -saxatile, 151
    -serpyllifolium, 139
American Horticultural Society Heat
    Zone Map, 122
Anagallis varieties, 134
Andromeda polifolia, 252
Androsace, 139-144
    -carnea, 141
    -lanuginosa, 142
    -sarmentosa, 142-143, f,
    -sempervivoides, 143
    -vandellii, 140
    -villosa, 143
    - x 'Millstream', 142
Anemone blanda, 232
annuals, and alpine gardens, 133
Antennaria
    -dioica, 144
    -parvifolia, 144
Antirrhinum varieties, 134

Aqilegia 144-146
    -jonesii, 145-146
    -bertolonii, 145
    -pyrenaica, 146
    -saximontana, 146
    -scopulorum, 146
Arabis, 146-148
    -alpina ssp. *caucasica,* 147
    -androsacea, 147
    -bryoides, 147
    - x kellereri, 147
Arcterica species, 252
Arenaria
    -balearica, 148
    -tetraquetra, 148
Aretian androsaces, 140-141
Armeria
    -caespitosa, 149
    -juniperifolia, 149
    - maritima 'Victor Reiter', 149
Artemisia
    -assoana, 149
    -caucasica, 149
Ashwood strain (*Lewisia*), 187
Asperula
    -arcadiensis, 151
    -gussonii, 150
    -nitida, 150
    -sintenisii, 150
    -suberosa, 151
Aubrieta species, 82
Aurinia saxatilis, 151
autumn, and planting, 126
Avent, Tony, 124
banks, 15
Barlow, Roger, 168
barrels, 81
bellflowers, 151-156.
Betula nana, 249
Bland, Beryl and Peter, 46, 51,
    gallery p. c
bluebells, 151-156
Books, on alpine gardening, 262-267
boulders, and design, 33, 34

269

brassicas, 166
bridging, 55
bulb frame, 117-119
Bulbocodium vernum, 233
Bulbs, 117-119, 225-241
    in flowerpots, 229-231
    planting of, 227-231
Burgel, Jan, 204
Buxus suffruticosa, gallery p. a
calcifuges, 64
Campanula, 151-156
    -carpatica, 153
    - cochlearifolia, 152, 154
    - formanekiana, 154-155
    -garganica, 152, 155
    -portenschlagiana, 81, 152
    - poscharskyana, 152
    -rotundifolia, 152
    -scabrella, 155
    -shetleri, 156
    - x haylodgensis, 152,
      gallery p. g
    - zoysii, 156
Carousel hybrids (*Lewisia*), 187
Chamaecyparis obtusa, 245
Chionodoxa species, 233
CITES, 238
clay flower pots, 85, 86
coir, 63
Colchicum species, gallery p. h
cold frames, 114-117
color, of concrete, 32
    of rock, 24
columbine, 144-146. See Aquile-
    gia.
compost, 62
    compost, making of, 132
    J. I., 71
concrete, 31, 32, 52, 80, 94
conifers, 244-249
containers, and alpine plants,
    77-97
    and bulbs, 229-231
Convention on International Trade

in Endangered Species
    (CITES), 238
Convolvulus
    -boisseri, 157
    -cneorum, 252
    -nitidus, 157
corms, 225
Corydalis, 157-158
    cashmeriana, 158
    -flexuosa, 158
    -solida, 158
Crocus, 233-235
    -ancyrensis, 234
    -chrysanthus, 234
    -laevigatus 'Fontenayi', 234
    -pulchellus, 234
    -sieberii, 234
    -speciosus, 234
    -tomasinianus, 224, 235
Crook, Clifford, 156
Cyclamen, 159-161
    -coum, 159
    -hederifolium, 160
    -purpurascens, 160-161
Daphne species, 253-255
    -arbuscula, 253
    -cneorum, 254
    -jasminea, 254
    -petraea, 254
    -retusa, 255
Davidson, Roy, 193
design, 16-22, 35-45, 46-60
    and containers, 80
    and planting, 128-129
    and rockwork, 23-33, 35-45
    of raised beds, 47-59
Dianthus, 161-165
    -alpinus, 162
    -deltoides, 164
    -erinaceus, 162
    -freyneii, 163
    -glacialis, 163
    -gratianopolitanus, 164, 165
    -haematocalyx, 163

- 'La Bourboule', 165
-*myrtinervius,* 164
-*pavonius,* 163
-*simulans,* 163
Draba, 165
   -*brunifolia,* 168
   -*dedeana,* 168
   -*densifolium,* 169
   -*incerta,* 169
   -*longisiliqua,* 167
   -*mollissima,* 166, 167
   -*oligosperma,* 169
   -*paysonii,* 169
   -*polytricha,* 167
   -*rigida,* 168
   -*siberica,* gallery p. d
   -*ventosa,* 169
   - x *salomonii,* 168
drainage holes, 86. See also weep
   holes.
drainage, 11, 13, 61
   and soil, 72-74
Elliott, Clarence, 88, 89
Elliott, Joe, 88
Enzian, 173
Eranthis hyemalis, 235
Ericaceae, soil mixture, 69
Erigeron, 169-171
   Erigeron aureus, 169
   Erigeron crysopsidis, 170
   Erigeron karvinskianus, 170
   Erigeron leiomeris, 171
   Erigeron scopulinus, 171
Erythronium, 171-173
   Pagoda, 173
   Erythronium revolutum, 172
   Erythronium tuolomense,
     172-173
   Erythronium 'White Beauty',
     173
exposure, 10
   for alpine houses, 105
Farrer, Reginald, 179
featherock, 29, 30

feet, for troughs, 93
fertilizing, of alpine gardens, 131
Foster, H. Lincoln, 202
Galanthus
   -*nivalis, 236*
   -*n.* 'Flore Pleno', 226
garden, sunken, 17
Gentiana, 173-179
   -*acaulis,* 174
   -*septemfida* 'Latifolia', 173,
     175-176
   -*sino-ornata,* 176
   -*verna,* 174, 175
Geranium, 178-179
   -'Ballerina', 178
   -*cinereum,* 178
   -*dalmaticum,* 178, 179
   -*farreri,* 178
   - 'Lawrence Flatman', 178
Gevjan, Roxie, 247, gallery p. b
glazing, of alpine houses, 104
granite, 28
gravel, 63, 75, 93
greenhouses, 98-114.
grit, 61
grooming, 130
gunnite, 32, 33
Gypsophila
   -*aretioides,* 180
   -*briquetiana,* 180
   -*cerastioides,* 181
   -*muralis,* 134
   -*repens,* 181
   -*tenuifolia,* 181
Haberlea rhodopensis, 181-182
habitat, 21
hardiness, of plants, 122-124
hare bells, 152
heating, of alpine houses, 101,
   106-110
herbaceous plants, 135-223
hot beds, 115
hypertufa, 89-93

Ingwersen, Will, 20, 165
Innes, John, and soil mixtures, 70-72
Iris
       -cristata, 182-183
       -lacustris, 183
       -reticulata, 236
Jans, Harry, 77, 205
Japanese style, 21, 22
John Innes Centre, 71
Jovibarba species, 214, 215
Juliana hybrids (*Primula*), 197
Juniperus communis 'Compressa',
      246
Kabsch, William, 202
Kabschia saxifrages, 100, 201
Kelaidis, Gwen, 65
keystone, 40
Klaber, Doretta, 194, 220
Kline, Boyd C., 192, 221
krummholtz, 243
Lambert, Mike, 98
leaf mold, 62
lean potting mixture, 69
Lewisia species and hybrids,
      183-188
      -brachycalyx, 184
      -columbiana, 184, 185
      -cotyledon, 184, 185, 187, 188
      -pygmaea, 184
      -rediviva, 184, 187
      -tweedii, 184, 187, 188
light, 10, 11,
lime, 64
limestone, 25
Limnanthes douglasii, 134
Linaria maroccana, 134
line level, 54
loam, 62
loam-based potting soil, 69
Lobelia varieties, 134
Lupp, Rick, 171, 193
Lychnis flos-jovis, 82
maintenance, of alpine gardens,
      129-131

Malby, Reginald A., 31
McDonough, Mark, 193
meadow, alpine, 34
mulch, 75, 76
Murfitt, Rex, about, 268
mustard family, 166
Narcissus
      -asturiensis, 237
      -bulbocodium, 237, gallery
        p. d
      -cyclamineus, 237
      -triandrus, 237
nature, and rock gardening, 9, 10,
Nemophila varieties, 134
North American Rock Garden
      Society, 261-262, 265
nun of the meadows, 151
nutrients. See fertilizing.
organic matter, 62
outcrops, rocky, 9, 23, 35
      construction of, 40-43
overhangs, 10
Papaver
      -alpinum, 189
      -nudicaule, 189
parking areas, and garden design,
      19, 49
pavement, 13
      and raised beds, 57-58
      and rock garden drainage, 74
peat, 61, 62, 63
Penstemon, 189-194
      -davidsonii, 191
      -hirsutis Pygmaeus, 194
      -pinifolius, 194
      -procerus, 192
      -rupicola, 192
pH, 64
Phlox, 194-197
      -alaskensis, 197
      -albomarginata, 197
      -andicola, 197
      -douglasii, 195
      -hoodii ssp. *muscoides,* 197

-subulata, 194, 195
Picea
    -abies, 246
    -glauca, 246
Pieris japonica, 255
Pinus mugo, 247-248
Plant Hardiness Zone Map (USDA), 122
planters, see containers.
planting, timing of, 125-126
plantings, foundation, 14
plants, and pot size, 83, 84
    for alpine gardens, 121-259
    for containers, 81
Porphyrion saxifrages, 201
Portulacaceae, 184
pot size, and alpine plants, 83, 84
potting soil, 68-72
preplanting, 127
Primula, 197-199
    -hirsuta, 198
    -juliae, 197
    -marginata, 198
    -minima, 81, 198
    - x pubescens, 198
Ptilotrichum spinosum. See Alyssum
    ptilotrichum.
pulhamite, 32
Pulsatilla
    -vernalis, 199
    -vulgaris, 199
pumice, 29, 30, 31
Puschkinia scilloides, 239
raised beds, 47-59, 67-68
Regenbogen strain (Lewisia), 187
retaining walls, 51
rhizomes, 225
Rhododendron, 256-259
    -calostrotum ssp. keleticum, 257
    -campylogynum, 258
    -camtschaticum, 258
    -hirsutum, 257

-impeditum, 258
-keiskii, 259
-radicans, 257
rich soil mixture, 69
Rock Garden Quarterly, 265
rock, 23-34, 35-45
    and construction, 39
    artificial, 32, 33
    nature of, 23-33
    outcroppings of, 9, 23, 40, 41
    purchasing of, 38
    types of, 25
    underlying, 15
rock garden, construction of, 35-45
rough fill, 59
safety, and rockwork, 36
Salix, 250-251
    -boydii, 250
    -herbacea, 251
    -lanata, 251
    -reticulata, 251
    -retusa, 251
sand, 61, 63
sandstone, 27
Saponaria
    'Bressingham', 200
    -ocymoides 'Rubra Compacta', 200
    -officinalis, 200
    - x olivana, 200
Saxifraga 201-208
    and containers, 79
    mossy types, 208
    older varieties, 203
    recent cultivars, 204
    silver types, 204-208
    -'Hi Ace', 208
    -callosa, 206
    -cochlearis, 206
    -cotyledon, 206
    -exarata ssp. moschata 'Cloth of Gold', 208
    -hostii, 4
    -oppositifolia, 206

-*paniculata,* 206-267
-'Rainsley Seedling', gallery p. c
-*sancta,* 203
-'Southside Seedling Boer-dum', gallery p. c
-'Whitehill', 208
-'Winifred Bevington',208
- x *apiculata* 'Gregor Mendel', 202
- x *burnatii* 'Emile Burnat', 207
- x *eudoxiana* 'Haagii', 202
Scilla siberica, 239
Scottish Rock Garden Club, 265
scree gardens, and *Androsace,* 140-141
Sedum, 208-211
-*acre* 'Aureum', 210
-*album,* 210
-*cauticolum,* 211
-*hispanicum* var. *minus,* 210
-*pachyclados,* 211
-*sexangulare,* 210
-*spurium,* 210
seeds, soil for, 70
semi-woody plants, 135
Sempervivum, 212-215
- 'Mayfair', 8
-*octopodes,* 215, gallery p. a
shade, 10, 11, 76
shading, of alpine house, 111-112
shrubs, and trees, 243-259
Silene
-*acaulis,* 215
-*alpestris,* 216
-*shafta, 216*
Sinks, 87
sites, for rock gardens, 11-19,
slab gardens, 94
slopes, 12, 15, 55-57
snow cover, and plant hardiness, 123
soil recipes, basic, 66
for containers, 68-72
soil, and drainage, 65, 66

and pH, 64, 65
components of, 63-65
for raised beds, 58-59
for rock and alpine gardens, 61-76
renewal of, in containers, 81
Soldanella
-*alpina,* 217
-*carpatica,* 217
-*montana,* 216, 217
-*villosa,* 217
stone. See rock.
Stonecrop, 117
stoneware, 80
strain, definition of, 187
strata, and rock gardens, 9. 10, 23
stream bed, 17
summer, and alpine houses, 110-113
sunrooms, 103
sweet woodruff, 150
tailing, 127
Tanacetum densum ssp, amanum, gallery p. a
terra cotta, 85, 86
Terraces. See raised beds.
Thymophylla tenuifolia, 134
Thymus, 217-220
-'Doone Valley', 220
-'Doretta Klaber', 220
-*neiceffii,* 218
-*polytrichus,* 218
-*pseudolanuginosus,* 219
-*serpyllum,* 218
topdressing, 75, 76, 93
topping, 127
travertine, 29
trees and shrubs, 243-259
Trillium, 220-222
-*nivale,* 220
-*rivale,* 220-221
troughs, 87-93, 213, gallery p. h
soil for, 68-72
Tsuga canadensis, 248-249
tubers, 225

tufa, 26, 27, 29, 89
       planting in, 95-97, 99
Tulipa 239-241
       -batallinii, 240
       -clusiana, 240
       -humilis, 240
       -kauffmanniana, 241
       -linifolia, 241
       -sprengeri, 241
       -tarda, 241
       -turkestanica, 241
       -urumiensis, 241
Ulmus parvifolia, 251
Verbena hybrids, 134
Veronica
       -armena, 222
       -bombycina, 222
       -pectinata 'Rosea', 222
       -prostrata, 222-223
       -spicata, 223
walls, construction of, 53-58
       retaining, 51
water, and rock gardening, 10, 21,
              128
weeds, 76, 129
weep holes, 58, 74
whitewash, 111
winter, and alpine houses, 107-110
       and plant hardiness, 122-124
wormwood, 149-150
zone maps, 122

A word of thanks. Many people assisted Rex Murfitt and me during the creation of this volume. We greatly appreciate Carlo Balistrieri's expert advice on the nomenclature in plant chapters eight and onward. Any errors are ours, you can be sure. We warmly thank Jean Mansmann for her editorial work, Anne Freeman for her eye for a good photo, and Jane Grushow and Joyce Fingerut for launching *Creating and Planting Garden Troughs*, which led to work on this volume. We thank all the photographers who contributed. We treasure our memberships in the North American Rock Garden Society. Above all, we thank Ruth Murfitt and Tom Mackey for their endless patience and support throughout the lengthy development of this book.

Betty Mackey, Publisher
B. B. Mackey Books
www.mackeybooks.com